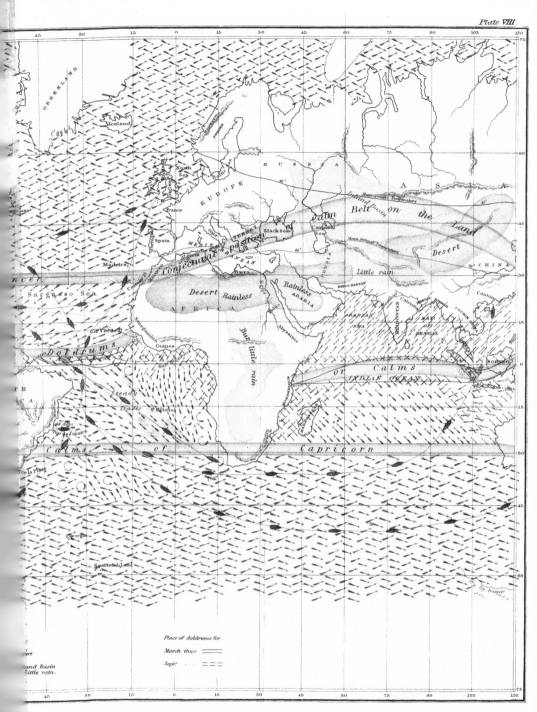

Plate 8, Winds and Routes, from Maury's 1861 edition of *The Physical Geography of the Sea*. See page 196.

TRACKS IN THE SEA

Matthew Fontaine Maury and the
Mapping of the Oceans

❧

Chester G. Hearn

International Marine / McGraw-Hill

Camden, Maine • New York • Chicago • San Francisco
Lisbon • London • Madrid • Mexico City • Milan • New Delhi
San Juan • Seoul • Singapore • Sydney • Toronto

International Marine

A Division of The McGraw-Hill Companies

9 7 5 3 1 2 4 6 8 10
First Edition
Copyright © 2002 by Chester G. Hearn

Library of Congress Cataloging-in-Publication Data

Hearn, Chester G.
Tracks in the sea : Matthew Fontaine Maury
and the mapping of the oceans / Chester G. Hearn.
p.   cm.
Includes bibliographical references and index.
ISBN 0-07-136826-4
1. Maury, Matthew Fontaine, 1806–1873. 2. Oceanographers—
United States—Biography. 3. Oceanography—History. I. Title.
GC30.M4 H43 2002
551.46´0091—dc21
2002007004

This book is printed on 55 lb. Sebago by R.R. Donnelley, Crawfordsville, IN
Design by Dennis Anderson
Production by Faith Hague and Dan Kirchoff
Edited by Jonathan Eaton, Dan Spurr, and Jane M. Curran

Photo Credits

Chapter opening art from the cover boards of the 1856 edition of *The Physical Geography of the Sea*; page 45 (top and bottom), courtesy U.S. Naval Historical Center; page 46, Library of Congress; pages 99 and 100, courtesy the National Archives, College Park, Maryland; page 109, courtesy U.S. Naval Historical Center; page 110, Library of Congress; pages 129 and 130, courtesy the National Archives, College Park, Maryland; page 131, courtesy U.S. Naval Historical Center; page 181, courtesy U.S. Naval Historical Center; page 182 (top), courtesy U.S. Naval Historical Center; page 182 (bottom), courtesy National Portrait Gallery, Smithsonian Institution; page 215 (top and bottom), U.S. Naval Historical Center; page 216, courtesy the Albert and Shirley Small Special Collections, University of Virginia; page 235 (top), courtesy National Portrait Gallery, Smithsonian Institution; page 235 (bottom), courtesy Valentine Museum/Richmond History Center, Richmond, Virginia; page 236, courtesy Valentine Museum/Richmond History Center, Richmond, Virginia; page 243, courtesy U.S. Naval Historical Center; page 244, courtesy Valentine Museum/Richmond History Center, Richmond, Virginia.

TRACKS IN
THE SEA

CONTENTS

To my wife, Ann,
who makes the interminable hours
of research and writing possible

PREFACE

I FIRST learned of Matthew Fontaine Maury at the age of twelve. During the winter, when Lake Erie iced over and there was little left for a boy to do with his boat until spring, I would take the city bus into town and stride over to the Erie County Public Library, an old building situated at the southeast corner of Perry Square. The square had been named in honor of Commodore Oliver Hazard Perry, who defeated the British on Lake Erie in the battle of September 10, 1813, and then sent the message: "We have met the enemy, and he is ours." The bones of his flagship, USS *Niagara*, still lay across Presque Isle Bay on a sandy neck of land we called "the Peninsula."

With America then at war with Germany and Japan, I developed a particular interest in geography and history. I cut maps and articles out of newspapers and magazines (but never from library materials!) and pasted them in a scrapbook while keeping a sharp lookout for something new. In a cart at the library I came across an old edition of Maury's *Physical Geography of the Sea*, which one of the workers was about to carry downstairs to the basement archives. I doubted the book would advance my knowledge of the war, but when I opened it, the book fell open to a colored map of the world. Arrows designated the flow of winds across the surface of the oceans, and having done a little sailing on Presque Isle Bay and Lake Erie, I was instantly drawn to that map. On page after page the arrows, cryptic notations, flowing curves, and finely wrought ocean basin margins spoke of deep secrets and vast geographies. Here was a key to the great world beyond Erie, if I could only learn how to read it.

It took several trips to the library to get my fill of Maury's illustrated geography. Hours melted away in that spell of rapt concentration quite natural to twelve-year-olds. I probably learned more about the world, and in particular about its oceans, from the *The Physical Geography of the Sea* than from any single book I have read since. Time passed, and I forgot the author's name, but a surprising residue of ocean knowledge stuck with me.

Years later I encountered Maury again while writing my first book, *Gray Raiders of the Sea*, about the Confederate raids on Union shipping during the Civil War. Still, nothing stimulated me to investigate him in depth until the day when, stopping at a bookstore in Farmville, Virginia, I happened across an old, battered copy of an 1890s juvenile edition of Maury's great work, which I bought for three dollars.

So more than fifty years after our first introduction, I returned to this enigmatic navigator who had taught me at the age of twelve so much about the oceans. *The Physical Geography of the Sea* is still one of the most interesting and entertaining books I own, but only after I began to study Maury's life in earnest did I come to appreciate his genius, not as a geographer but as a marvelous self-taught scientist who discovered patterns from chaos and disorder in events others saw only as random. In mapping the winds and currents of the seas he provided a rational framework for route planning that, with only a little exaggeration, can be compared with today's computer-generated trip maps for motorists. I discovered in this man of the nineteenth century a great talent who fought a multitude of obstacles to give the sailing nations of the world a new mastery of the seas—a system of navigation that was simple, yet grand.

Much of my research came from Maury himself in the form of his works and letters. He wrote frequently and profusely to friends and relatives, and the two largest collections of personal letters are in the Library of Congress and in Alderman Library at the University of Virginia. James Hutson, Barry Zerby, and Edward J. Redmond got me started on the documents at the Library of Congress, and archivists at Alderman Library sent me a pile of photocopies of Maury's family letters. I especially do not forget the immense help I received from Mary Goodrich, who on my behalf dug through folders of documents at the Library of Congress, Smithsonian Institution, and the National Archives in search of papers and records pertinent to this book. I am also indebted to Jan Herman, the historian at the Bureau of Medicine and Science in Washington, D.C., which has a substantial collection of Maury's maps, charts, and publications. Maury's official letters are in the Naval Records section of the National Archives, and some may now be on microfilm. The logbooks he used are bound in more than five hundred volumes—the number in each binding often exceeding twenty.

I also owe a debt of gratitude to Jean L. Hort and Ed Finney Jr. at the Naval Historical Center in Washington, D.C., and to Dr. Donald S. Marshall and Marla Gearhart at the Peabody Essex Museum and Phillips Library in Salem, Massachusetts, for directing and providing me with other sources of research. Ann Hassinger and James Cheevers at the U.S. Naval Academy have been especially helpful in providing publications and documents pertaining to Maury's work at the U.S. Naval Observatory. Thanks also to Diane B. Jacob, archivist at the Preston Library, Virginia Military Institute, for providing genealogical information about the Maury family.

I also owe thanks to the staff of the U.S. Naval Observatory, who provided assistance when questions arose on historical accuracies regarding the observatory: Steven Dick and Geoff Chester, historians; Brenda Corbin, librarian; and Annette Hammond, Jan Herman, and Gregory Shelton.

I can never get through a book without help from those at my local library. Evelyn Wesman at Erie's Blasco Library brought in more than forty books through the interlibrary loan system, many of them primary sources that came from university archives. I still do not know how she did it. Mary Rennie helped me borrow books from Erie's Maritime Collection, which under normal circumstances never leave Blasco Library. John Merrill, an old salt from Waterford, Connecticut, and an admirer of Maury, was also kind enough to share some of the research he had done over many years.

I am indebted to Jonathan Eaton at International Marine for his sound advice as to style and content, and for the enhancements he suggested in telling the story. The staff at International Marine, and especially Deborah Oliver, have been most helpful in providing professional editorial assistance and in tracking down art work.

To those whose names I have forgotten over the years, I apologize. My gratitude to each of you is absolute.

Chester G. Hearn
Erie, Pennsylvania

INTRODUCTION

MATTHEW Fontaine Maury's contribution to the science of the seas occurred at the precise time when the maritime industry of the United States experienced its greatest growth. Indeed, it was during the Golden Age of Sail that Maury's work on navigation identified the so-called highways of the sea and marked them with numeric "signposts" for the sailors of the world. Satellites and electronic devices map the way for the navies of engine-driven ships and the small sailboats of the twenty-first century, but the sailing ships of the nineteenth century had no such gadgetry. What they all relied upon was the inquisitive and industrious superintendent in the U.S. Naval Observatory whom the great sailing nations of the world came to know as Lieutenant Maury (pronounced *Morry*).

In most streams of scientific thought, one idea stems from another, developing and building toward a state of better understanding and perfection. But each such stream has to start somewhere. An accurate timepiece for calculating longitudes took six thousand years to develop; even after John Harrison's chronometer was recognized by an act of the British Parliament in 1773, it took another fifty years for the maritime world to adopt the chronometer for common use. Then Maury came along and created an entirely new science from a wellspring of curiosity. His was a practical science, an immense creation of immense value. Maury set before himself a challenge "to shape the course on voyages as to make the most of winds and currents at sea," thereby perfecting "the navigator's art." But Maury transcended art and made it a science.

Whether a sailor was an old salt with fifty years on the oceans or a neophyte commanding his first ship of sail, Maury wanted his path to be "literally blazed through the winds for him on the sea; mile-posts . . . set up on the waves, and finger-boards planted, and time-tables furnished for the trackless waste, by which the shipmaster, on his first voyage to any port, may know as well as the most experienced trader whether he be in the right road or no[t]."

His research came at a time when sailing ships were reaching the full, glorious pinnacle of their technical adaptation to the pursuits of war and commerce on the high seas, still unchallenged by steam. No better testament exists to the value of Maury's charts than the great achievements of the American clipper ships. They followed Maury's routes around the world and became a source of great and justified pride for all Americans. The enormous body of knowledge that he fashioned and dispensed during the mid-nineteenth century still survives and still is useful, despite the fact that power-driven vessels superseded sailing ships more than a century ago.

From a few seemingly simple questions—like why is the evening sea breeze so predictable?—Maury created a fountain of new knowledge. Today, every chart of winds, currents, and weather bears his fingerprints.

Maury's pioneering work on oceanography became the catalyst for a new and fascinating science. He discovered the heat pump for planet Earth, isolated its variables, condensed its consistencies, and harnessed this knowledge as a predictive tool for navigators. As a creative oceanographer he left much undone, but he opened the eyes of the world to the unknown wonders of the oceans. Never having been schooled in science, Maury had his limitations as a purist. In his classic text, *The Physical Geography of the Sea*, his assumptions were wrong as often as they were right, but he built the foundation for today's weather balloons, radar, international weather-monitoring stations, and tracking satellites poised high above the Earth. His was a highly individual book that nobody else at the time could have written. He borrowed facts from others when he could, and he tried to find answers that made sense when the technology for further investigation did not exist.

A series of coincidences shaped Maury's life and led him to his work. His prolific mind never stopped probing for answers, and he never stopped educating himself. If he came across a difficult problem, he assumed that everyone else in the world suffered in some way from its impact. If he solved the problem, he refined the solution in terms simple enough for a novice to understand. As a sailor, he understood the mariner's problems, and as a navigator, he understood the shipmaster's problems. Both were the same: how to get from one place to another swiftly and safely.

Coincidence cast Maury into the role of inquisitor by toppling him out of a careening stagecoach and rendering him unfit for sea. Had he remained a sailor on active duty, he would never have been thrust into a desk job, nor would he, as superintendent of the Depot of Charts and Instruments, have found the gold mine of old, neglected logbooks that provided his springboard to capturing the winds and currents of the seas.

Maury had a unique way of expressing his thoughts so that the everyday traveler could understand. Anybody looking across the vastness of the seas could not imagine it filled with invisible highways and byways put there for sailing ships. But Maury put them there in a form that could be understood by the seafarer. He described his work as mapping the seas for the sailor: "Thus the forks to his road, its turnings, and the crossings by the way, have been so clearly marked by the winds for him that there is scarcely a chance for him who studies the lights before him, and pays attention to the directions given, to miss his way."

Throughout his life Maury created new knowledge, opening vistas for others to explore in the fields of science. On the oceans of the world he created roadways for sailors to follow—and he called them "tracks in the sea."

One day as I passed through Richmond, Virginia, with a friend, he noticed three large statues in the center of the city. He immediately recognized generals Robert E. Lee and Thomas "Stonewall" Jackson, but he was puzzled by the third. He turned to me and asked, "Who is that guy?"

"That's Matthew Fontaine Maury," I replied.

"Why, he's right up there with Lee and Jackson," my friend said. "I've never heard of him. What did he do to be in such good company?"

So then I told him, not so much of the Civil War but of the man himself.

Chapter One

THE TRACKLESS SEAS

IN 1492, Christopher Columbus commanded three caravels across the uncharted Atlantic from Spain to the Bahamas. The voyage lasted sixty-nine days. Had he not first sailed south to the Canary Islands, below 30 degrees North latitude, the voyage might have taken much longer. Columbus's passage from the Canary Islands to Watling Island ("Guanahani," or San Salvador) took only thirty-four days during the height of what would later be recognized as the hurricane season. What he discovered, but refused to acknowledge even to his death, was an enormous continent blocking the westward sea route to Asia.

From the Portuguese, who jealously guarded their knowledge of the seas, Columbus had learned of the steady northeasterly winds that blow in the latitudes of the Canaries, winds that would carry him on what he believed to be a short, swift passage to Asia.

At the time of his historic voyage, Columbus, by his own reckoning, had "followed the sea for 23 years, without leaving it for any appreciable time." He had lived for a while in the Madeira Islands, north of the Canaries, and sailed on trading voyages to a Portuguese trading post on the Gold Coast of the Gulf of Guinea, only a few degrees north of the equator. He once ranged as far north as Iceland. During his voyages he experienced the northeasterly trade winds south of 25 to 30 degrees North and the prevailing westerlies farther north. In his log entry of August 25, 1492, as he struggled to repair the *Pinta*'s rudder at Grand Canary and begin the out-ward voyage in earnest with his recalcitrant crews, he wrote, "We will return from the Indies with the westerly winds, which I have observed first-hand in the winter along the coast of Portugal and Galicia. When I sailed to England with the Portuguese some years ago, I learned that the wester-lies blow year-round in the higher latitudes and are as dependable as the easterlies [of the lower latitudes]."

Though he shared his full knowledge with no one, then or later, he seemed to have learned his weather well, for he sailed far enough north on the return trip from the West Indies to pick up the prevailing wester-lies that carried him in forty-two days safely back to Europe. Such knowl-edge of wind patterns was neither widely known nor particularly precise.

In the decades after Columbus returned to Spain in 1493 and informed King Ferdinand and Queen Isabella that great wealth could be plucked from the world to the west, the maritime nations of Europe launched one of the greatest shipbuilding efforts in their collective histories. Over time, shipmasters sailing from Europe learned that the fastest routes to and from the West Indies were the very tracks Columbus had chosen for his daring first voyage into the unknown.

❧

NAVIGATORS shared their knowledge of winds and currents with other seafarers, passing down through generations a combination of wisdom and rumor. But it remained for Matthew Fontaine Maury, a self-educated lieutenant of the nineteenth-century U.S. Navy, to apply any sort of sci-entific discipline to the collection and analysis of meteorologic and oceano-graphic data. His research led to publication of wind and current tables for the Atlantic, Pacific, and Indian Oceans and later, in 1855, to the first textbook of oceanography, his *Physical Geography of the Sea*. In the centuries preceding Maury the success or failure of an ocean voyage often owed as much to luck as to seamanship and navigational skill. The winds and cur-rents were as constant as the Earth's rotation, yet until Maury no one had thought to make disciplined observations and from them codify the pat-terns. After Maury, there were fewer excuses for a long or difficult passage.

When out of sight of landmarks, navigation had always been a risky business, despite the fact that Columbus and Magellan proved to the sea-faring world that oceans could be mastered by using solar and traverse tables (which give the distance gained in both latitude and longitude for any course sailed at a certain speed) in combination with such instruments as compasses, quadrants, cross-staffs, astrolabes, hourglasses, theodolites, and a wooden log tossed overboard to estimate a vessel's speed. Still, existing knowledge and instruments were far from precise. The calculation of longitude, which coupled with latitude gives the navigator a far more accurate position than that derived from dead reckoning, could not be made with any accuracy until John Harrison's invention of the chronometer in 1761. In the meantime, mariners had no choice but to depend first and foremost upon visual landmarks for determining position. In the New World, no landmarks had been charted until the arrival of Columbus on an island he mistook for part of Asia.

There is more to navigation than position fixing. If one is to make a fast and comfortable passage—even in modern, power-driven vessels, great and small—one also must know the direction and speed of ocean currents, the direction and seasonal variations of the winds, and how to forecast changes in weather, for the mariner always is at risk of squalls, gales and hurricanes, foul tides, and contrary currents. A sextant, chronometer, and celestial tables can tell a navigator's location on Earth in terms of degrees North and South latitude, East and West longitude, but tell him nothing about the desirability of that location and course relative to his destination.

Columbus discovered the risks of plying unknown waters when in 1492 his flagship, the *Santa María*, wrecked on a bar in Charcoal Bay, near Cape Haitian off Hispaniola. Though a very experienced sea captain for his time, Columbus still lacked considerable knowledge about weather, winds, and currents, and especially such seasonal phenomena as hurricanes, which two years later flung two caravels, *Mariagalante* and *Gallega*, onto the rocks. In 1495, six more Spanish vessels succumbed to a storm, but an even greater disaster occurred in 1502 despite Columbus's reading the skies and warning the governor of Hispaniola of an approaching hurricane. The governor ordered Admiral Antonio de Torres to sea with a fleet of thirty gold-laden caravels. Two days later a tempest ripped the fleet asunder, destroying all but four vessels. The king, queen, and the church did not get their gold that year.

Two hundred and fifty years later, massive flotillas of richly laden Spanish galleons still navigated with rudimentary instruments, placing enormous dependence on landmarks. Their piloting charts had grown more detailed since the early days of Columbus, but they tracked sailing routes not so much by weather, winds, and currents as by latitudes and prominent features of nearby landforms. Once Spanish mariners learned the location of rocks, reefs, and other hazards, they sailed toward them on the theory that it was better to know where they were than not to know, even if the known location placed the vessel and crew at risk.

Working on this assumption, Spanish captains chose routes that followed the islands of the West Indies and the Caribbean, often traveling far out of their way just to keep in sight of land. They spent much of their time battling headwinds and currents, wrecking their vessels on the very hazards they used to guide them. Over time, navigators became familiar with the winds and currents along beaten paths, but no man or country had taken steps to organize the knowledge in a more useful form. It seemed that the importance of knowing a ship's position from landmarks transcended all other considerations. Although using landmarks provided obvious advantages, the practice discouraged navigators from plotting courses to avoid adverse winds or currents or to take advantage of favorable ones.

For the great flotillas carrying the wealth of the New World to Spain, the port of Havana, Cuba, became a central staging area. As many as a hundred galleons, heavily laden with gold and silver, sailed together, often armed and under escort. Their route home led directly to the Florida Keys, an area claiming more Spanish shipwrecks than any other location in the Western Hemisphere. After sighting and sheering away from the Keys, they made for the Bahama Channel and another series of obstacles. This channel, being no narrower than fifty miles at any point, would in later years encourage prudent navigators to steer directly up its center, but sailing directions in the seventeenth century called for a pilot to keep in sight as many known points of land as possible. Hence, a flotilla followed

Florida's east coast as far north as Cape Canaveral. After the ships passed the cape and veered eastward through the horse latitudes of Cancer, Bermuda became the next landmark, another graveyard for Spanish treasure ships, and after that the Azores, off the coast of Portugal. Had the flotillas followed Columbus's sailing directions and, after passing Cape Canaveral, sailed a few miles north of Cape Hatteras before tackling the Atlantic, they would have avoided a band of variable calms and contrary winds and picked up westerlies that would have carried them straight to Cadiz. In the centuries before the discovery of reliable chronometers, using landmarks to establish position took precedence over speed.

Barely a year passed without major catastrophes, and on each occasion the disaster involved weather, winds, currents, or a landmark. In 1733, two hundred and thirty-eight years after Admiral Torres lost his flotilla off Hispaniola, a descendant, Don Rodrigo de Torres, set sail from Havana with twenty-two vessels laden with gold, silver, and Chinese porcelain. Following the prescribed route, Torres sailed for the Florida Keys in the face of a brisk north wind. On reaching the Keys, he signaled the flotilla to stand for the Bahama Channel, but the wind suddenly shifted to a strong southerly, driving every vessel under Torres's command onto shoals lying between Key Biscayne and Vaca Key. Had Torres sailed directly into the Gulf Stream, he might not have escaped the storm, but once in the powerful north-flowing current his ships would have been in deep water with options before them.

In 1715 Captain-General Don Juan Estaban de Ubilla experienced no better luck in the Bahama Channel. Sailing from Havana on July 24 and following charts developed over a period of two hundred years, Ubilla passed the Florida Keys and headed into the channel. Instead of passing up the center and using the strong Gulf Stream current to speed his passage, he hugged the coast of Florida. A fierce storm struck the flotilla and wrecked all but one vessel, spewing 6,388,020 pesos among the sands and taking a thousand lives, among them Ubilla's.

After other nations began to settle in the New World, Spain began to look for other routes, not because of improved navigation but because of a different threat: fierce competition from other colonizing nations and an increase in piracy.

Eighteenth-century shipmasters guided their courses by a practice known as *latitude sailing*. They followed a certain latitude until they sighted a known landmark and fixed their position, and sailed either north or south to reach the next latitude of choice. They would then sail the new latitude, searching for another landmark and fixing the distance traveled by dropping a log overboard—by using a sand glass to measure time and a knotted rope (hence "knots") on a reel to measure distance, a navigator could calculate the speed of the ship before retrieving the log. As their understanding of the doldrums and trade winds increased, they sought latitudes with favorable winds without always finding them. The Portuguese called the fair winds "trades," because the breeze was so reliable in strength and direction that trade could be built upon its sure help in transporting goods.

Though latitude was ascertainable, the typical navigator could not fix latitude or longitude exactly because instruments were not sufficiently reliable, and lunar and celestial tables, as they became available, were beyond the comprehension of the average sailor and not always accurate.

Every time a ship went to sea, the crew gambled with the vagaries of the weather, never certain if they would see another sunrise. They zigzagged across the seas, following the parallels, and as long as the sun peeked through the clouds at the meridian, the stars twinkled at night, or a sliver of moon slid across the midnight skies, a good navigator could estimate—but not determine with certainty—the latitude of his ship.

Storms, however, often obstructed observations, blanketing the heavens with clouds, dropping torrents of rain, and pitching the vessel through towering seas. Fierce winds ripped sails to shreds, snapped masts, tore spars from aloft, and tumbled men into the froth below. For endless days and nights, ships bobbed about under short sail or no sail, carried by winds and currents in unwanted directions—sometimes into reefs, bars, or rocky outcroppings—never to be seen again.

※

IN 1765, one of the world's shorter trading voyages began off Sandy Hook, New Jersey, and ended at Fayal in the Azores. For *Peggy*, a typical sloop of the day, the voyage lasted forty days. By taking advantage of the well-known westerlies, the same that carried Columbus home from the New World in 1492, David Harrison, *Peggy*'s skipper, made the crossing in average time. There he loaded a cargo of wine and brandy, and on October 24 he sailed for home, never anticipating that the story of his eventual deliverance would one day be woven into a lurid novel by Edgar Allen Poe, *The Narrative of Arthur Gordon Pym.*

Had Harrison understood the clockwise pattern of the winds and currents in the North Atlantic, he might have first sailed a distance to the south, picked up the easterly trades, and enjoyed a fine voyage home. Instead, he waited at Fayal for the occasional southeasterly wind and returned by his outbound route, following a reciprocal course. Perhaps he was ignorant of the easterly trades he could find below 25 degrees North, though that seems unlikely. More likely he begrudged having to drop eight hundred miles south to find those trades, latitude he would have to regain off the American coast, necessitating two transits of the windless horse latitudes and possibly doubling his passage length. Maybe he gambled that his close-winded sloop could buck the westerlies. Maybe, like most sailors of the day, he failed to appreciate how, during the fall and winter, the mid-latitude westerlies dropped farther to the south and strengthened into gales, which were the exact conditions into which *Peggy* sailed. In any case, his nearly fatal error would not have been made following publication of Maury's *Sailing Directions.*

Five days out, *Peggy* encountered gale-force westerlies that tore away the jib and forced Harrison to heave-to against the wind. A week later another squall ripped away two pairs of shrouds and swept them into the sea. Winds stiffening out of the west-northwest then carried away more shrouds and laid the vessel's head to the east-southeast. Unable to find favorable winds, *Peggy* continued to be pushed farther to the east. Harrison wrote, "In this situation, we lay to, as before, under a ballanced [sic] reefed main-sail, the impetuosity of the storm still continuing, and the seas rolling mountains high, all of us expecting that the vessel would prove leaky, as she strained inconceivably hard."

Peggy eventually began to make headway. On December 1, thirty-eight days out of Fayal, Harrison estimated his position at 40 degrees North latitude and 58 degrees West longitude, placing *Peggy* about eight hundred miles east of Sandy Hook and halfway home. Harrison could not have been certain of his longitude without sighting a landmark, so he guessed, as did most skippers of the day.

Harrison had planned for a forty-day voyage, and supplies began to run low when another storm struck and carried away the foresail, leaving only the mainsail. All other canvas had been shredded by the winds or swept away where it fell, so once again *Peggy* hove-to. With rations dwindling, the crew's allowance diminished to two pounds of bread a week, washed down daily by a quart of water and pint of wine. When the water gave out, the crew drank from the bilge, and when that turned their stomachs, they seized the cargo, guzzled wine and brandy, and stumbled about the decks in a drunken stupor. Assessing the dismal prospects for survival, Harrison wrote, "Little less than a miracle could save us from inevitable destruction."

On Christmas Day lookouts sighted an island and then a ship, but the captain of the unnamed vessel gave them only a small amount of bread. With seas running high, he could do little more, and not liking the cut of *Peggy*'s half-starved crew, he sped away. Neither Harrison nor the skipper of the other vessel recognized the island, and it would not have been improbable for *Peggy* to have drifted back among the Azores. After feasting on the ship's cat and speculating on where they were, the crew encountered strong southerlies that carried *Peggy* back up the Atlantic to a latitude of 42 degrees North, only to be struck once more by gales from the northwest that ripped the mainsail to pieces and caused the vessel to drift to the southeast.

Still somewhere at sea on January 13, the mate came to Harrison's cabin and in a drunken state declared that "they could hold out no longer . . . that they had eaten up all the leather belonging to the pump,—and even the buttons off their jackets, that now they had no chance in nature but to cast lots, and to sacrifice one of themselves for the preservation of the rest." For this, they wanted the captain's permission. Though he refused to participate, Harrison could no longer control the actions of his crew. The mate returned a short time later and informed the captain that they had drawn lots and that a slave, aboard as part of the cargo, would be executed and eaten. The black man appealed to Harrison for his life, but the crew hustled the frightened victim into the steerage and shot him through the head. Harrison's log suggests he witnessed this act or its immediate aftereffect:

> They suffered him to lye but a very little time before they ripped him open, intending to fry his entrails for supper, there being a large fire made ready for the purpose;—but one of the fore-mast men, whose name was John Campbell, being ravenously impatient for food, tore the liver from the body, and devoured it raw . . . not withstanding the fire at his hand where it could be immediately dressed. The unhappy man paid dear for such an extravagant impatience, for in three days he died raving mad, and was, the morning of his death, thrown overboard,—the survivors, greatly as they wished to preserve his body, being fearful of sharing his fate, if they ventured to make as free with him, as with the unfortunate negro.
>
> The black affording my people a luxurious banquet, they were busy the principal part of the night in feasting on him, and did not retire to rest till two in the morning.

After consuming all they could, the crew carved up the remains and pickled the pieces, serving them for several days as "stakes" fried or broiled with a variety of wines. Though suffering by then from scurvy, Harrison refused a "stake" and, having no influence with his crew, expected to be murdered and his carcass placed on the roasting spit.

Sure enough, in late January the mate returned to Harrison's cabin, grumbling that the "black" had been fully consumed and that the time had come to again draw lots for their next meal. Harrison suggested that prayer might serve their purposes better than murder. Scorning that advice, the crew threw Harrison's name into the hat but drew the name of David Flatt, a foremastman and the only man on board on whom the captain still placed a measure of confidence. Killing Flatt troubled them more than executing the slave, so they agreed to let him live until 11 o'clock the following morning.

As the hour approached, a lookout sighted a sail approaching, and the weakened crew, with great effort, managed to lower a boat and row in the direction of the vessel. Not until Thomas Evers of the ship *Susanna* rescued the crew of *Peggy* did David Harrison learn that he had drifted to within a few hundred miles of the coast of England. Even Evers, who had been tumbled about in a winter storm, could not be sure of his position until March 2, 1766, when he sighted Land's End on the southwestern tip of Cornwall.

After four months and nine days at sea, the *Peggy* reached Dartmouth. During the short trip to England, Harrison recovered, but the inconsiderate mate died from "wallowing . . . in every mire of excess." Driven "out of his senses" by the experience, Flatt raved about his imminent execution and seemed unable to comprehend that his life had been spared. Of *Peggy's* six survivors, only two remained capable of performing any duty whatsoever.

❧

FOR nearly two centuries, nations had been at work to reduce the perils of long voyages at sea. Philip III of Spain, after losing incalculable treasure to the vicissitudes of the weather, recognized that shorter and safer routes must be found, but to utilize them required an accurate means of determining a ship's position, and this meant calculating one's longitude. In 1598, Philip III offered a reward of a thousand crowns to whoever solved the problem. Other nations upped the ante. In 1714, England's Parliament put up the fantastic sum of £20,000, payable to anyone who could develop a "practicable and useful" means of determining longitude. Many methods were posited, some preposterous, such as carrying aboard ship a wounded dog that would supposedly yelp whenever someone at home dipped a cloth soaked in the dog's blood into a bath containing the "powder of sympathy." Time passed—170 years since Philip's offer and 47 years since Parliament's—before an unlikely Englishman solved the problem.

The uneducated woodworker John Harrison of Yorkshire (no relation to the skipper of *Peggy*) believed that longitude could be determined by knowing the exact time at an agreed-upon meridian (set at Greenwich, England) as well as aboard ship. The time difference between Greenwich and the ship could be converted to distance measurable in degrees and miles. To match the times, however, only a good clock would do. In 1761,

Harrison perfected a reliable timepiece, later known as a chronometer, at a cost of £450. Harrison endured a great deal of cynicism as well as down-right prejudice from royal astronomers, who claimed to be the ruling authority on navigation, but eventually King George II awarded him the prize.

Five years later, Pierre Le Roy, the great French clockmaker, developed a design that became the basis for future chronometers, but the parts of his clock had to be handcrafted and were not interchangeable. A few years after Le Roy's work, Thomas Earnshaw modified the mechanism and reduced the cost to £45. Though Harrison gets credit for the original design, navigators benefited most from the chronometers of Le Roy and Earnshaw.

❧

TWO years after the deliverance of the sloop *Peggy*, the age of modern navigation began to emerge. During the years between 1768 and 1779, Captain James Cook undertook his voyages of discovery. Supported by England's scientific institutions, Cook became the first skipper to conduct systematic explorations at sea with the latest complement of navigational equipment, techniques, and knowledge. On his first voyage he carried a cumbersome astronomical clock, a "journeyman" clock, and a watch provided by the Astronomer Royal—but no chronometer. These devices, used together with the tediously complicated lunar distance method, enabled Cook to calculate longitude. He carried four chronometers on his second voyage, and though only the one built on Harrison's model worked, it enabled him to navigate his vessels with a precision unimagined by Columbus, Magellan, or, more recently, David Harrison of *Peggy*. During his third and final expedition between 1776 and 1780, while many of his fellow officers were engaged in the American Revolution, Cook traversed five oceans in HMS *Resolution*. Though he himself was killed in the Sandwich Islands (later the Hawaiian Islands) in 1779 in a petty altercation with islanders, his ship established a record for the longest sailing voyage ever made. For sailing master and navigator on that final voyage he chose twenty-two-year-old William Bligh, a man destined to become a subject of both fame and infamy, depending upon whether one accepts the judgment of the Royal Navy or relies on the classic *Bounty Trilogy* by Charles Nordhoff and James N. Hall.

At the time of Cook's explorations, astronomers had greatly advanced the science of navigation, though for most seafarers it still remained a rudimentary art. England published the first nautical almanac, sailing charts improved, and as scientists learned more about magnetic variation, compasses could be rectified at sea. Schools began using textbooks written to simplify the mathematics of navigation. And finally, accurate chronometers could be produced at prices that a few wealthy merchants could afford. By the time Bligh took command of *Bounty* in 1787, chronometers made by Kendall had shrunk in size to that of a large pocket watch.

In late December, Lieutenant Bligh sailed for the Society Islands (Tahiti) in the South Pacific on a mission to gather and transport breadfruit seedlings from Tahiti to the West Indies. There the transplanted trees would be developed as a cheap nutritional source for thousands of starving plantation slaves whose main source of food from America had been shut off by the Revolution. For the voyage, the Royal Navy purchased a rather small 215-ton ship, only ninety-one feet long on deck, and before turning HMS *Bounty* over to Bligh, they reduced the accommodations for the crew by modifying the decks to carry, greenhouse style, a thousand pots of young breadfruit plants.

Because of the urgency of the mission, the British Admiralty ordered Bligh to take *Bounty* around South America's Cape Horn, being thirteen hundred miles shorter than the Cape of Good Hope route around Africa. If Bligh experienced difficulty rounding the Horn, however, which would force him to beat to windward against the westerly gales of the "Roaring Forties" and "Furious Fifties," he had the Admiralty's approval to turn about and take the longer route. More than sixty years would pass before a lieutenant in the U.S. Naval Observatory, Matthew Fontaine Maury, explained to the Admiralty why the shortest route sometimes took the longest sailing time.

For instruments, Bligh took a Kendall chronometer, a sextant, charts, tables, and a recent copy of the *Nautical Almanac*. But Bligh had never been around the Horn, Captain Cook having chosen the Cape of Good

Hope for both the outward and homeward legs of the voyage he did not live to complete.

Charts and sailing directions for mastering Cape Horn were at best sketchy. Fifty years had passed since British Captain George Anson attempted to take seven ships around the Horn, and the miseries he experienced stuck in Bligh's mind. After two months of fighting storms, gales blew two of Anson's vessels back into the Atlantic, and he returned home. A third vessel wrecked, and four finally crossed into the Pacific, but at a huge cost in human life. On March 21, 1788, Bligh got his first look at Cape Horn's terrors while off the Strait of Magellan. A gale struck with sudden and unexpected force. Seas became mountains, and the atmosphere turned ice cold. Bligh continued south, working around Staten Island off the tip of Tierra del Fuego, but he could not make a westing. The deeper south he sailed, the worse the weather became. Snow fell, ice encrusted the rigging, and heavy seas poured over the decks. Sailors, their hands cut and bleeding, could not move about topside without holding onto a rope.

When Bligh reached a point 79 degrees West and 62 degrees South, he had driven *Bounty* beneath the Shetland Islands, crossed through the Furious Fifties, and come to the same latitude as the tip of Antarctica's Palmer Peninsula. He still could find no wind to carry him into the Pacific. Mindful of Anson's experiences, Bligh came about, picked up the Roaring Forties, stopped at the Cape of Good Hope for supplies, and continued his journey east to Tahiti. With the weather stacked against him at the Horn, Bligh reasoned that nobody should ever take that route if a better option existed. He had unknowingly sailed hundreds of miles too far to the south. Had he been told that Cape Horn would be conquered in ten days by the sailing ships of 1850, he probably would not have believed it.

Later, following the mutiny aboard *Bounty*, Bligh and eighteen others were deposited in a twenty-three-foot open boat in the middle of the Pacific. The mutineers never expected to see them again. They forgot about Bligh's exceptional skill as a navigator. With his chronometer and sextant, he took advantage of the easterly trades he remembered from his days of sailing with Cook. He led the boat through mostly uncharted waters until, after seven weeks at sea, he reached the tiny Dutch island of Timor, four thousand miles away. Bligh knew that if he sailed east in an attempt to reach Tahiti, a mere five hundred miles upwind, the trades would blow in his face and stop him in his tracks, so he sailed west, a desperate but smart move.

❀

THOUGH few commercial vessels could afford them, chronometers radically reduced the problems of finding a ship's position at sea. Old ways, however, changed slowly, even in the navies of Europe where chronometers first found homes. Not until 1795 did the British Admiralty form a hydrographic department to deal with the problem of reducing the bulkiness of what had become hundreds of old charts and sailing directions, such as those carried by Bligh on *Bounty*. By the beginning of the nineteenth century, ships could fix their positions at sea provided their owners could afford to purchase a chronometer—and too few of them could or did.

In 1790 the ship *Massachusetts*, the largest and best-equipped American merchantman of the day, did not carry a chronometer. With all her folios of charts and sailing directions, she missed Java Head in the East Indies. The vessel wandered about for three weeks lost at sea because, as one sailor recalled, "of our not having a chronometer on board, or any officer who knew anything about lunar observations."

But even if one had a chronometer, without accurate charts and sailing directions, astronomical tables, instruments for measuring distance and location, and manuals such as the British *Nautical Almanac*, the mariner was still left in a fallback position of dead reckoning, little better off than Spanish captains like Torres who wrecked their flotillas on the hazardous outcroppings of the New World.

Outcroppings were not the only problem, nor were hurricanes. Between the Bahamas and the Azores, bounded by the Gulf Stream and the North Equatorial Current in the horse latitudes of the North Atlantic, floated the weed-strewn waters of the windless Sargasso Sea. Once caught in the grip of this carpet of floating vegetation, according to lore a ship's hull could sprout grass and barnacles, and the borer worm of tropic waters would riddle its undersides.

When the American Revolution ended in 1783, Europeans dominated ocean trade, and their sailing vessels paid regular visits to the ports of the world. Two years later, 1,347 vessels sailed from Europe to the Western Hemisphere, attesting to the development of broader markets. America's vast forests of prime timber, coupled with a huge demand for foreign goods, lured merchants once grounded by war back into the carrying trade. Shipbuilders went to work replacing vessels destroyed during the war, and traders soon reestablished their import-export connections around the world. By the turn of the century, competition between American carriers and those of other nations began to have a telling effect upon the commerce of the world. Cost cutting became an important consideration when competing for cargoes in international markets. No two factors became more important to reducing costs than speed of delivery and the assurance that a shipmaster would reach his destination safely.

Independence not only brought the United States to the forefront of maritime commerce, it encouraged the scientific minds of the country to advance the knowledge of navigation.

Scientific advances seldom occur in quantum leaps, however. Two hundred years had been invested in the development of a chronometer. Once sailors could fix longitude, many thought the mariner's greatest problem would be solved, but captains had developed bad habits in their years of sailing by dead reckoning, and it would be many years before most merchantmen could afford to purchase the expensive chronometer and take the time to learn its use.

In the late 1790s, a young Salem man by the name of Nathaniel Bowditch was already at work on a remedy, but his would be only a swipe at the problem. Bowditch discovered many errors in the standard navigation texts of the day—John Hamilton Moore's *The Practical Navigator and Seaman's New Daily Assistant*, John Robertson's *Elements of Navigation*, and the *Requisite Tables* of Dr. Nevil Maskelyne's celestial work as Astronomer Royal at Greenwich, England—books issued to every ship of the Royal Navy. Bowditch corrected his predecessors' mistakes and published several editions of his own nautical text, *The New American Practical Navigator*, the first in 1802. His simplified approach to navigation became the new international standard. Worked with a chronometer, his tables pinpointed a ship's location at sea. Even without a chronometer, a mariner could shoot his position with some accuracy. More than 850,000 copies were printed in more than seventy editions, and in the early 1800s, Bowditch's text became the navigator's bible for the United States Navy. "Notwithstanding the work of Bowditch," historian Samuel Eliot Morison observed, "it took a generation or more to wean most . . . shipmasters from their dependence on dead reckoning, in which primitive method, they were adepts."

To satisfy the practical needs of the navigator required more than weaning, as Captain David Porter learned when he attempted to round Cape Horn in the frigate *Essex* during the War of 1812. Porter sailed with Bowditch's *Practical Navigator* and a chronometer, but neither helped him get to his destination—the west coast of South America—in good time. He followed the old conventional track south, crossing the Atlantic eastward to the Cape Verde Islands to pick up trade winds that would carry the *Essex* to Brazil, but the route compelled him to cross the Atlantic twice to get to Rio de Janeiro—the same circuitous route followed by just about every American sailor of the day. After failing to locate the squadron's flagship *Constitution* at a predetermined rendezvous, Porter set a heading for Cape Horn. His alternate orders directed him to enter the South Pacific and destroy the British whaling fleet.

No reliable directions existed for rounding Cape Horn, and for the passage skippers relied on their sailing skills. During the southern summer, usually a bad season of the year for tackling the Horn, Porter headed for the Strait of Le Maire off the tip of Argentina. Battered by contrary gales and immobilized by intermittent calms, Porter did not have the option to turn back, as did Bligh, so he struggled for nearly six weeks before reaching the Pacific. During one storm, a towering sea stove in the ports from the bow to the quarter, drove the weather quarter boat onto the wheel, took the lee boat off her davits, and sent tons of water pouring through the hatchways and flooding into the lower deck, causing the frigate to wallow in seas running mast-high. "This was the only instance," Midshipman David Glasgow Farragut recalled, "in which I ever saw a regular good seaman paralyzed by fear." Porter did not know that by pressing a bit further into the South Atlantic—but not as far as Bligh—he would find better winds and weather, and with no more than average luck, round the Horn in ten to fourteen days.

Neither the chronometer nor Bowditch's *Practical Navigator*, nor all the nautical science then on record, addressed Porter's problems—or those of any other mariner—when sailing the Atlantic, rounding Cape Horn, and finding the most favorable winds and currents for setting a course up the western side of South America. A chronometer could help sailors mark their position, but it could not tell them where to find the best winds to speed them on their journey. For more than three hundred years seafarers had crossed the doldrums and the horse latitudes, discovered the Roaring Forties, the trade winds, and become conscious of the sea's currents, but they never unified or condensed the knowledge in a useful manner.

Fifty years would pass before another scientist, Matthew Fontaine Maury of the United States Navy, began closing the final chapters in a search for nautical knowledge that spanned more than six thousand years.

Chapter Two

THE LURE OF THE SEA

ON January 14, 1806, on Richard Maury's four-hundred-acre farm west of Fredericksburg, Virginia, Diana Minor Maury gave birth to the seventh of the family's nine children. They named him after distinguished ancestors and prosperous relatives—Matthew Fontaine Maury—a good French name from Huguenot forebears.

The Maurys who brought Matthew into the world were neither sophisticated, wealthy, nor sailors, but through three hundred years the Maury family carried the proud heritage of being descended from Jean de la Fontaine, an officer who served under Francis I, Francis II, and Henry II and during the minority of Charles IX.

The Fontaines began falling on harder times when in 1535 Jean decided to shed his Roman Catholic faith and become a Protestant. Each generation that followed found life in France increasingly uncomfortable.

In 1694, James Fontaine moved his family to Ireland and established a profitable fishing business. The work put a little salt water into his sons' blood. They were, however, harried by French privateers who took special pleasure in attacking Huguenots, so in 1715 James's son John Fontaine journeyed to America to purchase a tract for the family in Virginia. A year later his sister Mary Anne married Matthew Maury in Dublin. In 1719 the two newlyweds, who would become the great-grandparents of Matthew Fontaine Maury, arrived in Virginia with their son, James. They settled

[23]

near Fredericksburg, built a beautiful plantation home, and named it "Fontainebleu."

James Maury, Matthew's paternal grandfather, became a highly regarded clergyman, possessed of a vibrant personality and an eager interest in all natural phenomena. Well versed in Latin and Greek, he founded in Virginia a small school for boys, where Thomas Jefferson began his education. Another boarder, James Madison, cousin of the future president of the same name, later would himself become president of William and Mary College.

Reverend James Maury proposed uses for the coal found in the earth of Virginia. The opening of the Mississippi River intrigued him, as did questions concerning another great river in the West, the hitherto unexplored Missouri. It is quite possible that James Maury first inspired Thomas Jefferson to consider the expedition that would become the journey of Lewis and Clark and the Corps of Discovery to the West Coast in 1804–6.

In attempting to resolve a more practical matter, James Maury became plaintiff in the famous Parson's Cause case, in which he sought to have his back wages as clergyman of the Anglican Church paid in tobacco, as stipulated by royal laws of the colony. As it happened, the price of tobacco had risen substantially, which made local officials reluctant to honor the agreement. Also, a movement by a group called the Dissenters advocated a break with the Anglican Church. They sought a change in the law, paying clergymen twopence in lieu of tobacco. James Maury sued. For their defense lawyer, the parish hired attorney Patrick Henry, who later achieved prominence in the American fight for independence. (It was Henry who exhorted the Virginia militia against the British army with the rousing refrain, "Give me liberty or give me death!") Though James Maury lost his case, his excellent character preserved his good reputation. In fact, Henry later apologized to Maury for words said in court.

Matthew's maternal ancestors—planters and justices of the court—were equally successful. The Minor roots reached back to a Dutch sea captain. In the mid-seventeenth century Maindort Doodes took an interest in Virginia and gave up being a shipmaster to become a planter. During the family's Anglicization in Virginia, Maindort's son's name became Doodes Minor. Through successive generations the energetic Minors evolved into wealthy planters, excellent administrators, and community leaders. Matthew's maternal grandfather, Major John Minor, fought in the war for independence. In Diana Minor's blood ran gifts of judgment and administrative ability—gifts she could pass to her children but not her husband.

Fortune did not smile so lovingly on Richard Maury, the twelfth of thirteen children born to the Reverend James Maury and his wife Mary Walker. Despite being a likable, God-fearing, good-looking fellow, he would never become a success. His father died when he was only three, leaving the family with no funds for his education. Having few other choices open to him, he became a plantation overseer. The great quest for knowledge and personal success so strong among his predecessors seemed to have skipped over Richard, but through young Matthew's blood coursed the intellect of the Maurys and the wisdom of the Minors, blending together into a special genius Richard and Diana passed to their son.

That Richard Maury did not prosper as a farmer became an embarrassment to him and his wife. The Maurys owned poor land (bought in 1797 from Henry "Light-Horse Harry" Lee—a friend of George Washington, and the father of Robert E. Lee, who helped suppress the Whiskey Rebellion of 1794) and lacked the funds to improve it. The land would not yield to him no matter what uses he sought of it. As biographer Patricia Jahns discovered, neighbors remembered Matthew's father mainly "for the volume and carrying quality of his voice; he could be heard yelling at his slaves from a mile away." Richard Maury also exerted a firm grip over his wife and family, because farming poor land left no allowance for luxuries.

For a boy like Matthew, being born on a farm in the early 1800s usually meant spending one's life wedded to the soil. But Matthew was no ordinary boy.

Events leading to the War of 1812 enraged all Virginians, and the Maurys joined the hue and cry against the British seizure of American shipping and the impressments of sailors. Such intrusions by the Royal Navy represented acts of war, and the Virginian who would become the fourth president of the United States, James Madison, who grew up in nearby King George County, thought so, too.

Being too young to comprehend his parents' heady discussions over politics, Matthew listened instead to his older brother John, who being ten years his senior provided the best family source on worldly affairs. John demonstrated a wave of patriotic ardor after British marines from the frigate HMS *Leopard* boarded USS *Chesapeake* off Hampton Roads, Virginia, on June 22, 1807, and declared four sailors British deserters. The *Leopard* carried the four men to Halifax, Nova Scotia, where British authorities hanged two of them. His Majesty's government, then at war with France and in desperate need to fill their crews, blatantly ignored the forthcoming American protest and issued general orders instructing their captains to accelerate their impressments of American sailors. Outraged, John stomped about the farm, vowing to take action. Matthew might never have been lured to the sea had his thirteen-year-old brother not received an appointment in 1809 to join the United States Navy as an acting midshipman. John's decision distressed his parents, but Matthew dearly wished he had been old enough to go with him.

Richard Maury worked the farm for thirteen years before he decided that if he owned all the slaves in Virginia, he could not make his acres pay. During the course of those years he changed from the happy, genial young man that Diana Minor had married to a disillusioned and grumpy farmer beleaguered by debts and a growing number of children, all of whom he intended to cultivate into farmhands.

Other members of the clan had already moved west, and when Richard Maury's tobacco crop failed in 1810, cousin Abram and brother Philip urged him to sell the Virginia farm and join them in central Tennessee. After settling debts from the sale of the farm, Richard Maury cleared less than $300. He packed the family in a Conestoga wagon and resettled near the crossroad village of Franklin, a few miles south of Nashville, where he once again began to farm. In the early nineteenth century, Tennessee represented the western frontier of the young nation. The University of Tennessee had just recently been established in Knoxville in 1794.

At the age of five, young Matt, as his family called him, listened in wonderment to the reading of his brother's letters. Midshipman John spun dreams of a sea Matt had never seen—a sea where great ships sailed under billowing clouds of canvas and where frothy white-topped waves crashed against the bow and washed the decks with the sharp sting of salt spray. Matt learned of a sea of mighty storms and tropical nights, and of faraway exotic ports. To a young boy already indoctrinated in the endless and dreary routine of drawing water, feeding chickens, milking cows, slopping hogs, hoeing corn, picking beans, chopping wood, memorizing the Bible, and listening to the stentorian voice of his father bellowing orders from the door of the barn, John's letters offered a different, more expansive world. As Matt grew older, the drudgery of farm work only grew more tiresome, building him physically but suppressing him mentally.

Soon after the Maurys settled in Tennessee, older brother Dick enrolled at the nearby "old field school," which provided elementary education for children of the area. Matt pestered his father until the family put enough cash aside to enable him to join Dick at the schoolhouse. The speed with which book-hungry Matt consumed knowledge amazed the schoolmaster. Though merely introduced to the most elementary rudiments of an education, Matt found his intellect awakened to every detail of life around him. When not at school or barred by chores, he and Dick often slipped away from the farm to roam the fields and woods. There they studied wildlife or lay on their backs to watch the clouds roll by. They predicted the weather as each season passed and, during the hot days of summer, skinny-dipped in the West Harpeth River.

Late in 1811 a letter arrived from John, now sixteen, who had been serving on the frigate *United States*. He had secured a furlough through a family friend, Lieutenant William Lewis, but chose not to come home. In those days, an officer drew half-pay while ashore, and one never knew if or when orders would come for another chance at active sea duty. So, like many junior naval officers on leave, John instead accepted the first attractive offer to come his way: a first officer's berth on the three-hundred-ton *Pennsylvania Packet*, a merchant ship armed with six small guns and manned by a crew of twenty-five. Lewis commanded the vessel and intended to take it on a trading voyage to China. Though the Maurys were proud of John, the news also worried them. With war in the air, John would be far from home and out of touch. Six months later their fears intensified when President James Madison precipitously declared war on Great Britain in what advocates called the "second war for independence." With little recourse but to wait and to trust John's fate to God, the Maury family prayed twice daily, early morning and evening.

Nothing fascinated Matt more than war news, but no word came from John. When the Maurys learned that Captain David Porter had sailed the thirty-two-gun frigate USS *Essex* around Cape Horn and into the South Pacific, they hoped to learn something of their son's whereabouts. Porter cruised off the western coast of South America and captured a number of British whalers, but two years passed before John emerged unexpectedly from an island in the South Pacific.

During the voyage to China, Lieutenant Lewis had stopped at the island of Nuku Hiva in the Marquesas and sent John ashore with a group of sailors to trade for a cargo of sandalwood. Lewis sailed on to China, promising to return. Months passed without any sign of *Pennsylvania Packet*. John gave up all hope of rescue.

Two rival tribes lived on the island, the Happas and the Typees. John became fast friends with the chief of the friendly Happas, but after losing several men to raids by the Typees, he no longer felt safe. In a desperate measure, the remaining sailors built a tree house for protection and took turns posting a guard. Months later a vessel appeared off the island flying the American flag. John and his crew dropped to the ground, dashed to the beach, shoved a canoe into the surf, and paddled out to the vessel. There they met an officer assigned to the ship from *Essex*, and from him John learned that this visiting ship had been captured as a prize by Captain Porter and that the country had been at war with Great Britain since 1812. As for *Pennsylvania Packet*, she had most likely been blockaded by the British in some port along the Chinese coast. Gaunt and bearded, John looked more like a deserter than an officer in the U.S. Navy. At last he succeeded in making his identity known, and when Porter finally sailed from Nuku Hiva, he named John Maury executive officer of *Essex Junior*, the fastest, largest, and best-armed vessel among the captain's many prizes. After two British warships forced Porter to surrender the *Essex* on March 28, 1814, off Valparaíso, Chile—two days before British and allied troops entered Paris and twelve days before Napoleon abdicated and was banished to Elba—the entire American crew received paroles and returned to New York in *Essex Junior*. The survivors included another Tennessean, Midshipman David Glasgow Farragut, who in 1862 would become the first rear admiral of the United States Navy.

During the summer of 1814, still some six months before war with Great Britain ended with the signing of a treaty at Ghent, Belgium, John received a brief leave. Five years had passed since he left home. He appeared on the doorstep dressed in the natty blue, gold-trimmed uniform of a lieutenant. With his family gathered round him, John commenced to spellbind his parents, brothers, and sisters with tales of his many adventures on the other side of the world. Matt pestered him to repeat his stories over and over, plying him with questions and redigesting every detail. When the visit ended, it continued to spawn far-off visions in the fertile mind of the eight-year-old boy. Matt decided the place to live life—to really live fully, with excitement and adventure—was at sea in the United States Navy, not on a farm in the backwoods of Tennessee.

Later that year, while Matthew relived his brother's experiences through maps and geography books, John joined Captain Thomas MacDonough's fleet on Lake Champlain, where the U.S. squadron captured the British flotilla. Prior to that time, Matt had never heard of the lake. The war ended in 1815 with Andrew Jackson's defeat of the British at New Orleans. Free of the war, John returned to Virginia and married their Uncle Fontaine's daughter Eliza. The newlyweds made their home in Fredericksburg and had two boys.

❧

SCIENTISTS seldom come from predictable backgrounds. They evolve from all walks of life, and just as some of the great scientific discoveries have been accidental, so have some of the great scientists. Mathematics often provides the stimulus that awakens latent genius. By a curious coincidence, Matt one day discovered x's and y's separated by arithmetic symbols scratched on the soles of shoes repaired by an elderly local cobbler. Determined to know what they meant, he asked the shoemaker, who replied that the characters were no mystery but a method for finding solutions to difficult problems.

Wanting to learn this arcane symbology—and wanting to learn more than the basic reading, writing, and arithmetic he had been taught at the old field school—Matt pleaded with his father to send him to Harpeth Academy, where Dick studied. Because of the expense, Richard Maury balked. With Dick at school he needed Matt's help on the farm. Disheartened by his father's refusal, Matt solved the problem quite literally by accident. He toppled forty-five feet from a tree, nearly bit off his tongue, and severely injured his back. For several weeks he lay in bed. The doctor ordered no more farm work until the boy recovered, which, he warned, could take several years. Relieved that their son would get better, the family began saving for his education. Perhaps as an incentive to speed his recovery, they told him he could start at the academy when well enough to ride a pony the six miles to school and back.

In 1818, at the age of twelve, Matt entered Harpeth Academy. Three capable teachers ran the school and taught Latin, Greek, and the classical sciences. Matt displayed a knack for learning foreign languages, but his interest soon shifted to such works as Hutton's *Mathematics*, Day's *Navigation*, and the *Elements of Ancient and Modern Geography*. Richard Maury's cousin, Abram Maury, one of the academy's trustees, lived near the academy and owned a small library filled with fascinating scientific titles. Instead of returning home for chores, Matt spent his time after school in cousin Abram's study, poring over maps of the world, the *Dictionary of Arts and Sciences*, Ferguson's *Astronomy*, Pinkerton's *Geography*, and other works of science. His comprehension of difficult scientific subjects advanced so rapidly that neither parent fully understood his supper table conversation.

When Maury reached the age of seventeen, he resumed the life of a farmer's son, spending part of each day doing chores. The injury to his back had healed, leaving him strong and robust again, but he never grew taller than five feet, six inches, and always blamed his height on the fall. His father expected him to remain in Tennessee to work the farm, but such plans did not coincide with the boy's hunger for more education. Matt's mother encouraged his efforts to learn. She had come from a family of great intellect and recognized the thirst for knowledge burning inside her son. Had it not been for her support, Matthew Fontaine Maury might always have been a farmer.

Elder brother John proved equally essential to Matthew's emancipation from the southern farmland. By 1823, at twenty-eight years of age, John Maury had become flag captain in Commodore Porter's pirate-chasing squadron in the West Indies—the youngest man of his rank and the most promising in the navy. His career had been a fourteen-year vicarious adventure for Matthew—the brightest star in his boyhood firmament, still beckoning with all its allure as he attained young manhood.

Matthew wished hard to escape the farming life and follow his brother John into military service. Like his grandfather, he fantasized about the myriad possibilities such a life offered for studying the fantastic physical world about him. Nothing could have prepared him, nor his parents, for the grim news that came on a midsummer's day. The family received official notice on June 23, 1824, that John, their twenty-eight-year-old son, had died of yellow fever while on the storeship *Decoy*. In those days the navy buried the dead at sea, and the grieving family were left with nothing but his memory.

The death of the family's eldest son struck Matthew's mother particularly hard, because she never wanted him to join the navy. Richard Maury's pride in his son quickly turned to inconsolable grief, and daily prayers took on a new and mightier meaning. Matt was heartbroken. How could a person so vigorous and alive as John be dead? The loss bit deeply. Matt began to imagine himself as a replacement for John, but how could he do that, consigned to a future of laboring on his parents' farm?

Apart from his mother, only two people understood Matt's burning desire for knowledge, James H. Otey at Harpeth Academy and William C. Hasbrouck, who in 1823 replaced Otey as principal. In the fall term that year, Hasbrouck mentored Matt, saw genius in the young man, and engaged him as a teaching assistant. Knowing Matt's aptitude for mathematics and science, Hasbrouck suggested he apply for an appointment to West Point, the military academy of the U.S. Army. Matt pondered the notion, not certain of the process. When he entered his final year at the academy in 1824, the suggestion took root, but the mere mention of it to his father produced an angry outburst of well-intentioned paternal disapproval. Richard Maury had already lost one son, and he did not want to risk the life of another. No more sons were to leave home for a career in the service. His final denouncement probably echoed across the fields and into the nearby meadows of his neighbors.

When Hasbrouck learned of Richard Maury's decree, he urged Matt to go to college instead. Matt took the proposal home and presented it as an alternative to West Point. His father flatly rejected the idea. Try as he might to understand his father, Matt deemed a life on the farm intolerable. After so many years together, the elder Maury had still not learned that suppressing his son only made him more determined; Matt would bear the cross of this righteous stubbornness throughout his life and adopt a little of the same for himself.

Casting aside any hope of help from his father, Matt conceived a plan. He would not go against his father's wishes by applying to West Point, which had been the central issue discussed at the supper table. Instead, he would follow in the footsteps of his brother and seek entry into the navy. Why he thought his father would feel better about a different branch of the service is difficult to understand. To cousin Rutson Maury, Matt confidentially wrote, "My Dad and Mom say I shall not go; but you can guess whether I will or not. I am as determined as ever for you to know I always intended going." With those words, one might wonder whether all the concentration on West Point had been merely a deception on Matt's part to hide his true interest and join the navy.

Without the knowledge of either parent, Matt wrote Congressman Sam Houston (whom he may have met at Abram Maury's house) asking for an appointment in the navy. The simply worded request contained no endorsement by a distinguished citizen or any evidence of political contrivance. Houston took immediate interest in Maury's background, finding it similar to his own. Matthew had no doubt his application would be accepted, and when a letter arrived with the conspicuous heading, "Washington, D.C., February 1, 1825," he knew what it contained: acceptance in the United States Navy as an acting midshipman. The joyous moment sank a bit when he faced the prospect of conveying the news to his parents. Richard Maury raged at his son's backhanded conspiracy, but Matt's mother, though she dreaded his going to sea, recognized that her nineteen-year-old son should not be averted from his chosen career. To a cousin, Matt wrote, "It disturbed the family very much and my father expressed his disapprobation of my conduct in strong terms. And, as I had proceeded without consulting him, he determined to leave me to my own resources."

If Richard Maury believed he could hold Matt at home by not supplying funds for the 750-mile trip to Washington, he did not understand the nature of his son. Matt took his problem to his friends, his relatives, and his teachers, and because his orders did not require that he report for duty immediately, he sent letters to anyone who might support him. With much effort, he finally scraped together the bare necessities for the trip, including an old mare borrowed from a neighbor to whom he promised to send seventy-five dollars the moment he sold her after reaching Washington. As for his lack of cash, he would have to make the trip without it. "The bitterist pang I felt on leaving home," Maury recalled, "was parting with my brother Dick, two years my senior. We two had hitherto been inseparable."

With barely a cent in his pocket, Matthew Maury rode into Franklin "intending to trust to luck." It came in the form of thirty dollars, which William Hasbrouck left for Matt at Harpeth Academy as a stipend for his help as a teacher's assistant. Then, still trusting to his luck, he took the road leading into east Tennessee. There he met two roving peddlers who, on hearing his story, took him in tow and crossed with him into Virginia. Traveling at a rate of twenty-five to thirty miles a day over the same route taken by his parents more than fourteen years before, Matt now had the opportunity to view in larger perspective the country in which he lived. As a sailor, he would not again see these fields and forests for many years.

The trip also gave him an opportunity to visit and get to know relatives he had not seen since his early childhood. Stopping in Spotsylvania County, Virginia, near the site of his birth, he visited the home of his father's sister, Elizabeth Herndon. She had taken in an orphaned niece and nephew, Ann Hull Herndon and Brodie Herndon, who filled the otherwise quiet home with fun and laughter. Though five years younger than

Matthew, Ann made quite an impression on him, and he on her. She thought him "very handsome with his wavy brown hair, highly colored cheeks, and alert blue eyes, often merry with laughter." Though rather short, he impressed her with his "broad square shoulders and a well-developed chest" and hands "small but powerful." When asked what she thought of him, Ann's eyes twinkled as she replied, "The young shepherd David straight from the fold." The visit to the Herndons' would not be Matthew's last. Indeed, the frustrated scholar also had within him the ardor of an impassioned suitor.

An early June mist blanketed the Potomac River on the morning of Matthew's arrival in Washington. After he disembarked from an overnight voyage on a steamboat—his inaugural trip afloat—he viewed for the first time the bustle of the nation's capital. In years to come, he would become a part of it.

To reach the Navy Department Matthew had to pass the recently rebuilt President's House, as people then called the White House, which had been destroyed by the British when they burned Washington during the War of 1812. Beyond it lay the Navy Department, a structure about 55 by 165 feet in size and identical to its next-door neighbor used by the army. During his recent stay with the Herndons he had learned that a cousin, Richard B. Maury, worked for the Navy Department. Richard B., soon to become the navy's registrar, took Matthew in tow and arranged an appointment with Secretary of the Navy Samuel L. Southard, who by his own order met all new midshipmen. Having studied Matthew's application, Southard conversed knowledgeably about his new midshipman's background. In those days, most midshipmen came from politically connected families, with whom a prudent secretary took pains to cultivate a good relationship. In accord with naval policy, he stated that Matthew would be reimbursed fifteen cents a mile for travel expenses. Matthew could not conceal his relief. The boat trip had drained his last cash. He quickly calculated that travel expenses came to a little more than one hundred dollars, enough to pay off his debts and hopefully fix him up with a fine set of regulation uniforms. The cost of good clothes, however, would cause him much dismay when the bill arrived.

Unfortunately, his navy pay of nineteen dollars a month, plus one ration a day, would not begin until assigned to a vessel, which marked the day he would officially become a member of the U.S. Navy. That is how the navy operated in the early nineteenth century—no base, no naval academy, and not much pay. All indoctrination and training took place aboard ship, and until a ship with officers became available to begin instilling sea knowledge, the government saw no point in paying its sailors.

During their meeting, Secretary Southard explained that after six months of service Maury would be elevated to midshipman. The arrangements sounded fine to him.

After meeting with Southard, Maury headed for the navy yard, located about one mile from the city on the Anacostia River, a tributary of the Potomac. There to his astonishment floated the largest and most graceful vessel he could imagine, the forty-four-gun frigate *Brandywine*, hauled alongside a dock to be fitted for sea. She measured 175 feet between the perpendiculars with a molded beam of 45 feet, depth in hold of 14½ feet, and a rating of 1,726 tons displacement. She cost $825,000 to build and had been designated by President John Quincy Adams to take the sixty-eight-year-old Revolutionary War hero Marquis de Lafayette back to France following his celebratory tour of America. While waiting for orders in Washington, Maury stayed with his cousin, Richard B., but he visited the yard almost daily to witness the intricate work of rigging *Brandywine*. He watched as workmen hung the rudder and strung the ropes. Taking aside anyone who would explain the purpose of the work underway, he quickly grasped the essence of a large sailing ship and what made her run, but one question always led to another, for Maury had a lot to learn.

On July 9, 1825, a most important event occurred. A liver-colored envelope arrived containing Maury's orders: "Proceed to Washington and report to Capt. T. Tingey for duty on board the *Brandywine*." Maury could not have been happier. He had been handpicked for the cruise because, unlike other "young gentlemen of the steerage" who obtained their appointments through the influence of their parents, Maury had come to the navy through his own efforts. Nobody had worked to secure his appointment, though thanks to brother John the name "Maury" did not come without credentials in the navy. In that sense, John's memory remained fixed in his thoughts, and in the years to come would remain so in unexpected ways.

Now officially ordered to sea, Maury hurried to purchase his uniforms, the full dress and undress, a heavy coat for winter deck duty, an enormous pile of clothing for every occasion, and articles such as vests, collars, gold lace, brass buttons, cocked hats, half-boots, black cravats, and a double-edged sword for ripping open the body of an enemy. Other requisite items included a quadrant (the forerunner of the more expensive sextant, which evolved from the quadrant about 1757) and a copy of Bowditch's *New American Practical Navigator*, standard issue for all officers. The cost of the uniforms staggered the young midshipman, and he found himself in debt to the navy for the near equivalent of a year's pay.

On August 13, 1825, Maury waited his turn to board the frigate *Brandywine*, burnished bright in glossy black paint with a yellow stripe running from stem to stern across the gun ports. In addition to her rating of forty-four guns, the ship carried a small battery of carronades, short-chambered ordnance pieces of large caliber especially suited for fighting at close quarters. A gentle breeze blew the fresh smell of paint and tar to the boat coming alongside that carried Maury, twelve other midshipmen, seven officers, and a boatswain, all immaculately dressed for the occasion. While standing in the boat and waiting his turn to board the frigate, he made a vow to "make everything [in my life] bend to my profession." His would become a promise well kept, but not in the career he envisioned the day he stepped on board *Brandywine* to become a sailor.

Attired in his new uniform, Maury felt quite proud of himself, and his turn to board at last arrived. For the first time in his life he stood on the holystoned deck of an American frigate, a remarkable improvement from the old frigate *United States* on which his brother John once sailed. The strangeness of his adopted surroundings created a burden of new learning, but it also energized him with a remarkable feeling of release from the limitations of the past. Unimaginable opportunities lay before him. For Matthew Fontaine Maury, the future had begun.

Chapter Three

THE EDUCATION OF A SAILOR

FOR all Americans, the administration under James Monroe (1817–25) had become known as the Era of Good Feeling. In 1819 the nation acquired Florida, a year later Congress agreed on the Missouri Compromise, and in 1823 John Quincy Adams, then secretary of state, wrote the Monroe Doctrine, placing the Western Hemisphere under the guardianship of the United States. The "good feeling" came from the absence of any serious wars, and in such a peaceful setting Congress chose not to make big expenditures to perpetuate a larger-than-necessary navy.

In 1825, when Maury stepped onto the deck of *Brandywine*, the golden age of the fighting ships of the War of 1812 had long passed. The total fleet consisted of only seven ships of the line; six frigates, first class, including *Brandywine*; three frigates, second class; and a few sloops of war, schooners, a galliot, and several smaller vessels. For Maury, *Brandywine* became a special ship. He watched her being built, the newest ship in the navy, and she became the steppingstone to a new life, one he could not even begin to fathom.

Maury soon discovered that *Brandywine*, though a beautiful ship topside, emitted a nauseating odor below from stagnating bilgewater. No longer could he enjoy the fragrant smells of field and forest or the luxury of space, for his new home—the steerage—contained but two small portholes. Every occupant lived out of a wooden footlocker two feet square and slept in a hammock of hempen cloth. They shared with others two crude washstands and basins. Though designed for a sailing complement of eleven midshipmen, Southard had yielded to political pressure and during the last days before sailing added fourteen more midshipmen to Brandywine, not so much to honor Lafayette as to appease influential parents.

Maury easily made friends among his peers, most of whom were much younger than he. Lads such as fifteen-year-old Samuel Barron had already seen five years duty at sea. Having been appointed a midshipman at the age of two, Barron almost qualified as an "old salt." Under Barron's tutelage Maury quickly mastered shipboard terms and naval lingo, processes that included such simple but peculiar matters as learning to tell time by the ship's bell. Another midshipman and fellow Virginian, William F. Lynch, would become a friend for life. Maury got along well with all the young men and from each learned something about sailing. Though naval regulations stipulated that "The commanding officers will consider midshipmen as a class of officers, meriting in an especial degree their fostering care," it surprised Maury to learn that the gunner, boatswain, master's mate, sailing master, and even the ship's carpenter all outranked him.

Probably nobody on board could explain the navy's peculiar time clock. The ancient Egyptians and Phoenicians adopted the practice centuries ago by measuring time using a half-hour sand glass. After the sand trickled to the bottom, a ship's boy struck a gong and turned the glass, striking one for the first turning, two for the second, on up to eight, which became the seafarer's watch of four hours. The navy, which adopted the practice without the sand glass but with a bell, decided that the age-old system had merit and wrote it into their regulations. If Maury ever questioned the practice, which was likely, he probably never received the right answer.

With Lafayette soon to be on board, Maury and his fellow midshipmen received a crash course in shipboard behavior. At all times one had to show proper respect to all officers and obey all commands. The requirements reminded Maury of home, where his father had not permitted the questioning of an order and demanded his son's deference to persons older than himself. Little about the navy had changed that part of his life. Other activities, such as climbing the rigging, became no more torturous than scampering up trees in his father's woods. The risk of falling remained about the same, and Maury still remembered his first scrape with death. But the basic elements of handling the ship, taking battle stations, and working the guns presented a new and challenging study all in itself. Not until August 14 did *Brandywine* weigh anchor to drop down the Potomac to a new anchorage where the river emptied into the Chesapeake Bay. By then Maury had mastered a few rudiments for handling a ship, but with actual sailing yet to come.

On September 5, 1825, Captain Charles Morris came on board to take charge of the frigate, which had already become another world of new experiences for Matthew Maury. Here he found all the rudiments of sailing—everything from charts to lunar tables with tidal data, and dates of eclipses. Copies of the British Admiralty's *Nautical Almanac* contained astronomical projections for the next three years so a navigator, anywhere on the globe, could determine his latitude and longitude through the sun, moon, or stationary celestial objects such as the North Star or the Southern Cross.

But for the moment the midshipmen concentrated on the distinguished captain, who had been the first among U.S. naval hero Stephen Decatur's boarding party to destroy USS *Philadelphia* after she had been captured off Tripoli by Bey Yusef's corsairs and imprisoned in the city.

On September 8 Maury first heard the roar of a ship's cannon when a detail of sailors rowed General Lafayette out to *Brandywine*. The seventeen-gun salute shook the decks, rattled the spars, and sent a cloud of smoke across the water. With great care, sailors helped the elderly general into a boatswain's chair. Others hauled him gently over the rail and placed him before Captain Morris, who gave Lafayette a salute as he came aboard. Secretary Southard came on board using the same conveyance, and for the next six hours the entire crew mixed with dozens of guests for a highly festive celebration. At 4:30 P.M. the secretary departed, followed by another seventeen-gun salute. The party ended and the cleanup began.

At dawn the following morning *Brandywine* weighed anchor. With every sail drawing, she stood down the Chesapeake, spurred on by a stiff north wind. Once outbound, the frigate pounded through heavy seas. By morning, officers discovered the mystery of the stinking bilge. A leak at the waterline required a work detail to jettison two thousand pounds of iron shot in order to float the ship high enough for carpenters to make repairs. The sickening odor of stagnant bilgewater soon cleared, only to be replaced by an equally foul smell.

Once at sea, Maury shared a common indisposition with the vessel's illustrious General Lafayette—the curse of seasickness. Before long, the malady attacked all the neophytes. Spray washed over the deck above, flooded the forward cabin, and showered down into the steerage. Maury could never remember being so sick, but if he had any regrets about joining the navy, the time to swim for shore had passed.

Maury's first voyage became as much a study of *Brandywine*'s captain as a training in gunnery or the process of scrambling aloft to reef the topsails. He observed that a U.S. naval officer in command of a vessel must be as adept at exercising diplomatic skills as he is at fighting his man o'war. A captain must also be kept informed of the constant changes in policy and protocol when dealing with European powers in order to fire appropriate salutes and avoid any act of discourtesy, no matter how innocent. Lieutenant David Farragut, who later would capture New Orleans during the Civil War (and be remembered for shouting, "Damn the torpedoes. Full speed ahead!" while leading his squadron into Mobile Bay), went ashore at Le Havre to clear the way for the general's return. The *Brandywine* exchanged salutes of twenty-one guns with the port's batteries. Captain Morris and Captain George C. Read accompanied Lafayette ashore, leaving the vessel under the command of the executive officer, Lieutenant Francis H. Gregory. While Morris and Read toured France, Gregory and *Brandywine* sailed for the Mediterranean. After their distinguished guest departed, the midshipmen got down to the more serious business of sailing.

Maury set his sights on becoming a navigator. Having studied Bowditch's *Practical Navigator* during the voyage to France, he found certain parts of the booklet vague and unable to answer the growing number of questions rambling through his thoughts. Bowditch did all the celestial mathematics for the shipmaster, but for the calculations to work well, the navigator had to know his latitude, know the accurate time, and be able to accurately shoot the sun, moon, or stars with a sextant. With that, the navigator had the basis for fixing his longitude . . . if he understood how to use Bowditch's tables. To reach that level of knowledge, a sailor required hands-on instruction from an experienced seaman, and most seafarers during Maury's time were not well educated.

Concluding that Bowditch's work, though helpful, lacked certain information important to navigators, Maury looked for other sources. During a brief trip ashore in England he acquired from a bookstore in Cowes a secondhand copy of Norie's *Epitome of Navigation*, which he carried back to the ship to study. The shouting, singing, and wrestling of fellow midshipmen in the steerage made it difficult to concentrate, but Maury blocked out the noise and went to work. After digesting the contents of both volumes and finding many contradictions, he concluded that a better system for navigation must be devised if shipwrecks were to be prevented.

From Sailing Master Elisha Peck, Maury learned the basic elements of navigation; from the boatswain, seamanship; and from the gunner, ordnance. Eight hours a day he stood watch, and he spent another two performing routine shipboard drills and exercises. Instruction for the midshipmen did not always conform to any logical or consistent standard. George Jones, a young civilian assigned to the ship as the midshipmen's schoolmaster, dolefully recalled, "We had a school in the *Brandywine* and the forward cabin for it . . . but its rules were not sufficiently strict and it did not amount to much. Larking," he added, "got the better of Bowditch and study."

Jones's task was to teach midshipmen navigation, but he questioned whether Bowditch's *Practical Navigator* worked as a textbook. "It is an excellent practical work, and does not pretend to more than this," he surmised, "but it is intended chiefly for Captains of merchantmen and he who uses it, wanders blindfolded through its labyrinths for there is little attempt at explanation except what is absolutely necessary." Maury had already read Bowditch and agreed with Jones that the methodology of navigation needed a better explanation to be understood by sailors. He also observed that getting an education in the navy fell far short of his expectations, but he remained hopeful.

Shore leave in the Mediterranean brought all efforts for study to a standstill. Captain Daniel Todd Patterson came on board to take command of the frigate and set all hands to putting the vessel in top shape. Jones abandoned efforts to hold school, moved ashore, and only came on board to report and collect his pay. Maury, however, continued to pursue his education. He studied privately, teaching himself navigation and, among other subjects, Spanish. He was disgusted by the absence of discipline and would later write, "The first ship I sailed in had a schoolmaster; a young man from Connecticut. He was well qualified and well disposed to teach navigation, but not having a schoolroom, or authority to assemble the midshipmen, the cruise passed off without the opportunity of organizing his school. From him, therefore, we learned nothing."

Maury made one observation that sparked his curiosity. Along the Spanish coast hundreds of vessels lay waiting for a brisk, favorable breeze that could carry them through the Strait of Gibraltar and back into the Atlantic. Asking a fellow officer why a ship needed so strong a breeze to work through a strait seven miles wide, he learned that sometimes a thousand sailing ships could be weather-bound for weeks on end because of a strong surface current that swept into the Mediterranean from the Atlantic. He then asked where all the water flowing into the Mediterranean went, and the officer could not tell him. If the constant inflow of water all evaporated, the Mediterranean would have become a vat of strong brine or cubic crystals millions of years ago. Many years would pass before Maury discovered the answer: for every surface current there is an undercurrent, and through the Strait of Gibraltar, that undercurrent flows back into the Atlantic several hundred feet below the surface current.

On February 21 Captain Read returned from his tour of France, relieved Captain Patterson, and made preparations to set sail for New York. *Brandywine* sailed from Gibraltar on March 8, and though the crossing was marked by a series of frontal gales, the midshipman rejoiced at the prospect of going home. Had *Brandywine* sailed for New York a bit farther to the south, she would have encountered more easterlies and fewer westerlies. But in 1826 such knowledge as "tracks in the sea" had not been well developed, much less recorded, even though mariners had been using trade winds for centuries. The person who would one day uncover nature's secret, however, now served on board his very first cruise, and the question of whether the sea contained natural courses would not excite his curiosity for another sixteen years.

Maury continued his efforts to learn anything new that lay within his grasp. "If I went below only a moment or two and could lay hands on a dictionary or any book, I would note a sentence, or even a word, that I did not understand, and fix it in my memory to be reflected on when I went on deck." Though the effort improved Maury's vocabulary, it fell short of providing the education he sought by joining the navy. His mind operated like an enormous absorption chamber that gave him no rest unless constantly engaged in the pursuit of knowledge.

On April 30, 1826, *Brandywine* anchored off the Brooklyn Navy Yard, where Maury received his official warrant making him a midshipman, dating from February 1, 1825. Always serious in matters of his career, Matthew wrote a letter of acceptance to Secretary of the Navy Samuel Southard. He then said good-bye to his friends and took the customary leave granted sailors returning to port from an extended cruise. He could not find time to make the long trip home to Tennessee, but nothing prevented him from going to Laurel Hill, Virginia, where he hoped to catch another glimpse of cousin Ann. She had never left his thoughts, but a five-year age difference impeded any notion of an open courtship. Though less than a year had passed, he found Ann blossoming into womanhood, which made her even more attractive.

On June 1 he returned to *Brandywine* in Brooklyn, and though short of cash, he spent his liberty hours watching ships being built in civilian yards. When the paymaster closed the ship's books at the end of June, Maury expected a few dollars, but none came. He had devoured his pay in rations, and the other half had been forwarded to his sister, so he passed the days walking among the shipyards girding the East River. The noisy work fascinated him, and his quick eye caught the elements of construction and the different design characteristics of vessels on the stocks. A short stroll down the waterfront brought him to the yard of Henry Eckford, who in 1820 had built the huge 750-ton *Robert Fulton*, the first ocean steamer. David Dunham and Company bought the experimental vessel and used her in the expanding trade between New York and Cuba, with intermediate stops at

New Orleans, Louisiana, and Charleston, South Carolina. After five years of trying, Dunham could not make the steamer pay. Passengers disliked the choking smoke that swept the decks, the immense racket created by the engine, and the frequent breakdowns. Five years later the company sold the steamer to Brazil. After trying to convert her to a warship, the Brazilian government removed the machinery and refitted the steamer as a second-class frigate. Poor sailing wrecked the vessel on the coast of Brazil. Another dozen years would pass before steamers began to make inroads into the ocean carrying trade, yet as Maury roamed among the shipyards strung along the East River, he spotted paddle wheelers under construction and envisioned a future of steam-driven ships of war.

A walk down Fourth Street to the East River brought him to the shipyard of Smith & Dimon. Old-style brigs and barks had given way to the construction of faster packet ships that carried mail and passengers on regular schedules. The shipyard buzzed with activity. In 1825, barely a year prior, Smith & Dimon had launched *Liberator*, a large double-decked forty-four-gun frigate built for Greek revolutionists seeking independence from Turkey, and the ship was still alongside the dock being fitted out. The Greeks could not pay for her, so the navy bought the vessel and renamed her *Hudson*. Maury had the good fortune to never sail on the frigate, because she had been built of poor timber and lasted one cruise. The same could not be said of Smith & Dimon's packet ships, which were among the finest afloat.

By 1826 New York had become a booming metropolis of two hundred thousand inhabitants, much of the growth due to its burgeoning commerce. Shipyards had sprung up all along the East River. David Brown and Jacob Bell owned a yard at the foot of Stanton Street, once a part of Henry Eckford's enterprise where famous sailing ships such as the *William Tell, Canada, John Jay, Congress*, and dozens of others had been built. Eckford soon engaged in steam technology, upon which Brown and Bell expanded; in 1840 they built the *Lion* and *Eagle*, the first two ships intended exclusively for transoceanic commerce. Finding no domestic buyers, they sold them to Spain for use as warships. In America, the early steamboats would operate only on inland and coastal waters until 1847, when the

The forty-four-gun frigate Brandywine *(foreground) in the Mediterranean with USS* Concord. *When nineteen-year-old Midshipman Matthew Fontaine Maury reported for duty aboard the newly built* Brandywine *in 1825, he vowed "to make everything [in my life] bend to my profession."*

The sloop-of-war USS Vincennes, *on which Midshipman Maury completed a four-year circumnavigation of the world in 1830.*

The Smith & Dimon Shipyard on the East River, New York, at Fourth Street. This painting was done by James Pringle in 1833, seven years after twenty-year-old Maury roamed the East River yards.

Ocean Steam Navigation Company formed in New York and with two side-wheel steamers, *Washington* and *Herman*, began regular service between the United States and Europe.

Isaac Webb, the father of William H. Webb, who later became one of the great builders of clipper ships, operated a yard that extended along the waterfront from Fifth Street to Seventh Street. Maury could not walk along the East River without stopping at Webb's yard, which he found jammed with new construction. Every reputable builder had at least one packet ship—the precursor of the clipper ship—on the stocks, but there were also steamboats, men o'war, ferryboats, canal boats, yachts, schooners, and sloops all in various stages of construction.

During the weeks prior to leaving on his next cruise, Maury's time spent nosing about the shipyards became an education in itself. There he watched New York's contribution to building the nation's great fleet of commerce. And when he had nothing better to do, he walked down South Street, where shops sold navigational instruments. He recognized hundreds of those whose names he now knew: quadrants, compasses, chronometers, and barometers. He found articles he wanted to buy—a beautiful polished brass telescope in one shop, a brass trumpet for shouting commands in rough weather in another—but he had no money. On occasion he stumbled across something old or something different and assailed the storekeeper with a flurry of questions. He never closed his mind, and his capacity to fill it seemed infinite.

On board *Brandywine* the crew worked assiduously preparing the frigate for a three-year voyage to the Pacific Ocean. *Brandywine* would be the flagship of Captain Jacob Jones, who had orders to relieve Commodore Isaac Hull in command of the Pacific squadron. His mission was to maintain friendly diplomatic relations with the countries of South America and sustain a presence in the countries where Americans had established business relationships. Jones's service dated back to the early wars when he trained as an officer under Edward Preble. He remonstrated unsuccessfully against the Navy Department for crowding so many men onto his vessels, but the secretary did not have enough vessels to keep enough of his sailors at sea, so he squeezed them on board wherever he could.

Maury did not mind the crowding. When he read the muster roll for the cruise he discovered that many of his shipmates had been assigned to other vessels, but two good friends, William Irving and John Willis, would be with him. During the summer months the crew filled to overflowing, cramming 480 officers and men onto the frigate. Jones again complained, but the Navy Department remained adamant. When it reached the Pacific, *Brandywine* would relieve USS *United States*. *Vincennes*, commanded by Master Commandant William Bolton Finch, would relieve the sloop-of-war *Peacock*. After much delay, *Brandywine* finally headed for sea on September 3, 1826, and Maury, always anxious to get to underway, planned to use this second cruise as an opportunity to expand his knowledge of the sea.

He hoped to learn more about navigation from the frigate's new schoolmaster, Inocencia De Soto, but to his dismay he soon discovered that the instructor had been assigned to teach Spanish, not navigation. De Soto's methods proved so boring that nobody listened, and Maury came away having learned almost no Spanish from the inept schoolmaster, De Soto.

For Maury, the most impressive lesson came from the change of the latitudes and the role of the weather. He noticed the way the air became humid as the ship approached the equator, and how after passing it and sailing south, it again freshened and became rarefied and stimulating. The heavens at night took on a startlingly different character. The North Star dropped behind the Earth, surrendering its role to the Southern Cross and the Magellanic Clouds, two galaxies nearest our own. Deck watch became a pleasure, because he could study an entirely new array of celestial bodies. During the day, for those who still guided their lights by dead reckoning, there were new landmarks, such as the up-thrusted mist-covered summit of Cape Frio and the Sugar Loaf at Rio de Janeiro.

The uneventful voyage to Brazil changed quickly after *Brandywine* anchored at Rio. War between Brazil and Argentina over the control of Uruguay threatened to disrupt relations with the United States. Captain Jones had orders to patrol coastal waters to protect American shipping deemed to be at risk, given the revolutions overtaking many South American countries. When the Brazilian emperor, Dom Pedro, became aware of the captain's intentions, he refused to sign an order permitting the frigate to leave. Jones threatened to sail the next day, with or without permission, but the local American consul warned that should he try, Brazilian forts posted around the harbor would fire upon him. Jones matched threat with threat, and three days later, on November 18, he sailed without incident, taking *Vincennes* with him. Maury watched the firm stand of the navy with interest as Jones resolved a sensitive diplomatic issue, and he tucked away the lesson for future reference.

As *Brandywine* approached Cape Horn, Maury was about to experience a violent phenomenon of wind and waves that would set his mind to thinking in ways he never expected. When off the Falkland Islands, Jones gave orders to prepare the vessel for the sudden onslaught of tremendous storms. The weather had already worsened, with wind slapping the yards and whining through the rigging. Gales shrieked in the face of the crew, rain stung their fingers, hail pelleted their oilskins, and through it all Maury and his fellow midshipmen spent hour upon hour in the tops reefing sails, furling sails, raising sails, and repeating the process over and over again during the same twenty-four hours. Life on deck became equally harsh. Cold seas washed through the scuppers, chilling the sailors who worked with cut hands, cracked fingers, and festering torn-out nails. Even during the summer, men suffered from frostbite in the higher latitudes. Abandoned ships became hazards, and some wrecks could on rare occasion be seen drifting about in the combers without a soul on board. Not even the hardy Falkland Islanders would venture forth to salvage them.

When rounding Cape Horn, the vessel plunged southward, staying well to the windward of land, tumbling back and forth against the Furious Fifties, looking for any break in the wind direction to carry it around Cape Horn. On many occasions the men never saw the cape, having swung a hundred or more miles to the south in search of a favorable breeze. Not only were the winds fierce and unpredictable, but during the summer months icebergs, blown north from the polar region and carried by the currents, appeared without warning and accompanied by a maze of fog.

In describing his first experience doubling Cape Horn, Maury wrote that when *Brandywine* "found the wind varying from N.W. to S.W., she ran up the usual westing without crossing the parallel of 57° 30′. When the winds freshened so that she could not beat to windward, she lay to with her head to the south, giving the land a much wider berth." Stump masts had already been sent up, along with storm sails, and all spars had been secured with preventer rigging because "the waves run to a height which, in other seas, they seldom attain. In the calm they cause no less damage than in the gale, by distressing the ship with labor." Sudden storms had been known to cause vessels to "roll their masts away." The thrill and experience of surviving such perils engrossed Maury's curiosity, causing him to ponder whether such dangers could be mitigated or entirely averted. His growing list of questions having no answers had begun to crystallize into challenges for his mind to conquer.

Vessels beaten back by Cape Horn storms often sought shelter among the Falklands, but the islands had neither docks nor repair facilities. Damaged vessels had to limp back to Rio or Montevideo, both expensive and often embarrassing time wasters. But *Brandywine* beat the storms and on December 26 sailed into Valparaíso.

Maury's arrival at the port gave him cause to reflect on his brother John, who twelve years earlier had anchored *Essex Junior* in the same harbor. Eleven days later, on January 6, 1827, Captain Isaac Hull arrived with the thirty-year-old frigate *United States*. For Maury, the occasion produced another remembrance of the past: John had served on that ship before the War of 1812. For a young man who wanted to follow in the footsteps of his brother, Maury had made a good start. But he could not appreciate that the combination of his native inquisitiveness and a series of coincidences in years yet to come would dramatically change his life and push him in directions entirely his own.

While *Brandywine* remained in port, other vessels of the squadron patrolled the coast. Though Maury enjoyed the sights, the people, and the climate of Chile, he privately celebrated when he received orders transferring him to the twenty-four-gun *Vincennes*, commanded by William Bolton Finch. At 127 feet long and 33 feet, 9 inches in beam, *Vincennes* had been designed for speed in cruising and for maneuverability when fighting. Though still on her maiden voyage, she had become the fastest sailer in the navy. Maury especially liked the change because the smaller boat carried fewer midshipmen in the steerage, giving him more opportunity for quiet study. He also hoped to have a better instructor in navigation, but, he soon learned, "The schoolmaster was a young lawyer who knew more about jetsam and flotsam than about lunars [a phrase referring to tables of numbers for various declinations of the moon, its phase, the date, and the hour, by which a navigator can fix the ship's position] and dead reckoning. . . . He was not on speaking terms with the reefers, ate up all the plums for the duff, and was finally turned out of the ship as a nuisance." Maury admitted learning more about the Spanish language from the daughters of prominent Chilean families than he had from his schoolmaster on *Brandywine*.

The climate and sea breezes at Valparaíso fascinated him. Everybody seemed to wait impatiently until ten o'clock each morning, when the onshore breeze began to blow away the sultry city heat and bring in a delightfully fresh wind off the Pacific. At sunset the onshore breeze subsided, followed by a brief period of calm before the land breezes returned. In the intertropical countries, Maury noticed that the rotation of breezes occurred each day, while in the extratropical countries north and south of the horse latitudes (the Tropics of Cancer and Capricorn), the phenomenon presented itself only in the summer and early fall. But Valparaíso, located as it was on the very southern edge of Capricorn's calm belt, went through the same daily cycle of winds, but with one exception. When the sea breeze set in, it created a gale that swept through the city, tore up pebbles, and whirled dust and debris through the streets. The swirling wind interrupted business, drove people indoors, and cut off all shoreside communication with ships in the harbor. Then, as if someone had thrown a switch at sundown, the wind instantly stopped, and a mild, soft breeze, which seemed to come straight off the Andes, began blowing through the city.

What caused this daily occurrence puzzled Maury, because the shift in winds near shore defied the constant trades. He recalled sitting by a fireside, and the closer he came to the flames, the stronger became the draft at his back. Applying this observation to the breezes at Valparaíso, he concluded that "the land is the hearth, the rays of the sun the fire, and the sea, with its cool and calm air, the room; and thus we have at our side the sea-breeze in miniature. When the sun goes down the fire ceases; then the dry land commences to give off its surplus heat by radiation, so that by dew-fall it and the air above it are cooled below sea temperature. The atmosphere on the land thus becomes heavier than the sea, and consequently, there is wind seaward . . . the land-breeze." At the time, Maury did not fully realize that he had discovered the answer to a long-standing navigation problem, one he would later share with the sailors of the world.

Farther north, in the harbor at Callao, Peru, Maury found himself among amazing fogs. Sometimes the fog would lie like a heavy, impenetrable blanket one or two feet above the surface of the water, the atmosphere being completely clear above it. At times, especially in the early morning, the fog would encapsulate a boat being rowed to shore to such an extent that the heads of its occupants could be seen as clear as day but the rest of their bodies remained buried in the vapor, leaving "nothing visible but two rows of trunkless heads nodding catenaries at the oars, skimming through the air and dancing on the fog in a manner at once both magical and fantastic." At times, when the thick cloud stratum moved higher, men in the tops could see three masts coming into port with topgallant sails and royals set, but no ship. "These sails, nicely trimmed, and swelling to the breeze in the sky," said Maury, "skim over the clouds and seem like things in a fairy scene." At the time Maury made these observations he did not know that the cool waters of Humboldt's Current flowed into Callao and mixed with warm, sultry air, but he scratched a note to add to his growing list of unexplained wonders and stuffed it into his seabag.

Maury's quest for an education absorbed most of his free time. On neither of his two cruises had he learned anything from shipboard instructors, but on *Vincennes* he discovered two works by Riddle: *Investigations of the Rules and Principles of Lunar and Other Observations* and, for him, the more interesting *Spherical Trigonometry*. Like Bowditch, who carried a slate and a pencil wherever he went, Maury developed the habit of chalking problems in spherical trigonometry on round shot racked on deck. He then worked out solutions as he paced back and forth during watch. He also developed two other interests: the geography of South America and the study of international relations, the latter arising from a perpetual state of civil unrest sweeping across the southern continent. Just a few years earlier, in 1821, Simón Bolívar had liberated Venezuela from Spanish rule; Colombia and Ecuador had followed in 1822, Peru in 1824, and had a new country—Bolivia—named for him in 1825.

Unlocking the mysteries of the sea, however, became Maury's personal quest, and it so intrigued him that on June 18, 1829, he informed a friend of a wish to sail across the Pacific and then come home by way of the Cape of Good Hope. If not, he wrote, "I think it quite probable that I shall go that way in an Indiaman in case this vessel does not." Maury began to suspect he had a mission in life, but the strands of his thought were not yet ready to be woven into form and substance.

No vessel of the U.S. Navy had ever circumnavigated the globe, and Maury could have turned cartwheels on deck when orders came for *Vincennes* to clear for Canton, sail through the South China Sea to the Indian Ocean, round the Cape of Good Hope, and cross the Atlantic for home.

Earlier, USS *Congress* had sailed to China but returned home by way of South America. Andrew Jackson, who in 1829 became the seventh president of the United States, hatched the idea of sending a naval vessel around the world when it became apparent that the sailing nations of Europe intended to establish more colonies and plant more of their flags in Africa, Asia, and the Pacific. For the United States, the time had finally come for an American ship to do what merchant vessels and whalers had been doing for a century—show its colors around the world and prove to all nations that the navy of the United States was a force to be reckoned with anywhere in the world.

Captain Finch picked a capable crew, among them four experienced lieutenants, one of whom, Thomas A. Dornin, became one of Maury's lifelong friends. On July 4, 1829, *Vincennes* set sail on the evening breeze and eased through Callao's harbor. The sloop's small band blared a few strains from "Home, Sweet Home," and the sailors manning the yards gave a whoop and a holler as they passed three American warships anchored in the harbor. For Maury, the adventure had begun, and no part of it would he ever forget.

The first leg of the cruise brought *Vincennes* to Nuku Hiva, where Captain Porter had raised the Stars and Stripes in 1813, and where John Minor Maury had lived in a tree house under virtual siege. With help from an English interpreter who lived among the Happas, Maury attempted to learn the language in an effort to obtain information about his deceased brother. He pried a few facts from an old Happa chief, Gattenewa, who purported to have known John, and from him learned the approximate location of his brother's home in the trees.

Not much had changed since Porter's visit. The Happa and Typee tribes on the island continued to war against each other, and trips inland or around the island could be taken only at the risk of one's life. Nonetheless, Maury went exploring, fully aware that a band of raiding Typees had recently stormed a Happa village and abducted three children. A rescue party recovered only two, the third having been eaten. But Maury wanted to search for the remains of his brother's tree house in a nearby valley, so he strapped on a revolver and started into the jungle with a few of his friends. Several Typees, heavily tattooed and dressed in feathered war bonnets, appeared overhead on the rim of a cliff and began hurling war clubs at the intruders. Maury and his companions expected to engage in a desperate fight to avoid the roasting skewer, but after the Typees discharged their weapons, a few shots from the Americans dispersed them into the jungle.

One day while *Vincennes* stood becalmed in a bay off Nuku Hiva, Maury observed a phenomenon that had puzzled mariners for centuries. A tremendous current, setting dead on shore, pushed the ship toward a wall of rocks scattered beneath a high cliff. With the water too deep to anchor, nothing could be done to maneuver the ship, and the dual action of the onshore swell combining with the current seemed determined to destroy the vessel. Maury probably had visions of swimming to the island, there to resume the life of his brother in another tree house. Captain Finch saved the day by ordering out the spars, and the crew fended off the cliff until the vessel cleared. The cause of such a swift and sudden current baffled Maury, and as with other puzzles collecting in his thoughts, the day would come when he sought to solve them.

Another experience awaited Maury when five days later *Vincennes* anchored off Papeete, the capital of Tahiti. Finch intended for the Tahitians to understand that American whalers, who made frequent stops at the island, were to be provisioned and protected. The island also had a reputation for harboring deserters who preferred the beauties of Tahiti to the drudgery of sea duty. Though the navy had lost no seamen to the sirens of the island, whalers had. What captured the attention of Maury were not the beguiling glances of the island women but the great distances whalers traveled to collect oil and the enormous amount of sailing experience they accumulated during their four- and five-year voyages.

While in the heated waters of Polynesia he noticed a tropical drift southward, but he did not discover until many years later that this broad, warm current carried planktonic coral polyps south to eastern Australia, building the Great Barrier Reef, and to both shores of New Zealand's two main islands. He made another note to tuck into his seabag.

Two weeks later, on a voyage north to the Hawaiian Islands, *Vincennes* passed through the Pacific doldrums. Much to Maury's surprise, he discovered a strong current (probably the South Equatorial Current) that he did not understand. One measurement recorded a rate of ninety-six miles a day, flowing from east to west. Another reminder went into his seabag, but twenty years would pass before such mysteries began to reveal themselves.

A month later, when *Vincennes* stopped at Hawaii, Maury learned that more than a hundred whalers and dozens of merchantmen called at the islands each year. Once again he watched as the captain played a diplomatic role with Hawaii's king, settling claims of fellow Americans. Before *Vincennes* departed, Finch collected several deserters from American traders and put them to work on the ship. Few of them objected. They had seen enough of island life.

On New Year's Day, 1830, after a long and tedious voyage from Hawaii, *Vincennes* dropped anchor off Macao, a Portuguese colony near the coast of China. Finch dispatched a letter to John S. Grosvenor, the U.S. consul at Canton, inquiring into the conditions of trade with China. Grosvenor replied that hundreds of American merchantmen visited the port each year. Unscrupulous local officials often abused the upstart Yankees, demanding bribes and making their trading efforts as difficult as possible, and shipmasters brought a steady flow of grievances into the consulate. Because Americans operated without armed protection, Grosvenor urged that the navy make regular goodwill missions to show a presence in China's waters.

Later, Finch hired a boat to take a small party up the Pearl River to meet the consul at Canton. Maury went with him. Never had he seen such congestion on a waterway. As the boat approached the walled city, a tight clutter of factories, pagodas, and warehouses rimmed the river. Merchants reminded Finch that prior to *Vincennes*, the only visit to China by an American warship occurred in 1819 when the thirty-six-gun USS *Congress* made a brief appearance. They urged that more warships be sent to Asia. What impressed Maury was the presence of so many Americans in Canton. Grosvenor claimed that during the trading season, no fewer than fifty U.S. merchantmen could be counted in the area at any one time. Until reaching China, Maury had been unable to grasp the true size of the world's carrying trade.

On January 22 *Vincennes* sailed for the island of Luzon in the Philippines. Maury took in the sights and traveled through the countryside with Chaplain Charles S. Stewart, whose chronicle of the cruise provided deep insight into Maury's capacity for learning and his evolving interest in the science and geography of the seas. Maury did not know that he would never get another chance to sail around the world.

Leaving Manila on February 9, 1830, *Vincennes* began to retrace, though not intentionally, the voyages made by Nathaniel Bowditch some thirty years earlier. The ship cruised down the South China Sea, passing between Borneo and the tip of Malaya, and entered the Strait of Sunda. Then, after passing Java Head, Finch anchored for two days to take on water. During this leg of the voyage a fellow officer, William Leigh, noticed Maury's small library. He confessed amazement that the midshipman had managed to acquire a course for personal study beginning with the rudiments of Euclid and extending to the higher mathematics of Laplace. Maury showed him that during off-duty hours he also had started work on his own set of lunar tables. These efforts did not go unnoticed by Captain Finch, who regularly invited Maury to his cabin for dinner and to pass the evening in conversation.

On one occasion, however, Maury nearly ruined his chances for promotion. The captain, perhaps having had one glass too many, insisted
that Maury also have another glass. When Maury declined to exceed the
modest amount of alcohol he allowed himself, the insistent captain approached him with a full glass in hand. Maury accepted the glass and then
threw it to the floor and left the cabin. Fortunately, Captain Finch overlooked the incident.

When passing down the east coast of Africa, *Vincennes* struck the equatorial calms off Somalia. Light breezes blew from both directions and the
crew constantly worked the tops to catch the wind and claw through.
Maury observed that the calms on one side of Africa were no different than
those on the other side, and along the calm belt ran a light surface current
that became stronger as the vessel bent southward and approached the island of Madagascar. The same current intensified and became quite strong
as the vessel approached Mozambique in the South Indian Ocean. By observing the drift in the sea, Maury noted that a current (the Mozambique
Current, sixteen hundred miles wide, nearly as broad as the entire length
of the Gulf Stream) flowing down the east coast of Africa seemed to blend
with another warm current (the Agulhas Current), setting westward round
the Cape of Good Hope. There he observed a northward-setting current
(the Benguela Current), one seemingly put there by Providence and augmented by southern trades to speed a vessel up the coast of Africa. Maury
did not know at the time that *Vincennes* was being carried along the coast of
Africa by currents almost as strong as the Gulf Stream, but he made a mental note of the curious change in the color and temperature of the water.

The ancient Phoenicians made the first known voyage around Africa
for Egyptian Pharaoh Necho. They sailed down the Red Sea and, after
reaching the Indian Ocean, passed around the thirteen-thousand-mile
African coast using a major portion of the same route later followed by
Vincennes. They discovered that Africa, because of winds and currents, was
more comfortably navigated east to west. Not until these early seafarers
started passing around the hump of West Africa did they strike the northeast trade wind, the Guinea Current, and the Canary Current, all of which
set against them on the return journey. The fifteenth-century Portuguese

rediscovered the same winds and currents three thousand years later, and though Columbus noted their value to the navigator, not until after Maury swung around the Cape of Good Hope in 1830 did anyone attempt to more accurately chart them.

On April 7 *Vincennes* doubled the Cape of Good Hope and entered Table Bay, dropping anchor a mile from Cape Town with an excellent view of Table Mountain. Maury took a carriage through the wharves and the countryside, examining the scenery while enjoying the hospitality of the people. Ships from every nation, bound for home or stretching their canvas for the East Indies, stopped at Cape Town for supplies and a respite from long days at sea. The visit lasted twelve days. By then the crew chafed to get home. The bilgewater had turned putrid and cockroaches infested the ship, and though an interim stop at St. Helena gave the crew an opportunity to stretch their legs, nobody wanted to remain on the delightful island longer than necessary.

During the voyage north from the Cape of Good Hope, *Vincennes* fell in along the west coast of Africa with a set of winds that blew directly north and remained steady right up to the equator. Maury thought this rather unusual because trades usually blew from a quarter. Twenty years later he would call the constant flowing southerlies a "Gulf Stream in the air" because he discovered that they blew with a regularity and consistency rivaling that of the Gulf Stream and were the only winds on the planet that maintained a truly northern set.

On June 8, 1830, *Vincennes* reached Sandy Hook on the New Jersey coast and brought a pilot on board to guide the ship to the quarantine station. Despite odors from the bilge and a cavalcade of fleet-footed cockroaches, the inspector gave the vessel a clean bill of health. All the men were robust and the ship otherwise spotless. Her arrival off New York harbor created quite a sensation among the press, as she had been expected for several months. Two steamboats carrying city officials and friends of the sailors circled the sloop-of-war as she came to anchor off the Brooklyn Navy Yard. The band welcomed the greeters with "Hail, Columbia," thereby provoking another round of cheers. After almost four years, the much-traveled *Vincennes* had come home—the first vessel of the United States Navy to circumnavigate the planet—and Midshipman Maury was on it.

⊰⊱

WHEN joining the navy in 1825, Maury did so to expand his education. None of his schoolmasters on *Brandywine* or *Vincennes* taught him a thing about mathematics, science, navigation, or sailing, but two cruises had given him time to educate himself. So disillusioned had he become over the navy's careless approach to education that he wrote home urging his younger brother Charles to stay out of the navy and try for an appointment at West Point.

But Maury thoroughly enjoyed his voyage around the world. Though he grumbled about his lack of education, he learned more about the Earth and its inhabitants than any college could have taught him in the same span of time. He had witnessed the practice of protocol in matters of international relations, made lasting friendships among his shipmates, and earned the respect of fellow officers. More importantly, he witnessed widely differing climates, the role of the weather in different seasons, the change of celestial observations in the latitudes, and how the winds and currents play tricks upon the seafarer over every section of the globe. Through hands-on experience he learned seamanship, and though his self-directed studies enhanced his knowledge of mathematics, astronomy, and navigation, he craved more.

What Maury wanted from the navy, navy schoolmasters could not give him. In mathematics and astronomy, he had already surpassed the more learned minds in the navy, but he did not know it. In navigation, he still had much to learn about the sea. Twelve years would pass before doors would open that would speed him to the threshold of his potential. The years between and after would be fraught with frustration, deep emotional pain, and great personal difficulty. A sailor's life is never easy, but in the early summer of 1830, he could not foresee how different his life as a sailor would become.

Chapter Four

A THIRST FOR KNOWLEDGE
UNHEEDED

IN 1830 the secretary of the navy assigned Maury to the New York Navy Yard's school for instruction, where midshipmen studied for the examination all young officers were required to take to become "passed midshipmen." Most senior navy officers, however, placed little value on a lengthy formal education. From their perspective, an officer learned the sea by first becoming a sailor. A few men such as Jacob Jones, Maury's former commanding officer aboard *Brandywine*, studied law and medicine before joining the navy. But prior to 1830, most captains went to sea as midshipmen, gained their knowledge of navigation from sailing masters, and placed little confidence in classroom studies. Maury looked forward to attending the school, but he used his accumulated three months leave to visit his parents, whom he had not seen for five years. On the trip to Tennessee he took along his sister-in-law Eliza (John's widow) and her two children. His parents had never seen their grandsons. The happy reunion with the family brought another small blessing—his father forgave him for joining the navy.

Maury's itinerary also included a trip to Laurel Hill to visit cousin Ann, who had grown into a lovely nineteen-year-old woman with sparkling blue eyes and lustrous auburn hair. Their five-year difference in age seemed to have diminished during Maury's absence, but he still had bills to pay and no money to support a wife. With solemn regret he said good-bye but promised to return, temporarily suppressing his matrimonial urges in exchange for the practical necessity of getting ahead in the navy.

Maury reported for school on October 6, 1830, and received for study such familiar works as Bowditch's *Practical Navigator*, Euclid's books by Playfair, McClure's *Spherics*, Bourbon's *Algebra*, and texts on mental and moral philosophy, seamanship, and Spanish or French—he chose the former. But Maury had already read and mastered the books on science and mathematics during his cruise around the world. Dissatisfied with the quality and content of teaching at the navy yard, he told his superiors he would be better prepared for the examination through self-study than by attending class. On December 22 the navy granted him unlimited leave and excused him from attending classes.

Release from the navy yard gave Maury an opportunity to once again roam Manhattan's waterfront. During his four years at sea tremendous changes had occurred, but cows were still being pastured around 23rd Street, and nothing had changed along the filthy sidewalks of the bawdy financial district. He noted a remarkable increase in the number of steamers working the river. In the years to come, efficient steamship lines would thrust aside the sailing ships at the very apex of their evolution and condemn them to the lowliest of cargo trades, but not during the working lifetime of Matthew Maury.

On his walks through lower Manhattan, the immense growth in the merchant trade amazed him. Out in the harbor yesterday's privateersmen, the old wall-sided, lofty-pooped Indiamen from the War of 1812, still swung at anchor with gun ports bristling. Mingled among them could be seen deep-waisted droughers from Canada, a few Dutch galliots, here and there a snaky felucca, also turpentine-sided vessels, bright-waisted ships, red ships, green ships, yellow ships, and pea-soupers, ships of every color and of different ages and vintages all mixed together. Sinewy, pigtailed sailors, exhausted from a night on the town, hung around Cherry Street and exchanged stories with wide-eyed youngsters looking for work.

But speed had become the fetish for American traders and created new criteria for building packet ships and merchant ships. Maury observed that the designs of ships were in rapid transition from the old full-bellied traders to vessels with sleek, narrow hulls topped by clouds of canvas. New yards had been wedged in between older yards to such a degree that room for more could not be found. During Maury's cruise around the world the Merchant's Exchange had been erected, and one of the fastest growing businesses occupying the interests of both shippers and brokers involved the insuring of ships and their cargoes. The number of commission merchants, ship agents, chandlers, sailmakers, clothing stores, liquor brokers, hotels, and grocers along South Street had tripled, testifying to the enormous expansion of American commerce. New Yorkers bought and sold shares in ships, and the transactions on South Street between the 1830s and the 1850s eclipsed the trading of stocks and bonds on Wall Street. There were three million tons of shipping on the American register, more than three-fourths of it roaming the free ocean lanes of the world, and in the mid-1800s, the Stars and Stripes flew from more ships than ever before in the nation's history. The bustle and excitement energized Maury, and his walks gave him a vision of the future. His personal role remained obscure, though he knew he wanted to be a navy man.

While preparing for the passed midshipman's exam he left New York and moved in with Richard Maury's family in Georgetown, where he taught two of the children and studied his texts. Astronomer and mathematician Pierre-Simon Laplace's rules and reasons fascinated him, and he soon fell into the habit of studying books that occupied his interest—not the textbooks provided by the navy. Forever anxious to expand his knowledge, Maury turned to peripheral fields of science. Doing so validated what he already believed—that each area of scientific study connected with others, and that mathematics provided the adhesive that tethered them all together. With spherical trigonometry he made an exciting discovery because he could apply it to both navigation and astronomy. But Maury wanted more than just knowledge; he wanted to find a way to use it. For the present, he settled for also tutoring several midshipmen who each day beat a wintry path to Georgetown for instruction.

The other matter occupying his thoughts had nothing to do with science. As time permitted, he made short visits to Laurel Hill and soon fell

hopelessly in love with Ann Herndon. Now twenty years old, she recipro-
cated by traveling to Georgetown to visit, further cementing their relationship.

On March 3, 1831, Maury appeared before the dreaded examination
board. One look told him that the examiners were ancient line officers who
had long ago learned their navigation from doing it the Bowditch way.
Passing the examination meant memorizing Bowditch's formulas for finding lunars—nothing more and nothing less. When one examiner questioned Maury on a lunar problem, instead of reciting Bowditch he boldly
went to the blackboard and developed his answer using spherical trigonometry. The professor of mathematics conducting the examination "got lost in
trying to follow him and declared the demonstration wrong." Maury dis-
agreed. The officers of the examining board, knowing even less than the
examining mathematician, caucused and decided after an embarrassing
consultation to side with their colleague. The penalty for being smarter
than the professor almost cost Maury two more years at sea as a midshipman. The examiners then had second thoughts and passed Maury twenty-
seventh in a class of forty. Midshipmen tutored by Maury passed with
higher standings. The lesson had its benefits. He would not demonstrate his
knowledge again before ignorant superiors.

Being warranted a passed midshipman on June 24, 1831, to rank from
June 4, gave Maury a few more dollars to spend each month. He could now
pursue his own interests until placed on active duty. Ann Herndon, his first
interest outside the navy, pleased him in every way. He could not afford
marriage, but engagements were cheap, and since they both were in love,
Ann accepted his proposal. Maury then received orders to report to the
sloop-of-war *Falmouth* as acting sailing master, a post that would give him
an opportunity to demonstrate his ability as a navigator. He could not have
been happier.

The navy placed Francis H. Gregory in command of the two-year-old
Falmouth, an officer under whom Maury had served on *Brandywine* and a
person he respected. There were many other officers from *Brandywine*, including Lieutenants Thomas A. Dornin as the executive officer and Elisha Peck. The twenty-gun *Falmouth*, a twin of *Vincennes*, made Maury

quite comfortable as sailing master, and the cruise to the Pacific would once again take him around Cape Horn and up the west coast of South America. For Maury, the voyage would be a practice and study of navigation and sailing, but it could mean another three or four years of absence from Ann.

The role of sailing master involved numerous duties, and Maury knew exactly what materials he needed to perform them. In the weeks before sailing he began a search for information on winds and currents. After finding none among the naval records, he broadened his search to the merchant houses of New York, whose vessels rounded Cape Horn with regularity. He spoke with several experienced "Cape Horners," only to learn that each shipmaster attacked the cape differently, leaving their tactics to chance and nothing to science. Amazed at the absence of printed information, he considered it a serious deficiency that needed to be rectified.

On July 5, 1831, with a crew of 232 men, *Falmouth* cleared the bar off Sandy Hook and set sail for South America. Maury took his role as sailing master seriously. For the first time in his career he had charge of an important department of a vessel. His duties included the maintenance and accuracy of navigational equipment, the inspection and care of sails and rigging, and the disbursement of provisions. He also kept the logbook, recording the course steered, the distance traveled, the set and velocity of the winds, weather changes, the results of astronomical observations made to determine the ship's location, and compass variation. In addition, he needed to record the longitudes of places visited and, when traveling close to the coast, prominent features that could be used as landmarks. Also into the logbook went the rise and fall of tides and the force and direction of currents.

When the cruise began, Maury planned to emphatically demonstrate his skill as a navigator. He expected the cruise to be *his* opportunity to establish a reputation, so he took a keen interest in the winds and currents. Why such information was not available to seafarers baffled him, so he began keeping remarkably precise records of his daily observations. What the navy did with all this information Maury did not know, but he envisioned its potential usefulness.

Cape Horn presented a problem for sailors any time of the year, but when *Falmouth* arrived in October, the usual spring gales struck with expected ferocity. A vessel approaching the tip of South America had three options: to round Cape Horn in the open sea, to cut through the shorter but dangerous Strait of Magellan, or to take the more popular passage through the Strait of Le Maire off the southeastern tip of Argentina. Too many vessels had been cast upon the rocks when using the straits, so Maury chose the longer route across the open sea. Standing south and then west, he found better winds and twenty-four days later sailed up the Chilean coast. He set no records, but rounding the Horn in twenty-four days looked better on the books than the forty it often took to sail from 50 degrees South on the eastern side of the continent to 50 degrees South on the opposite side. Maury later learned that during the same season the British *Volage* took the inshore passage, spent thirty-eight days to reach the same latitude, and then lost another twenty days making repairs. Comparing the time consumed by each vessel to reach the same destination, Maury concluded that a better understanding of Cape Horn's winds, currents, and weather would have benefited both vessels. On the occasion of the two vessels making the passage at the same time, *Falmouth* just happened to be the luckier.

The incident made Maury curious, and curiosity, once implanted in Maury's mind, resided there in perpetuity. The lack of wind and current information and the absence of reliable sailing directions put sailors at risk by sending them into storms and ice fields they could not predict. But how to collect and arrange such information required an exhaustive study without the means available to conduct it. Yet Maury began, using his own log and hundreds of notes he stuffed into cubbyholes in his small, cramped cabin. He spoke with the sailing master on *Volage* and compared observations, concluding that the inshore passage should be used only when the winds were favorable; when finding contrary winds off the cape, a vessel should "stand boldly to the south . . . keeping near the parallel of the Cape." He also concluded that when sailing from the Pacific into the Atlantic, "The ratio of winds with westing in them to those with easting is as three to one," making the return trip "less dreaded and shorter than the outbound trip."

Maury's experiences rounding Cape Horn in 1834 formed the basis for his first scientific paper. He wrote it while on *Falmouth*, and it contained more than just a commentary on winds and currents. He provided specific sailing directions for each leg of navigating the cape. From South America he mailed the manuscript to the *American Journal of Science and Arts* in New Haven, Connecticut, one of the most prestigious scientific publications in America. The journal's editor, Benjamin Silliman, noticed that the article came from a mere passed midshipman, but he also recognized that the data had been systematically collected, professionally presented, and contained new information. When published, "On the Navigation of Cape Horn" would become the catalyst that launched Maury's career as both an author and a budding scientist on subjects such as meteorology and navigation.

In faraway places like Valparaíso, Chile, Maury began to fret about his future. Promotion came slowly, as did increases in pay. Being confined to patrol duty for two or three years did not help his state of mind, especially knowing that Ann waited patiently for his return to America. Having no money for marriage—he earned a mere $700 a year—he questioned the fairness of tying her to him by engagement when he could see no prospect of ever becoming financially capable of providing for her and for children, should they have them. He could not change his situation in the navy, and he doubted whether he could improve his status out of the navy. Many of his shipmates shared his concerns over poor pay and slow promotion and talked of leaving the service. Maury suspected that once he returned to Virginia, relatives would press him to try a different career. While worrying over the prospect of having to choose between two loves, Ann or the navy, he wrote brother Dick, rather decisively, "If on my return . . . I am not promoted, I think I shall go . . . right off to sea again." He did not mean to abandon his obligation to Ann, but he could earn twice the pay serving at sea and save much of it while waiting for promotion.

As dejected as Maury sounded in his many letters home, he wasted no opportunity to improve himself during the long months of patrol off the coast of Chile, Peru, and Ecuador. Whenever an opportunity occurred for survey work, he asked for it. He enjoyed poking around outcroppings, taking instrument readings, measuring the flow of currents, recording the direction and force of winds, and discussing navigation with the many commercial shipmasters who hauled into port for supplies and relaxation. From them he collected a wealth of information showing that every shipmaster followed as his guide his own inclinations and accumulated experience.

In 1833 Maury began compiling data for a new text on navigation, the type of book he would have liked to own when he first joined the navy. Bowditch had done the same with his *New American Practical Navigator*, which every officer in the navy adopted as the "Holy Writ," the one possible exception being Maury. He wanted more—a textbook that "would so clearly present both the practice and the theory of navigation that a midshipman could truly understand it and not just learn the rules by rote," as had been the practice. Maury's duties on *Falmouth* precluded such a project, but he started making notes, knowing a day might come when he could use them.

On August 21, 1833, Maury transferred to a smaller ship also in the harbor of Callao, Peru, the schooner *Dolphin*. His assignment as her executive officer did not last long, however, for on October 23, 1833, the frigate *Potomac*, a sister ship of *Brandywine*, arrived at Callao, homebound for the United States. The highlight of her west-to-east voyage around the world had occurred at Sumatra, where she burned a village to avenge the plundering of the American ship *Friendship* and the murder of her crew. Maury received orders to report to the *Potomac* commander, Captain John Downes. On February 10, 1834, *Potomac* sailed out of the harbor and, with Maury on board, headed for Boston.

The homeward voyage gave Maury a closer look at the ravages of Cape Horn. A strong gale struck on March 10, sending icebergs into the path of *Potomac*. Floes seemed to be everywhere, with great pieces of ice and five enormous bergs bobbing about in towering seas. On March 13 gale winds drove the side of *Potomac* into a mass of ice, and the crunching sounds against the wooden hull sent shudders through the crew. The vessel escaped with little damage, but one near-disaster led to another. On March 14 fog spread across the sea, diminishing visibility to near zero, but the wind subsided, lessening the risk of the ship being driven hard into a monolithic iceberg. Not until March 16 did the skies clear and sailing return to normal, and Maury would recall the incident in later years when writing about the world's navigational hazards.

On May 24, 1834, *Potomac* anchored off the Charleston Navy Yard at Boston. Three days later Maury went ashore for a three-month leave. He planned to go to Fredericksburg to see Ann, but a most frustrating and humiliating problem continued to distress him: he still had no money.

Maury reached Laurel Hill in early June and found Ann as anxious to be married as he. Neither could wait any longer, and on July 15, 1834, Matthew married cousin Ann at the home of Edward Herndon, where the bride and groom had first met. Having no funds, the newlyweds circulated through Virginia and spent their honeymoon enjoying the hospitality of relatives. When the honeymoon ended, the Maurys returned to Fredericksburg and "went to housekeeping" by boarding with other relatives. As a passed midshipman on leave, he received forty dollars a month, barely enough to buy groceries.

As an unexpected wedding gift, Maury became a published author. In July 1834, the *American Journal of Science and Arts* published his article "On the Navigation of Cape Horn." The same issue contained a design he had submitted, entitled "Plan of an Instrument for Finding the True Lunar Distance." Seeing both subjects in print provided a strong stimulus for him to begin a more extensive project—the text on navigation he dreamed of developing from notes he had collected while serving as *Falmouth*'s sailing master.

Maury did not know whether the book would sell, and he desperately needed money. Though chronometers were becoming more affordable, many merchantmen and a few naval vessels still sailed without them. Finding longitude at sea by lunar observation continued to baffle most sailors, and Maury wanted to simplify the process, whether the observer used a chronometer or not. He had midshipmen in mind when he wrote in the preface the book's objective: "It is not pretended that new theories are set forth or that new principles are established in this work; but it is believed that those which have already been established are here embodied in such a form that the means of becoming a theoretical as well as a practical navigator are placed within the reach of every student."

As a robust, twenty-eight-year-old passed midshipman, Maury had many career options more lucrative than writing a book on speculation. When his relatives prodded him to find a commission on a merchant vessel while waiting for orders, he stubbornly refused, for when Maury joined the navy, he made a commitment to serve body and soul. With similar determination, when he made the decision to write the book, the idea evolved into a challenge from which he could extract himself. To his family circle, he explained, "I do not expect much direct profit from [the book] though it may be of some collateral advantage in making my name known to the [Navy] Department and to my brother officers in a favorable manner." Maury's lack of cash probably had little effect on his standard of living. Fredericksburg contained many relatives who became accustomed to visits from the newlyweds around suppertime.

Maury worked assiduously on the book. Every day became a new struggle to simplify terminology and laboriously restructure tables. In November he wrote his uncle that he would complete the work by spring if "not interrupted by a call into service." He got his wish. The navy did not need his services, and relatives kept quiet while he worked.

To promote his manuscript, Maury sought endorsements. One inquiry went to Professor Alexander Dallas Bache in Philadelphia, another to Nathaniel Bowditch in Boston. Bache had already heard about Maury from two brothers, Richard and George, the latter having served on *Brandywine*. He affirmed the book as being of immense value to midshipmen and concluded that it would be in the navy's best interest "to sanction it." Bache may not have been so generous with praise had he been able to foresee the future, for Maury would one day become a formidable competitor whose scientific achievements would eclipse those of Bache. Another icon, Nathaniel Bowditch, whose *Practical Navigator* had become required reading for all midshipmen, wrote, "A work of the kind you are preparing for the press, containing the demonstrations of the formulas of *Nautical Astronomy*, would be very useful to those who have a taste for the subject and would like to examine the demonstration of the rules." Positive references from authorities like Bache and Bowditch were like money in the bank.

Late in April 1835, Maury mailed the completed manuscript, with both endorsements cleverly embedded, to Key & Biddle, a Philadelphia publishing company. In mid-June two events happened almost simultaneously. Maury learned that his manuscript had been accepted, and a few days later Ann gave birth to their first daughter, Elizabeth, whom they called Betty. With this joyful addition to the family came another mouth to feed.

About this time Maury finally prevailed in a long-standing dispute with the navy over back pay, and he received enough cash to rent a plain, two-storied clapboard house on Charlotte Street in Fredericksburg. There were always Maurys to fill available space, and others of the clan soon moved in, among them John's widow Eliza, whose small pension helped ends meet, and her two children.

With everyone comfortably settled, Maury turned his attention to Key & Biddle, whose slow progress in publishing the book distressed him. Being an unknown author, he worried that the publishers had lost enthusiasm for the text. With all the cash he could raise, Maury took a stagecoach to Philadelphia in the autumn of 1835 to expedite the project. Key & Biddle had not lost interest; they simply needed more work done to prepare the proofs. Maury remained in Philadelphia for six weeks, living in a tiny garret and eating cheese and crackers while preparing the book for print.

He also deluded himself—as twenty-nine-year-olds sometimes do—thinking the stodgy old navy would honor his work by granting him unprecedented laurels. His optimism emanated from at least one fact: no nautical work of science had ever come "from the pen of a naval officer," and upon its merits, wrote Maury to his brother, "I intend to base a claim for promotion." He envisioned himself placed above the heads of others but warned Dick not to mention his private machinations to anyone, because "for many of those over whose heads it is likely I would be placed would, if they knew I contemplated such a thing would use every exertion to prevent it." Maury's impoverished state got the best of him when he suggested, "I shall ask to be made a lieutenant of ten years' rank. If this is done, besides the advantage of making me old in rank, it will entitle me (I think) to back pay, as though I had been a lieutenant for these ten years; and this will . . . amount to some $4,000 or $5,000." There were no precedents for expecting such unlikely emoluments. In peacetime the navy never tampered with seniority, and petty jealousies operated with more persuasiveness than personal achievement.

During the mid-1830s the navy had too many officers and too few ships, forcing some men to stay ashore on half-pay for as long as four years. Maury found himself among that number and bided his time studying mineralogy and geology. He laid out courses of study for himself while waiting nervously for his book to come out. When in late spring 1836 a package arrived in the mail from Philadelphia, he tore away the wrappings and stared at his prize. Inside, the title page read, "A New Theoretical and Practical Treatise on Navigation by M. F. Maury, passed midshipman, U.S. Navy." It contained 216 pages of text, 174 pages of tables, 9 plates, and sold for $4 in bookshops or $2.50 from the publisher.

Now thirty years old and with publishing credentials, Maury traveled to Washington to collect his promotion. Seeking the most expeditious course, he arranged an interview with President Andrew Jackson. That he could do so was not as unlikely as it might seem today, for Jackson and Maury were both from Tennessee, which counted for much in the early years of the United States, and Maury's relatives included several men of prominence in that state. Andrew Jackson listened intently to Maury's proposal and concluded that some form of recognition, though not necessarily promotion, was worthy of consideration. Like a good executive, he referred the matter to Mahlon Dickerson, secretary of the navy, suggesting that Maury be reimbursed "out of the contingency fund" for all expenses incurred while preparing the book. But Dickerson, whom Maury called "a very old granny," denied the request, saying "the book brought its own reward" and that should be enough. Consolation came in 1837 when the secretary placed copies of Maury's *Navigation* on every ship in the navy, but in 1836, nothing haunted Maury more than his hunger for promotion and the compensatory rewards that came with it.

Unlike "granny" Dickerson, a number of open-minded senior officers praised the book. When comparing it to Bowditch, Commander Irving Schubrick found it "far superior as a book of instruction." Two competent professors of mathematics, recently hired by the navy to instruct midshipmen, eagerly adopted the text and added their praise. When in 1843 E. C. Biddle published the second edition, it included dozens of new endorsements, this time from navy men, and those endorsements meant more to Maury than all the others, which included a favorable review by the poet Edgar Allan Poe, writing for the *Southern Literary Messenger*. That publication carried essays and articles, but also reported on Washington politics (including army and navy appropriations), the southern economy, and people in the news.

On July 10, 1836, Maury received notification of his promotion to lieutenant, dating from June 10, but no orders came assigning him to sea. His work on navigation gained for him no special privileges from the navy, but his independent study of geology and mineralogy led to a temporary opportunity. Distressed by living on half-pay, he accepted a position as superintendent for the United States Gold Mine Company, a privately owned operation located about three miles from his birthplace. The company president quickly recognized Maury's talent and offered him the post of mine engineer with pay double that of a lieutenant on active duty. Maury rejected the offer, convinced the vein of gold would soon be depleted, but he encouraged the president to give serious attention to an abundance of local brown hematite iron ore, which, he said, might prove far more profitable than gold. Had Maury stayed with the mine, it might well have become an iron producer, but after three months in the mines, he lost interest in the venture and returned to Fredericksburg. He had been on shore for more than two years, and his growing impatience for active duty made him more resolute than ever to find a way to gain a berth.

Since 1828 the navy had been discussing the prospect of sending a squadron on an exploring expedition to the South Pacific. For eight years the project languished in red tape while other nations of the world continued to expand their influence around the globe. In 1835 President Jackson appointed Captain Thomas ap Catesby Jones to command the expedition, but friction developed between Jones and Secretary Dickerson over the selection of captains for the supporting vessels. Jones wanted Josiah Tattnall, Charles H. Bell, Thomas A. Dornin, and A. B. Pinkham as his commanders. Dickerson wanted Alexander Slidell MacKenzie and Charles

Wilkes, men whom Jones believed less fit. While officering the expedition remained in limbo, Maury spoke with Jones, who promised him a berth. Knowing that Jones wanted him, Maury applied for active duty. The captain immediately made a formal request to the department asking that Maury be assigned to the expedition. As soon as Dornin heard that his old friend would be available, he asked the secretary to transfer Maury to the storeship *Relief* as his executive officer. Jones could not have picked a more capable and inquisitive scientist than Maury for the expedition, and Dornin could not have picked a better navigator as executive officer if *Relief*, or any ship of the expedition, sailed into trouble.

In the muddle of political turmoil over the expedition, Maury learned that influential friends in Tennessee were lobbying the president to assign him command of a vessel. He knew this would not happen and desperately wanted to escape the troublesome secretary's spotlight because, he wrote, "The Honorable Secretary and I have had almost too many sparrings." Maury also feared the expedition would disintegrate into a "bungling" affair by the mistake of "sending out for such service so large and unwieldy a ship as a frigate," which he viewed as "an encumbrance." But he wanted to be a part of the expedition. Not only would he enter an uncharted section of the globe, but the voyage would provide an invaluable opportunity to continue his research in various aspects of the ocean and to seek answers for long-standing questions.

Maury worked with Dornin to find the best young officers in the navy, only to have his hopes shattered in late September when Secretary Dickerson decided to assign two more lieutenants to *Relief*, thereby bumping Maury from executive officer to third lieutenant. Though bitterly disappointed, Maury accepted the bad news as officers must. With the squadron soon to rendezvous at Norfolk, he boarded his wife and child with relatives and prepared for the long voyage. Days later, politics over command of the expedition again erupted in Washington, causing a last-minute postponement and another long delay. So for Maury, another fall and winter passed, and he used the time to advance his knowledge of astronomy. The decision proved timely.

With the spring of 1837 came the revival of the expedition. Dickerson, whether by intention or mistake, reassigned Maury to the frigate *Macedonian*. Furious with "that imbecile Secretary," Maury declined the post and demanded a furlough, even though he needed the extra pay with Ann expecting a second child.

On June 25 Ann gave birth to their second daughter, Diana, whom they nicknamed Nannie Curly, and the happy occasion was immediately followed by a letter from Dornin urging Maury to forget his differences with the Navy Department and come on the expedition. Dornin said he had spoken with Jones, who agreed that Maury would be elevated to the post of acting astronomer. Maury could not resist the opportunity for a purely scientific role, so in September he traveled to Philadelphia to further his knowledge of the subject.

Never trusting Dickerson to keep his word, Maury stopped at Washington on the way home from Philadelphia. The secretary confirmed the appointment as being signed, and when Maury reached Fredericksburg, he found his orders in the mail. As of September 5, his pay advanced from $1,200 a year to $2,500. With all of his problems suddenly solved, Maury could even find a few good words for Dickerson. He wanted to make the voyage more than a narrow study of astronomy. Writing with cautious enthusiasm, he asked the secretary to expand his scientific role to include other subjects, such as "observations on ebb, flow, and other tidal phenomena; on the set, rate, breadth, depth, and the like of currents at sea; on the prevailing winds of . . . sea; on the variation of the needle; on the longitude and latitude of places already known, or which may be discovered; and on any other subjects of general interest to the navigator . . . which may serve to guide mariners in the navigation of whatever seas the expedition shall visit." Maury recognized the importance of expanding the scientific study of the sea by using systematic observations, but would Dickerson?

For the beginning of the most cherished work of his life, Maury waited for an answer from the secretary, not knowing that Captain Jones had unintentionally thrust him into the center of a controversy involving Lieutenant Charles Wilkes. Wilkes had recently returned from Europe, where the secretary had sent him to purchase chronometers and the most advanced scientific instruments available for such an expedition. Jones ordered Maury to obtain the instruments from Wilkes, but the latter would not give them up. Maury explained the problem to Jones, who then complained to Dickerson, writing, "I again send Lieutenant Matthew F. Maury to Washington, for the purpose of receiving the chronometers and other instruments said to be in the depot." Jones undiplomatically accused the secretary of conspiring with Wilkes to detain the instruments, and a few days later confided to Maury that Wilkes's "conduct in reference to the expedition . . . has been such that I should not be willing to trust him to make any selections or calculations whatsoever for the expedition."

On November 29 Maury finally received the instruments, but in checking the list of Wilkes's purchases he found many of them missing. Once again, Jones complained to Dickerson, who instructed Wilkes not to take USS *Porpoise*, to which he had been assigned, to sea until Maury received all the instruments. Wilkes did not have the instruments, but he had intentionally muddied the waters by sending them off to the naval store in New York, knowing that other commanders would requisition and remove them to satisfy their own needs.

Many years later Wilkes revealed that he had personally stonewalled the expedition because he believed that Jones "was not equal to the task." Nor, according to Wilkes, did Jones have the ability "to organize the expedition and . . . was inadequate to accomplish it." Regarding the instruments, he admitted locking them in storage at the New York Navy Yard and keeping the keys. Upon returning to New York, he said, he found the storage area "broken open and their contents examined by those entirely unacquainted with them." The only person in the navy who knew more than Wilkes about astronomy and the use of instruments was Maury. Wilkes knew it and resented it. In his autobiography, Wilkes wrote, "I was very desirous of showing the uses and mode of handling the Instruments to the person who was going out in Charge of the Astronomical & surveying department, but there was no one ordered . . . to perform the duties." Wilkes simply lied, and in the year he wrote this, most of the men who could have refuted it were dead. Wilkes did all in his power to undermine Jones because, though only a lieutenant, he wanted to head the expedition.

The battle between the secretary and Jones, now in its second year, ended on December 6, 1837, when the latter, apparently wanting to rid himself of the problem, complained of a chest cold. Dickerson obliged by relieving Jones as commander of the expedition. Then, when searching for a senior officer to replace Jones, Dickerson found no one interested in the command because of the agonies Jones endured dealing with the secretary.

President Martin Van Buren, who inherited the problem of the expedition from his predecessor, took hold of the matter in December 1837. He excused Dickerson from any responsibility for the expedition and transferred the project to Joel Poinsett, the secretary of war. Poinsett, who knew little about naval affairs, asked Maury to prepare a list of recommended candidates. Poinsett then held interviews with officers to help choose a commander. Among others, he interviewed Maury himself, who had not put his name at the top of the list but at the bottom. In the end, Poinsett chose Lieutenant Wilkes, who Maury believed from the very beginning had conspired with Dickerson to obtain the command. Wilkes's appointment rankled dozens of senior officers who had been passed over. They flatly refused to go on the expedition because they held a higher rank than the squadron leader. Though Maury could not complain on the basis of seniority, he asked with much regret to be detached because Wilkes's behavior over the instruments did not make for a compatible relationship. Poinsett agreed, and though Maury requested active duty in any other form, he returned once again to Fredericksburg "on waiting orders."

Meanwhile, Wilkes held several interviews with Nathaniel Bowditch on the subject of navigation. Having once been in charge of the Navy's Depot of Charts and Instruments, Wilkes did not lack scientific credentials. Had he wished, he might have sought the advice of fellow officer Maury, who had already superseded Bowditch on the subject of navigation, but doing so would have been an admission that another lieutenant in the navy had as much or more knowledge than he. It is interesting that in Wilkes's 930-page autobiography, he never once mentioned Maury, whom he knew well and adroitly avoided as a scientific competitor.

In the eyes of the public the hassle over the expedition made the entire navy from secretary to ordinary sailor look ludicrous. Maury remained faithful to the navy but critical, blaming the mess on Dickerson more than Wilkes. On July 1, 1838, President Martin Van Buren finally replaced his inept secretary with James K. Paulding and told the latter to restore the prestige of the navy. Maury no longer trusted civilian administrators and conceived a way to induce the new secretary to consider needed reforms. Using pseudonyms such as "Harry Bluff" and "Will Watch," he submitted a number of editorials to the *Richmond Whig and Public Advertiser* criticizing the failings of the old naval bureaucracy and demanding changes.

The newspaper editorials caused an enormous stir. The public believed a high-ranking captain had written them, and Paulding went on a fishing expedition to find the author. For many years Maury remained undiscovered, and by the time his authorship became known, everything in the navy had changed.

Dornin excused himself from the expedition and eventually became a captain. The Wilkes expedition proved controversial, because a lieutenant led it, as well as successful, because it represented the nation's first scientific expedition into the South Seas. The six-ship flotilla departed Hampton Roads, Virginia, in August 1838, visited several islands in the South Pacific, and in early 1840 sighted the Antarctic continent. Wilkes claimed to have discovered Antarctica, though its existence was already known. Whalers had hunted there, and previous expeditions had been stopped by ice. The four-year expedition gathered every conceivable form of scientific data related to weather, climate, and astronomy, and charted a section of the world extending from Antarctica through the Fiji Islands, Hawaii, and the far North American coast in the Pacific. The ships returned by way of Honolulu, Manila, Cape Town, and Brazil. But Wilkes's accomplishments were overshadowed when the secretary of the navy publicly reprimanded him following a court-martial for improperly punishing members of the crew. Wilkes's reputation suffered further when some of his claims of discovery proved to be untrue.

Six months passed after Maury withdrew from the expedition led by Wilkes and before he received orders for duty on *Engineer*, a small survey steamer commanded by Lieutenant James Glynn. Like Maury, Glynn resented Wilkes and had resigned as hydrographer for the exploring expedition. While Maury and Glynn took soundings off harbors in North Carolina, Georgia, and along the Gulf Coast, Lieutenant Dornin worked on a scheme that would take him and Maury into the Pacific Northwest to survey the mouth of the Columbia River. When no mission materialized, Maury returned to Fredericksburg to await orders. After learning that the brig intended to replace *Engineer* would not be ready until October, he decided to take his family to Tennessee for the purpose of persuading his parents to come live with him and Ann in Fredericksburg. His parents had become frail, and he had not seen them for nine years.

The trip to Tennessee changed Maury's life, but not as he expected. While making arrangements for his parents' care, he received orders to report to the brig *Consort* in New York. Maury departed from Tennessee, traveling by stagecoach. When passing through Ohio on October 17, 1839, the coach stopped at Lancaster, where the agent overloaded it with three more passengers. Maury gave his place inside the coach to a woman and joined the driver on the top. The stagecoach, top-heavy with passengers, baggage, and luggage, moved at a rapid clip over a dark, narrow, and meandering soft-shouldered road. On a sharp curve it began sliding off the track, careened suddenly, and turned over. Flung from the top, Maury somersaulted in the air and landed hard, fracturing his thigh bone and dislocating his knee. The local doctor snapped the knee into place but improperly set the thigh bone. Days later a doctor from another town rebroke the bone and reset it—all without an anesthetic.

Maury could not be moved. He spent seven weeks lying in a shoddy tavern that served greasy soup before he could take a few painful steps with his leg strapped in a crude cast. Maury finally got into a sleigh with help from cousin John Minor and started for New York. When he arrived, *Consort* had sailed without him.

In late January 1840, Maury returned to Fredericksburg. He could not dress or undress himself, and he could not get out of bed without help. He applied for pay to cover money loaned to him by his cousin, but the nagging question in his mind, and that of his family, was whether the injury would end his career in the navy or, worse, leave him incapable of performing any work whatsoever.

Chapter Five

SETTING THE NAVY STRAIGHT

WITH muscles atrophied, ligaments ruptured, and the main tendon torn, Maury recognized the importance of building strength to support his knee. He could not keep the joint in place, and when he tried to walk, the pain emanating from the dislocation paralyzed him. What he feared most was being unable to go to sea. As he did throughout his life in times of trial, he turned to his faith, praying to God for the understanding and the grace to accept his fate.

In mid-February he shared his fears with his first cousin Ann Maury in New York, a woman more intellectually inclined than his wife and with whom Maury enjoyed discussing issues of politics, science, and self-development. He wrote to her in detail of his disability, wondering whether he would be compelled to content himself "with cultivating a few little patches of knowledge." He admitted that his mind had become a "wilderness" of knowledge, and he sought answers as to how to direct it—to "light or heat?—storms or currents?—ship building or ship-sailing?—steam or trajectiles?. . . winds or tides?"—and so on. For Maury, the desperate search for a scientific role had begun.

By March he felt well enough to hobble about on crutches. With strength slowly returning to his shattered thigh, he wrote Secretary James K. Paulding asking to be assigned a duty that could be performed on crutches. Paulding chose not to respond, so Maury set to work reviewing his fifteen years in the navy, nine of which had been spent at sea. The more he thought about it, the more angered he became about chronic problems in the navy, problems that with little difficulty could be corrected. The service had been in a slow decline, building fewer vessels and ignoring rapid advances in steam technology. The fighting force afloat had diminished in size, and Maury believed the navy's ships and ordnance had become so outdated that a European power could sweep it from the sea in an instant. He understood that peacetime politicians responded mostly to public pressure, so while nursing his injury, he contrived a way to stir up civilians with a series of straightforward articles. The country had already heard from Harry Bluff, and now they would hear from him again. With characteristic wit, Maury titled the articles "Scraps from the Lucky Bag," naming them for a shipboard receptacle used to collect odd lost items found on the ship. With such a title, Maury could roam through the multitude of issues that troubled him.

Few people knew the identity of Harry Bluff: Maury's wife; his publisher, Thomas A. White of the *Southern Literary Messenger*; and his cousins in New York, who sometimes critiqued the articles before they went into the mail. Maury's first article attacked the navy's inability to defend the country and protect the nation's fast-growing carrying trade. Only six frigates had been built during the past forty years. Worse, Maury argued, the navy had no plan, no mission beyond the status quo, and little self-respect. As an example, he showed that because the navy provided only three ranks—lieutenant, commander, and captain—officers were often embarrassed at sea and in foreign ports by being overshadowed by men of higher rank from other countries. After the article appeared in the *Messenger*, the *Army-Navy Chronicle and Scientific Repository* reprinted it, thereby ensuring that Harry Bluff's opinions would be read at the highest levels of government.

In another article he implored the navy to improve the nation's seaboard fortifications and take steps to prepare for the eventuality of war. He also criticized past and present secretaries for not keeping pace with the army in the education and intellectual development of their officers; there should be a school where midshipmen could receive training commensurate with West Point. Without a library in Fredericksburg to supply him with news, Maury drew his insights into the problems of the navy from a combination of his own experiences coupled with letters from fellow offi- cers who acted as unwitting informants. It is not clear from their letters to Maury whether they knew the identity of Harry Bluff, but it is clear from Maury's letters to his friends that he cleverly baited them for the informa- tion he sought.

Months passed without word from the navy. His leg, which seemed on the mend, reached a plateau, worsened for a while, and confined him to doleful meditation. When the navy refused to pay for his medical expenses, he sought restitution from the stagecoach company and collected dam- ages of $2,325—financial salvation for a lieutenant drawing half-pay. But the navy he loved continued to ignore him, and he languished in Freder- icksburg with little hope for the future.

Not until late August of 1840 did he hear from the Navy Department, when orders came summoning him to Washington for a physical examina- tion. Six months earlier, surgeon John C. Mercer had examined the leg and pronounced Maury totally disabled and unable to perform any duty what- soever. Two more navy surgeons, John A. Kearney and Bailey Washing- ton, now reexamined the leg and rated Maury's condition as "three-fourths a degree of permanent disability." Still, the change in status to partial dis- ability gave Maury an additional $12.50 a month, retroactive to the date of the accident. The extra money arrived in Fredericksburg about the same time as Richard Launcelot, the couple's first son and third child, whom they nicknamed "Goggen," though most of the family called him Dick.

While in Washington, Maury hobbled over to the Navy Department and chatted with Secretary Paulding, who promised to assign him to hy- drographic work, but after two months of hearing nothing further on the subject, Maury gave up any expectation of being called to duty and re- turned to his persona as Harry Bluff.

This time the mysterious Mr. Bluff pressed for a school for midshipmen with full-time naval instructors and not teachers plucked temporarily from civilian vocations. He laid out a four-year course of study, followed by two years at sea before standing examination for commissioning. Though he advocated using a school ship, he later changed his mind, realizing that the navy needed an academy equal to West Point. Maury's article won the approval of most navy personnel. He later learned that the officers on the seventy-four-gun *Delaware* took a collection, printed copies at their own expense, and distributed one to every congressman. Even civilians could see the logic of Harry Bluff's argument and harried their Washington representatives for action. Four years passed before anything happened, and though George Bancroft took the credit for starting the school and Franklin Buchanan became its first superintendent, Maury's service to naval education is indelibly inscribed on the west wing of the main academic hall of the U.S. Naval Academy at Annapolis.

So popular had Harry Bluff's articles become that the publisher pressed him for more, but Maury now found reasons for caution. This man Bluff had rankled old-line officers such as Commodore Charles Morris, who vowed to discover the identity of the bothersome author who rocked not just the boat but the whole hierarchy of the navy. Warned by fellow officers that he was under suspicion, Maury nonetheless brought out his most condemning article. Pointing to examples of graft among the navy's shipbuilders, he blamed the Board of Navy Commissioners for squandering the public's money. Maury showed figures to prove that "one sloop which originally cost $85,000 was repaired at a cost of $120,000." By blaming the navy commissioners for allowing such graft to continue, he forced them to publicly deny the charges. Maury expected the rebuttal, and in future articles he presented facts and figures to substantiate his claims. Embarrassed and angered, the commissioners wondered where this man Bluff obtained his information. When Maury went a step further and recommended that the commissioners be replaced by a more efficient system consisting of competent officers, they stormed in protest.

Most navy men agreed with Harry Bluff, and they circulated the articles throughout the service. When Maury began to receive encouraging letters from navy friends, he knew the identity of Harry Bluff had been exposed. He expected repercussions, but his articles attracted too much public support for Congress to duck the issues stressed by Harry Bluff. In the next session, Congress held debates on major reforms. Even the old sea dogs began to admit that something needed to be done. Some now claimed to have said so themselves, but it took a junior lieutenant on three-quarters disability, landlocked in Fredericksburg, Virginia, to wake up the country. So supportive had the officers of lesser rank become that one suggested that Maury, being the only person who clearly articulated the defects of the service and offered a well-conceived plan for solving the problems, be named secretary of the navy. The national press picked up the idea and endorsed it, advocating that Maury resign his commission, become a civilian, and then be made secretary. Paulding, the secretary of the navy, could have spared himself and his Board of Navy Commissioners untold grief had he simply ordered Maury to Beaufort, South Carolina, to perform hydrographic work, as promised. There, Maury's fertile mind would have become immersed in some new scientific endeavor, and Harry Bluff would never have emerged to disrupt the secretary's tranquility.

At the age of thirty-five, the last thing Maury wanted was a cabinet post, and he meant it sincerely. His articles had clearly spoken to the lamentable condition of the navy and aroused the attention of the country. Old-line officers who had lapsed into administrative roles chafed at being challenged by a lieutenant for practicing and protecting obsolete methods. One of their number who chose to remain anonymous sent a lengthy rebuttal to the *Southern Literary Messenger*. The editor published it, but commented that it proved nothing to the contrary and more than substantiated the charges in Bluff's "Scraps from the Lucky Bag."

By July 1841, everybody in the navy knew the identity of Mr. Bluff. As a tribute to the man who had done so much to improve his publication's circulation, the editor of the *Messenger* printed a brief biography of Maury, written by an anonymous "Brother Officer." Though the article praised the lieutenant, Maury referred to it as his obituary and believed an enemy had authored it.

With the cat out of the "Lucky Bag," Maury found he had many friends, among them Captain Thomas ap Catesby Jones, who still waged a private war with the Board of Navy Commissioners. Jones had been given command of the Pacific Squadron and wanted Maury to go with him as flag lieutenant on the frigate *United States*. Maury longed for active duty and wrote the secretary of the navy, admitting to his crippled condition but feeling quite capable of performing "the lighter duties at sea." Four months passed before orders came, but Jones advised him to remain in Fredericksburg until the vessels were ready to sail. The delay proved fatal to Maury's plans.

Maury's friends, fearful that he would permanently cripple himself, first tried to dissuade him from going to sea. Ann disapproved as well. When they failed to change his mind, a well-meaning local judge secured from three of Fredericksburg's leading physicians written statements attesting to Maury's inability to serve at sea on a warship. The judge tucked the message in an envelope, added his own comments, and mailed it to the new secretary of the navy, Abel P. Upshur. On November 15, 1841, the secretary wrote to Maury, advising that he had received the letters and asked if the lieutenant still intended to participate in the cruise. Maury had no knowledge of the physicians' statements until he opened the envelope from Upshur. After much soul-searching and inner distress, he concluded the doctors were correct and asked to be relieved from duty at sea. Upshur complied, and all of Maury's friends and family expressed grateful relief. But Maury, faced with the prospect of never again going to sea, shuffled about Fredericksburg in silent despair.

Maury knew little about Upshur, who had been a bright, successful lawyer in private life, but he would learn more about him in the coming months. When Upshur became secretary of the navy in 1841, he did so saying, "For twenty years past the navy had received from the Government little more than a step-mother's care. It was established without plan, and has been conducted upon no principle fixed and regulated by law. Left to get along as well as it could, the wonder is, that it retains even a remnant of character which it won so gloriously during the last war." When taking office he found that Paulding, his predecessor, had made it a mess. "I might as well have left my intellect at home," he lamented. In many respects he agreed with Harry Bluff's "Scraps," which continued to gather momentum in Congress. Upshur understood his role and, having the authority to implement changes, said, "I will reform it or else the country shall know that I am not to blame for my failure."

Meanwhile, Maury's scientific efforts were beginning to bring him recognition among members of the National Institute for the Promotion of

Science. A board of distinguished fellows elected him a corresponding member, and he suddenly found himself in company with men such as Joseph Henry, a professor at the College of New Jersey (later Princeton University) who would later become director of the Smithsonian Institution, and Alexander Dallas Bache, president of Girard College of Orphans in Philadelphia and one of the nation's emerging scientific minds. The institution also brought Maury into contact with distinguished foreigners such as L. Adolphe J. Quetelet, the Astronomer Royal of Belgium, and Professor Charles Wheatstone of King's College, London. Both Quetelet and Wheatstone would become particular supporters of Maury, whereas Henry and Bache would join forces to become Maury's competitors for scientific recognition. But for the moment, they were all friends, and Maury now had another vehicle for promoting scientific themes, the National Institute *Bulletin*. He made quick use of this publication to advance his views, writing an article to urge an exploration of the bottom of the sea.

Upshur soon discovered that everything Maury, as Harry Bluff, had said about the uselessness of the Board of Navy Commissioners was true. He found the commissioners to be indecisive, deliberate, unresponsive to new ideas, and derelict in their efforts to learn or understand new technologies. He also discovered that the exorbitant cost of building ships for the navy was even worse than Maury's estimates, some being on the stocks for as long as twenty years because the board regularly asked for superfluous design changes. And as Maury had claimed, Upshur found partisanship and graft especially pervasive in New York's shipyards. When Upshur asked the board why more vessels using steam had not been built, Commodore John Rodgers admitted knowing too little about the subject to write specifications. Frustrated by old fogies, in 1842 Upshur disbanded the board of commissioners and created six bureaus reporting directly to himself—one being the Bureau of Hydrography.

Dismayed by the inbred incompetence of navy personnel, Upshur considered hiring a civilian to head the small hydrographic bureau, but the idea of putting a civilian into the post when so many naval officers had nothing to do astounded Maury. He wrote the secretary, asking that if the navy formed such a bureau, he be considered for it.

Because Congress muddled Upshur's proposal for reform, four months passed before the secretary replied. Congress wanted Upshur's six proposed bureaus reduced to three, each assimilating two of the proposed functional oversights. In its infinite wisdom, Congress paired Hydrography with Equipment and Repairs. Upshur resisted because he knew that one had nothing to do with the other, and he wanted the Hydrography Bureau to operate independently from the others. He also wanted time to weed out incompetents. Meanwhile, he knew exactly what to do with Maury and ordered him to report to Washington as superintendent of the Depot of Charts and Instruments. This time there were no letters from friends and well-meaning doctors to obstruct the assignment. Had it not been for his bad leg, Maury might have jumped with joy. Here at last was a chance for scientific study in Washington, the hub of the nation from which most important decisions emanated. With Ann in the final term of pregnancy with their fourth child, Maury decided that she should remain in Fredericksburg until the baby came. Also, Maury's parents were now living with them, having recently moved from Tennessee, and because of their age and frail health it seemed best that they not be moved again so soon. Maury made arrangements for his family's care, packed his bags, and departed on the fifty-mile journey to the nation's capital to begin his new position.

On Independence Day, 1842, Maury arrived in Washington to take charge of the navy's Depot of Charts and Instruments. Despite its unimpressive name, the depot acted as the navy's center for the maintenance of its instruments and for the collection and publication of all the department's nautical and astronomical research. After more than thirty months of injury-imposed inactivity, Maury felt released from bondage. He soon discovered that although Washington had changed, senior officers of the navy still resisted steam, the exceptions being men such as Alexander Slidell MacKenzie, Matthew Calbraith Perry, Robert P. Stockton, and young John A. Dahlgren. Ancients such as Commodore Isaac Chauncey, one of the navy's annoying martinets, believed that steam would never be perfected. The pride of the service continued to be sixty ships of sail, of which only thirty-seven remained capable of performing active duty at sea.

It would be the sailing ships that engaged Maury's attention, because their problems were quite unlike vessels powered by steam.

Since its formation in late 1830, the Depot of Charts and Instruments had passed through the management of three lieutenants—Louis M. Goldsborough, Charles Wilkes, and James M. Gilliss—each of whom possessed a measure of scientific ability. Because Wilkes had located the depot in his home and was expected to soon return from his exploring expedition, Maury moved the records and equipment to a double house at 2422–2424 Pennsylvania Avenue NW. Each side had two rooms on the first floor and ample bedrooms on the second floor for his family, who planned to join him as soon as circumstances allowed. Into the two lower rooms of one home he moved the charts and records, and into the corresponding two rooms of the connecting home he moved the astronomical, meteorological, hydrographic, and navigational instruments used and serviced at the depot. That Maury could jam all the records and instruments into the lower level of his home and still have room for his family on the second floor indicates how modest the Depot of Charts and Instruments was in 1842.

Because of his injury, Maury had been out of circulation for three years. There had been no evening walks to lower Manhattan to witness the great changes in commercial shipbuilding. New designs emanating from the old Baltimore clipper ships such as the *Ann McKim* (built in 1833 and ascribed by some as the first of the modern clipper ships) appeared on the stocks of New York shipyards. The lucrative China trade produced the impetus behind the thrust for larger and faster ships. In 1844, Brown and Bell launched the 600-ton *Houqua*, William H. Webb launched the 500-ton *Montauk*, and in 1845 Smith & Dimon, located at the foot of Fourth Street on the East River, launched the 752-ton *Rainbow*, all large packet ships with sharp lines. *Rainbow's* distinguishing characteristic was an extremely hollow bow, a feature other shipbuilders later copied when designing the huge clipper ships. Maury could not have come into the Depot of Charts and Instruments at a more propitious time for the maritime industry, but he had not yet defined his role, nor could he during his first months as superintendent.

Officers at the depot determined time using the combination of a telescope mounted at right angles to a horizontal axis, a clock, and a chrono-graph. The staff made observations at noon, during the time of transit of the sun over Washington, and again at midnight, using prominent stars to determine solar and sidereal time. They compared time secured from ce-lestial observations to a standard clock and thence to all the navy's chronometers. Errors in the chronometers were recorded as variation from absolute accuracy. If the navigator did not know the rate of variation, his calculations would result in errors that could throw his position off by countless miles. Once set, a chronometer was never adjusted, and when it went to sea, its recorded rate of variation went with it. The depot kept comprehensive records on every chronometer, and if one showed signs of increased variation, it would be replaced.

Maury found no challenge in checking chronometers or in the mundane task of caring for sextants, quadrants, barometers, and thermometers. Me-teorological studies, however, intrigued him. The navy placed emphasis on wind force and direction, a subject Maury had long wished to study since the days of childhood when he and brother Dick would lie on their backs in fields and watch clouds form ahead of a storm. The depot also maintained a library of charts and nautical books issued to departing vessels and re-turned at the end of each cruise. Although hydrographic work also fell un-der the purview of the depot, when Maury took command he found no work in process, nor had Wilkes or any of his predecessors initiated any.

When Maury had urged the importance of an observatory in one of the "Scraps" from Bluff's "Lucky Bag," one of his predecessors, Lieutenant Gilliss, had used the article to persuade his superiors to seek an appropria-tion for a building to house both the depot and an observatory. As-tronomers and mathematicians agreed with both Maury and Gilliss that the crude observations being made at the Depot of Charts and Instruments could not be confirmed without corresponding observations validated in Europe, and to do so required a fully equipped observatory. The project had been under discussion for more than twenty years, and Upshur continued to press the matter with Congress. Never had the legislature been con-fronted by so many navy bills. In a final rush to adjourn and go home, the House and Senate on August 31, 1842, met Upshur's demands and passed an appropriation of $25,000 for an observatory. The secretary dispatched Lieutenant Gilliss to Europe to purchase the most advanced astronomical instruments available and put him in charge of building the country's first national observatory, which in 1854 would officially become the U.S. Naval Observatory and Hydrographical Office.

In early 1843, construction of the U.S. National Observatory began on a site selected by Commodore Crane and known as Braddock's or Camp Hill in Foggy Bottom. The site was ninety-five feet above the high-water mark on the Potomac River and about a mile west of the White House, between D and E Streets and 23rd and 25th Streets. Marshy flats lay between the river and the new brick building taking shape on the hill.

Because so many of Upshur's actions seemed to have originated from Harry Bluff's scraps, Maury expected to suffer a few cuffs from members of the ousted Board of Navy Commissioners, but only Commodore Charles Morris showed outward resentment. Maury now had the support of Upshur, and when Congress compelled the secretary to unify the departments of Ordnance and Hydrography into a single bureau, he made Maury's Depot of Charts and Instruments a part of it. By placing Commodore William M. Crane, also a former navy commissioner, at its head, he spared Maury a confrontation with Morris.

Crane had become a midshipman in 1799 and participated in the first bombardment of Tripoli in August 1804. As a lieutenant during the War of 1812, he had the unhappy experience of serving on the frigate *Chesapeake* during its ill-fated battle with HMS *Leopard*. Before becoming a commissioner, Crane held a variety of important commands, including the Portsmouth Navy Yard and the U.S. Mediterranean Squadron. His men liked him, and his actions had always been dignified and honorable. He respected Maury and never manifested a single expression of animosity toward his subordinate. With concerns over reprisals removed, Maury could begin his work unfettered. Upshur could not have provided Maury with a better boss.

Soon after moving the depot into his own quarters, Maury made a shocking discovery. When examining the navy's sailing charts, he found most of them useless and some as old as a hundred years. Others came from foreign countries, including charts for sailing the coast of America, and Maury noticed that most of these were wrong. For portions of the Gulf of Mexico there were no hydrographic data at all. In a candid letter to the new secretary of the navy John Y. Mason, Maury reported his findings, making the final point that "The charts used by an American man o'war when she enters the Chesapeake Bay, on her way to this city are English and we are dependent upon the English Admiralty for them."

During his months as acting sailing master on *Falmouth*, Maury had become acutely aware of the importance of providing navigators with accurate information. But after two months at the Depot of Charts and Instruments, he found little of value for the navigator, only heaps of disorganized data and a thousand dusty logbooks that had been kept since the birth of the United States Navy. His predecessors referred to the logbooks as depot rubbish, but Maury began to slog through them. The more he read, the more excited he became. Although some logs offered little information of value, other logs contained enormous detail. They might be dead storage to the navy, but to Maury they represented a treasury of priceless information, for they contained records of weather and sea conditions for every month of the year in all parts of the world.

Sailing masters entered data haphazardly, using no system and little consistency in their record-keeping methods. Logs often contained cartoons, sketches of sea life, silly limericks, or anecdotal information having more to do with a person's escape from boredom than with navigation. All sailors seemed possessed by omens, one writing in his log that an instance of "really bad weather" operated as a "prelude to, some great change, perhaps an earthquake, who knows?" For a person accustomed to deciphering puzzling problems, the logbooks offered a challenge equal to mastering spherical trigonometry—though not at all like it. Maury decided to take the logs as they were, and by applying scientific methods, extract only data pertaining to navigation.

His own experience sailing *Falmouth* provided the starting point. Maury began with the route between New York and Rio de Janeiro, which he had traveled during the summer of 1831. He pulled from the boxes only those logbooks containing entries about cruises made between the same two points. He reviewed his own logbook, one kept with meticulous records on winds and currents, and adopted its format. For his staff of midshipmen, he laid out a simple program for excising data on the force of winds, rain, fog, unusual ocean currents, the distance covered during a daily run, all natural or unusual phenomena observed, and any other detail that might prove significant or insightful in finding the fastest route. To coworkers he explained that he hoped to organize from the mass of data collected simple sailing directions that would provide average conditions prevailing for each season of the year for any vessel sailing from the eastern seaboard to Rio de Janeiro, Brazil.

Because of the time-consuming nature of the work, Maury applied for more men. To accelerate the project, he asked Commodore Crane for four lieutenants—among them Maury's brother-in-law William Lewis Herndon, eight passed midshipmen, one clerk, and one draftsman. Maury's current quarters could not hold all the personnel requested, but he looked ahead, hoping to occupy rooms in the unfinished observatory at Foggy Bottom. Herndon arrived for his new posting in late summer 1842, and he and his wife, Mit, shared meals in Maury's quarters, where the three made a happy company.

The analysis of old logbooks began to reveal trends. On voyages between New York and Rio de Janeiro the typical navigator, instead of using nature to hasten the voyage, fought with it. But Maury needed more data. If vessels sailing the route could provide enough additional information to validate his conclusions, he could produce an entirely new type of chart. To this could be added sailing directions, giving the navigator both the safest and fastest course to follow for each month of the year. He began to observe the possibility that sea lanes—the natural flow of winds and currents—could be determined and their seasonal variations defined. There were also belts of calms in the horse latitudes and doldrums as the navigator approached the equator. Some vessels slipped through them quickly while others lay becalmed for weeks, and Maury concluded that good or bad luck played more of a role than skillful sailing. He began to ask himself, could there be doorways through the calm belts?

He believed that the only way to collect data quickly would be to get it from the nation's shipping firms. With only thirty-seven naval vessels at sea, data collection would take decades to collect without help from merchant vessels. The type of chart he envisioned looked nothing like the ones then in use. He intended to depict the patterns of wind and currents as tracks in the sea. For centuries the lack of accurate sailing charts had caused enormous loss of life and property, but Maury envisioned more than port-to-port or point-to-point charts to increase safety. Such charts also could make sailing faster. If he could persist in his work, he believed he would find those routes and make them available to every ship that sailed the seas. Doing so would enhance the competitiveness of the nation's merchant enterprises, but Maury looked beyond the shores of America. He wanted his work to be of service to the world.

Maury harbored concerns. After all, he dealt with the navy, an institution slow to change. Would the navy, he wondered, have enough faith in him to provide the necessary funds to support his work? Turning to the Bible, he read Psalm 8: "Thou madest him to have dominion over the works of thy hands . . . and whatsoever passeth through the paths of the seas."

Chapter Six

TRACKING THE WINDS
AND CURRENTS

THE musty, water-stained logbooks of the depot would never be enough to complete the exhaustive study Maury had in mind. They yielded compelling guesses but not conclusions. Ships sailing the same course during the same period of the year experienced similar wind, weather, and current conditions. Ships sailing between the same two points but on different courses experienced different conditions. To Maury, same and different conditions each suggested a form of potential consistency, but how could he be certain?

Having drafted his conception of a chart, Maury laid it before Commodore Crane. To capture the data needed for making charts, he presented his own version of how the navy could help. Crane listened with interest, asked a few questions, and approved the project. Orders went out from the Bureau of Ordnance and Hydrography instructing naval officers to collect and send all navigational, hydrographic, and meteorological data to the superintendent's attention at the depot. Then the wait began.

With what would become the work of his life now underway, Maury set his staff to laboriously compiling data from the depot's repository of hundreds of old logbooks covering more distant voyages. As time permitted, the staff worked at the chore in bits and pieces, classifying each logbook by its voyage, such as New York to Rio de Janeiro, New York to Liverpool, Philadelphia to Gibraltar, Baltimore to Valparaíso, and so on. Long voyages to places such as India, China, and Australia were put in separate stacks and set aside because Maury wanted first to focus on the North Atlantic, Brazil, and Cape Horn. He had asked Crane for more men, and now he badly needed them. The larger responsibilities of the department still involved the maintenance of navigational instruments, daily weather reports, and a set of routine celestial observations.

Months, even years, would pass before fresh data became available, but it was a time of exciting research.

Maury returned to Fredericksburg in time for the birth of a fourth child and second son, John Herndon Maury, on October 21, 1842. Three days after the birth he set out again for Washington, but in November Ann was sufficiently recovered to join him there with their children and Maury's parents, filling the house with family. The reunion was soon saddened, however. On January 30, 1843, Maury's father died.

Maury had been working at a furious pace, as many as sixteen hours a day, when the sad event occurred. In a letter to his cousin Ann, he wrote, "The doctor has said I was destroying myself with over much headwork and in consequence I have had to hold up somewhat. But it is a hard case that one's brains will not stand the work of one's will." Sheer will and a self-imposed workload kept Maury going. The cause of "over much headwork" may have had less to do with his labors at the depot and more to do with Maury's revisions to his *Navigation* book. New knowledge required a new edition, and he immersed himself in preparing it. Heeding the doctor's instructions, Maury eliminated a large amount of night work, but he continued to divide his days between emendations to *Navigation* and extractions of data from old ships' logs.

He drove his staff as hard as he drove himself. He and his brother-in-law, William Lewis Herndon, worked well together, but the pace would eventually tell on Herndon.

❧

ONE of his daughters (not identified but most likely Diana) later recalled that during their residence at the depot her father spent all of his time writing or walking around the room like a sailor pacing the deck of a ship. Guests came and went. Maury enjoyed them all, but he especially liked young people, and, she recalled, "his humor and gentle sympathy were very pleasing to them." Being a man of great patience, he "never seemed annoyed by the interruptions of visitors or the noise of his [eight] children," and even when in the midst of his most intense work, he would lay down his pen and join in the laugh of a good joke, and he always allowed the fun to go on. His greatest books, she recalled, were written in the parlor while surrounded by his family. "He never had a study," she recalled, "or anything like a sanctum, where his wife and children could not come, preferring to work in the midst of them wherever they congregated." Whatever he wrote he reread, and how he shook his head conveyed to the family whether or not he approved of what he had written.

She also remembered that in these years her father became stout and his curly hair thinned. However, his complexion remained fresh and ruddy, his hair brown, and his blue eyes clear. She recalled his chest as deep and full and his arms as long and strong; he used his small and well-formed hands in a graceful manner when talking with others.

❧

HIS young subordinates found the labor of charting voyages from old ships' logs tiresome and tedious. Maury noticed they worked harder when he worked with them. He had just finished the revisions to the first edition of *Navigation* and was at the point of relaxing when in May 1843 his mother died, leaving him with the difficult and sad burden of settling his parents' estate.

Soon after Maury introduced his project to the navy, long-forgotten logbooks, charts, antiquated sailing directions, and other nautical papers packed away in the trunks of old salts began flowing into the depot. Many of the documents predated the navy, some being hundred-year-old relics from merchantmen and privateers, often worthless or no longer legible. But among the old logs Maury found valuable records of distant voyages to regions seldom, if ever, visited by ships of the navy. He compiled enough data from journeys made by merchantmen to the East Indies to publish in the March 30, 1843, issue of *Army-Navy Chronicle and Scientific Repository* one of his first articles since joining the depot, titled "Directions for Approaching the West Coast of Sumatra," a place he had been but once.

The deeper Maury plunged into the details of his self-chosen program, the more information he wanted. He conceived a new abstract log for the navy, which clearly and in an organized manner laid out all the important observations required for his analysis. But to get data faster, he needed to recruit help from the merchant service, so he prepared for commercial ships a modified log requiring fewer observations and less detail. Both logs contained blank forms with spaces designated for the class and country of the vessel, name of captain, composition of vessel (iron or wood), ports of call, and other salient information. Each section of the log contained spaces for the daily recording of latitude and longitude, direction and speed of currents, compass variation, air pressure, air and water temperature, direction and force of winds, and other meteorological data.

He did not expect to get cooperation from shipmasters of merchant carriers as easily as from naval personnel, so he sought help from the National Institute for the Advancement of Science, an organization for which he now served as a director. Its members included the secretary of the navy, the secretary of the army, chief of engineers of the army, and several members of Congress. And there were other distinguished men of power and influence, including former president John Quincy Adams, a self-trained scientist of considerable merit. At a gathering in July 1843, Maury laid before the institute's members his "scientific project" and sought their support. He introduced his standardized abstract log and asked the board to endorse his program. He then asked the members to encourage every shipmaster to use the log and to send it to the depot at the conclusion of their voyage. He promised to provide all participating merchantmen with copies of his charts and *Explanations and Sailing Directions to Accompany the Wind and Current Charts* (widely known as *Sailing Directions*) free of charge in exchange for receiving the data specified on the *Abstract Log for the Merchant Service*. He encouraged everyone to use this more comprehensive log adopted by the navy, but he would be content with either. In his appeal to commercial shippers, he wrote:

Course.	Dist.	Diff. Lat.	Dep.	Lat. by D. R.	Lat. by Ob.	Varia.	Diff. Long.	Long. in	Long. by Ob.

H.	K.	H.K.	Courses,	Winds.	L.W.	Remarks.

Course.	Dist.	Diff. Lat.	Dep.	Lat. by D. R.	Lat. by Ob.	Varia.	Diff. Long.	Long. in	Long. by Ob.

Hourly entries (above) and daily summaries (next page) from the logbook of the whaling ship George Champlain, which became volume 241 in Maury's logbook archives. From the florid penmanship in the hourly entries for Wednesday, January 3rd, 1848, emerges a complaint of stomach cramps.

(continued next page)

A Passage From Japan Towards...

The daily summary in a neater hand from Tuesday, September 27, reads, "All these 24 hours Moderate gales and thick weather from NW... steering... with all sail set and a heavy heavy swell from NW..." These were the lodes mined with such care and labor by Maury's staff.

This Bureau is making arrangements for collecting, with the view of rendering accessible to navigators, all that valuable information relating to the navigation of distant seas, which is collected by our enterprising commanders of merchant vessels in their various pursuits and much of it hitherto, for the want of some channel of communication, has been lost to the public at large. To enable it to bring this undertaking to a useful issue, the Bureau relies much on the public spirit and intelligence of American owners and masters of ships. It takes this opportunity of inviting their cooperation, and of requesting the favor of you to communicate any information of general character, that you may now or at any time possess, relating to the following subjects.

Maury listed the details of his abstract log and added other observations, such as the discovery of islands, rocks, shoals, shifting bars, and other navigational hazards. He also sought reports of any errors in charts currently in use, of tidal phenomena, the discovery of new anchorages, information on wood and water, sightings of icebergs, tracks of unusually short passages, and any other information that might be helpful to commerce and navigation. His interest in the geography of the sea induced him to add a space for remarks, where he requested information on such things as sea birds, whales, water discoloration, seaweed, and "all atmospherical and other phenomena" observed by the mariner. He even asked that sealed bottles be thrown overboard at specified times and allowed to drift until picked up by other seafarers, who would obligingly note the direction and distance of drift in the Remarks section of their logs. The institute appointed a committee to meet with the secretary of the navy and to urge that all naval vessels be issued Maury's blank charts. The secretary adopted Maury's expanded program and told the committee the charts would be implemented. For the present, many merchants remained skeptical, uncertain of the benefits, and left the decision of cooperation up to their shipmasters.

Setting bottles adrift had already enjoyed a curious history. Captain Frederick W. Beechey of the Royal Navy, a contemporary of Maury's, once kept a bottle chart that tracked the voyages of one hundred bottles cast from different locations in the center of the Atlantic. Some turned up in Europe and Africa, but a large number of them found their way to the Gulf Stream and made a circuit around the North Atlantic and came ashore on the

British Isles. Of two cast overboard in a southern latitude near the coast of Africa, one found its way to Trinidad and the other turned up at Guernsey in the English Channel. The problem with bottle experiments was the inability to discover where they had been on their travels or whether some prankster had picked one off the sea and carried it off course several hundred miles before throwing it back. Nonetheless, Maury believed that in the North Atlantic all drift materials not becoming bound by land would eventually work their way into the Gulf Stream, circle through polar waters, and find their way to Europe, as did the bottle that came ashore at Guernsey. Commenting on the Gulf Stream, one modern historian observed that "More drift bottles, oceanographer's nets, scientific instruments, and thermometers have been thrown into it than into any other current anywhere."

Not all navy captains responded with enthusiasm to the department's new directive. To those who complied, Maury wrote letters of thanks. To those whose efforts did not meet expectations, he coaxed them to do better by praising those who did best. Maury never expected to collect all the information he wanted, but he wanted all he could get.

He feared the program would die if he could not swiftly demonstrate its value. He needed to concentrate on one section of the ocean at a time, and after experimenting with the New York–Rio route, he started work on the busier tracks of packets traveling the North Atlantic between Europe and the United States. By September he had collected enough data to create a track chart for the North Atlantic. He wisely kept Commodore Crane informed, asking for authorization to begin the chart and to keep it at the depot "so that corrections of every ascertainable error may be made as soon as needed." Maury foresaw the need to make continuous refinements and did not want too many copies distributed until he could compare and verify the chart by using logbooks from future voyages. He again reminded the commodore of the country's hydrographic inadequacies, emphasizing "how little we have as a nation done for navigation that we, at this moment, are dependent on a foreign government even for the charts of our own lakes and inland seas." The commodore approved the charting project, knowing that the more encouragement Maury got, the harder the lieutenant would work.

Maury's remarkable ability to track winds and currents was well known:

shortly after the second edition of *Navigation* reached bookstores in the fall of 1843, mariners stripped the shelves of copies, and the book became so popular that the navy began to consider replacing Bowditch's *Practical Navigator* with Maury's *Navigation*, using the latter as the preferred textbook for training midshipmen. As soon as Maury learned of the navy's intentions, he immediately went to work on a third edition, adding more spherical trigonometry and dozens of new diagrams. He simplified everything for the reader. Knowing the average sailor's difficulty in understanding spherical trigonometry, he created a wooden globe cut into sections in such a way that the reader would be able to physically manipulate the methodology of the subject. On September 4, 1844, Secretary of the Navy John Mason signed an order making the third edition of Maury's *Navigation* the primary textbook for training midshipmen, whether at sea or in school at one of the navy yards.

In 1844 Maury began to hit his intellectual stride. He went to work on ocean phenomena, an interest developed during his first cruise on *Brandywine*. The Gulf Stream represented one of the most fascinating and least understood of all the powerful currents circulating the seas. In 1512, Ponce de León, when sailing between Florida and the Bahamas, had tried to set a course southward, and despite the fact that his ships enjoyed a fresh favoring wind, he found the current against his squadron so strong that his fleet actually lost way. On September 13, 1492, Columbus also observed a northern equatorial drift, which today we regard as the southern arm of the Gulf Stream. A. J. Findlay, whose contemporary directories of the oceans included a study of the Gulf Stream, believed that Columbus's discovery of the drift provided the first record of a mariner's ocean-current observation anywhere.

For more than three and a half centuries men such as Benjamin Franklin had studied the Gulf Stream flow and presented their theories, but in 1844 it still remained an unsolved mystery. During the second day of the first congress of scientific men held by the National Institute for the Advancement of Science, on April 2, 1844, Maury delivered the main speech of the day, a paper titled "The Gulf Stream and Currents of the Sea." It became an important speech for him. Early theorists such as Peter Martyr tried to show that the north-flowing waters stacked up and disappeared into a hole in the Earth somewhere in the north polar regions. Maury knew better. Not accustomed to public speaking, he appeared "as pale as ashes for the first few minutes but soon recovered and elicited great applause." With Maury, adulation always worked as a positive stimulant.

Maury kept his presentations captivatingly simple. When talking of currents, he used as his theme words that would one day catch the attention of millions of readers in a book yet to come:

> There are rivers in the sea. They are of such magnitude that the mightiest streams of the land are rivulets compared to them. They are either of warm or cold water, while their banks and beds are water of the opposite temperature. For thousands of miles they move through their liquid channels unmixed with the confining waters. They are the horizontal movements called currents.
>
> The mariner can sometimes detect them by the different color of their stream, while, if they give no such visible sign of their existence, he can trace them by testing their temperature with his thermometer.
>
> There is an equatorial current sweeping from east to west all along either side of the equator, and well nigh encircling the globe. There are polar currents setting from polar regions toward the equator; and there are return currents setting from the equator toward the poles.

Three-quarters of a century later, in 1922, the coast guard cutter *Tampa* would test Maury's theory by lying athwart the edge of the Gulf Stream in the upper North Atlantic with her bows in the cold current and her stern in the warm. A thermometer dropped from the bow read 34 degrees Fahrenheit while the thermometer dropped from the stern—240 feet away—read 58 degrees Fahrenheit. Then, overnight, the track of the current shifted slightly, but the clear "wall" between the warm and cold water remained. In 1950, another survey discovered that the Gulf Stream shifted course as much as eleven miles a day and affected the water "for a thousand fathoms [6,000 feet] down," something that Maury believed but at the time could not verify. He also believed that wind had no influence on the major currents of the seas, which he later confirmed as also being true of the Japan Current in the Pacific.

Some early scientists postulated that the Gulf Stream had as its source the Mississippi River, but Maury explained that the volume of water emptying from the river into the Gulf of Mexico was "not equal to the one thousandth part of that which escapes from it through the Gulf Stream." Its current, he said, "is more rapid than the Mississippi or the Amazon," and he described its indigo blue tint as being so distinct that "one-half of [a] vessel may be perceived floating in Gulf Stream water, while the other half is in common water of the sea."

In studying the Gulf Stream, Maury found it to be slightly dome-shaped in the middle and about two feet higher than the littoral water along its edges. Although the current runs north, boats lowered onto its center would slough off to either the east or the west and join patches of seaweed and driftwood already collected along the rim. Because of the sharp distinction, navigators would be able to see whether they were traveling in the current or beside it, either of which could improve their speed, depending upon their bearing.

He refuted many theories about the origin of the current and added to the knowledge of the Gulf Stream's circuit into the higher latitudes of the North Atlantic, where it meets a cold (Labrador) current from Baffin Bay that dives under it. The warm upper water continues an eastward flow toward Great Britain. He also discovered that the Gulf Stream experienced a seasonal shift, running closer to Newfoundland during the summer months, farther south in the winter.

Maury thought of the Gulf Stream as a great flowing mass of warmed-up water, emerging from the Caribbean by way of the Straits of Florida and then, after sweeping northward along the Atlantic seaboard, rambling toward Europe on a broadening, weakening front. The Gulf Stream sloughed off great chunks of itself as it traveled, mixing at the edges and in the middle also, containing within itself both a powerful jet stream and a countercurrent that went the opposite way and created eddies in the ocean. He further believed that this gigantic and complex system formed a part of a greater circulatory movement that pushed a large part of the North Atlantic round and round in a clockwise and ceaseless flow. More than a hundred years would pass before modern science discovered that Maury was right: in the eastern North Atlantic the Gulf Stream bifurcates, with one arm continuing north of the British Isles to Norway, while the other blends with the Canary Current. This branch swings southward down the Portuguese coast and becomes the west-setting North Equatorial Drift, which in turn completes the circuit back to the Caribbean.

Maury became an instant authority on the subject of marine research, and other organizations began to inundate him with invitations to speak. On May 14, 1844, six weeks after his speech to the National Institute for the Advancement of Science, he appeared in Washington to deliver a paper before the Association of American Geologists and Naturalists titled "On the Currents of the Sea as Connected with Meteorology." While there Maury did a bit of lobbying in an effort to advance his own plans. Afterward, a committee of seven scientists ambled over to the Navy Department to urge Secretary Mason to take more interest in the data Maury needed to continue his study of the Gulf Stream or, for that matter, any other ocean phenomena the lieutenant chose to investigate.

❧

TWO years had passed since Congress appropriated money to build an observatory with space to house the Depot of Charts and Instruments, and still no individual had been named to head it. Maury, who no longer walked with a cane, often visited the elevated site at Foggy Bottom to witness the building's progress. In late August 1844, as the observatory neared completion, speculation spread through the halls of the Navy Department as to who would be appointed superintendent; that the legislation creating the observatory allowed civilian staffing opened the field beyond the navy. Several names had been cast into the hat, among them Lieutenant James M. Gilliss, who supervised the depot prior to Maury. Gilliss had drawn the assignment of purchasing astronomical instruments in Europe, installing them in the observatory, and supervising the construction of the building. He wanted the appointment and felt entitled to it. However, some in Congress believed a civilian scientist with distinguished credentials should be chosen. Maury coveted the assignment, wanting the superintendency even more than promotion. After being in the navy nineteen years, he was still a lieutenant drawing a salary of $1,500 a month, the same pay as a lieutenant on shore duty.

Secretary Mason did not like the idea of a civilian running the new National Observatory, so the selection of a superintendent came down to two lieutenants—Gilliss or Maury. By the fortune of good timing, Mason's order on September 4 making Maury's *Navigation* the standard textbook for midshipmen provided the political impetus. Advocates pointed to Maury's pioneering work on hydrography. None of his predecessors, including Lieutenant Gilliss, had elevated the depot to an institution of science. Though Gilliss was better known as an astronomer, Maury had been the man assigned to the exploring expedition under Commodore Thomas ap Catesby Jones as acting astronomer. He had traveled to Philadelphia for additional training and after being attached to the depot had continued to educate himself on the subject. Maury's industry and administrative skills, combined with his great ability in mathematics, placed him several rungs above Gilliss. Scientists such as Alexander Dallas Bache lobbied for Gilliss, partly because the two men had become close friends and allies in matters involving scientific research. Bache viewed Maury as a rival who paid him no fealty: a rival who had begun to attract too much favorable attention for his oceanographic work. Bache could control Gilliss, but not Maury, and this troubled him. Such egos led inevitably to conflicts.

On October 1, 1844, the partially completed building at Foggy Bottom opened and Mason appointed Maury superintendent of the new National Observatory. A week passed before Maury learned of the appointment. He had been on an extended trip through the Northeast looking into the various types of nautical instruments used by commercial ships in the harbors. His plans to pull the merchant marine into his enterprise required an up-to-date awareness of the type of detail shipmasters were capable of providing, and this depended upon the various brands of instruments carried on their ships.

It was a short and pleasant ride from Maury's home at the Depot of Charts and Records on Pennsylvania Avenue to the new observatory. Over the door hung a marker, still there: "Founded A.D. 1842. John Tyler, President of the U.S. Abel Upshur, Secretary of the Navy." When Maury took possession of the observatory in 1844, the right-hand wing was not yet built, nor the lower dome in the rear. The structure, designated a National

Historic Landmark in 1966, is on what are now the grounds of the U.S. Navy Bureau of Medicine and Surgery; the marshy flats to the west have given way to the John F. Kennedy Center for the Performing Arts. (Within fifty years the "new" observatory at Foggy Bottom would be deemed inadequate, and in 1893 the current incarnation of the Naval Observatory would open on Massachusetts Avenue, N.W., in the neighborhood known as Embassy Row.)

For the next decade, the National Observatory would be also variously known as the Naval Observatory and the Depot of Charts and Instruments. Every astronomical publication produced at the observatory during Maury's tenure as superintendent would carry dual title pages, one reading "National Observatory" and the other "Naval Observatory." In 1854, the name would be formally changed to the U.S. Naval Observatory and Hydrographic Office. For simplicity, we will use the term "Naval Observatory" regardless of date.

The observatory presented an expansive appearance totally different from the cramped quarters occupied by the depot in Maury's rented dwelling. The observatory had four rooms on each floor in the main section of the building. The elevated, copper-sheathed observation dome rose prominently from the center of the building, under which a central hall opened into a circular area having hallways that led into the wings, each having stairways to the second floor. Four wings, two on each level, flared east and west, each wing containing two rooms seventeen feet square. A shorter wing to the south provided additional work space. It connected to a subterranean passageway that led to an underground observatory, separated from the main building, for studying the Earth's magnetism. Maury separated his staff into distinct departments of hydrography, astronomy, and meteorology and placed navy professors in areas where they could be most useful.

Twenty-three feet across, the dome revolved on cannon balls rolling in a groove of cast-iron rail. The astronomical instruments mounted in the dome included a 9.6-inch achromatic refractor, made by Mertz and Mahler of Munich, Germany—it was the best in the U.S. Navy. The west wing contained a vertical transit, 4.9 inches, and the east wing held a 4.1-inch

The U.S. Naval Observatory (center) was completed in 1844, and Maury began his duties as its first superintendent on October 8. The following April he was authorized to seek bids for construction of the superintendent's house (left), into which he moved his family in 1847. The observatory site was a low hill about a mile west and a little south of the White House, from 23rd to 25th Streets N.W., between E Street and the swampy, mosquito-infested shore of the Potomac. The Naval Observatory remained there until 1893.

Lithograph views of Washington and Georgetown, circa 1849. Note the Naval Observatory (right, second from bottom). The new Smithsonian Institution (top, third from left) is depicted as it would look when completed, though construction had only begun in 1849. The large central view is from the portico of the Capitol. Foreground in the bottom center view toward Georgetown is an elevated aqueduct of the Chesapeake and Delaware Canal, crossing the Potomac.

telescope, a comet seeker with a 3.9-inch glass was mounted in the equatorial room.

While the staff settled into new workrooms, Maury began an examination of the astronomical instruments purchased by Gilliss. He found, to his dismay, that many had been installed before the building settled. Some of the delicate instruments had suffered damage, and others had to be remounted or recalibrated. When Gilliss had mounted the instruments, he used a cement containing sulfur, and Maury discovered that the substance emitted an acidic gas that corroded the bases of the delicate instruments. He began immediate repairs and reported the damage to Commodore Crane, but he avoided any reference to Gilliss as the responsible party. The cleanup took much longer than Maury anticipated. Months later he was still making apologies for being unable to determine and compare the difference in longitudes between the Naval Observatory and observatories at Harvard College and the University of Alabama. Even when in working order, the impressive observatory manifested drawbacks due to its Foggy Bottom location. Mists and fog, rising with regularity from nearby wetlands, too often obscured the heavens and made observations difficult. Had Gilliss rather than Crane been allowed to have chosen a different site, it would not have been within the District of Columbia.

Former president John Quincy Adams, an amateur scientist himself and now seventy-eight years of age, took an active interest in Maury's projects. From time to time he would visit the observatory to view the heavens with the lieutenant. They became good friends, which led to a discussion between Adams and George Bancroft, the new secretary of the navy, as to why Maury should be compelled to walk from his home to the observatory at all hours of the night. He suggested that Maury have a home on the same site. Bancroft approved the idea and authorized funds for the construction of a superintendent's house connected to the east wing of the observatory. The new building would be a spacious home and a timely one, because on November 13, 1844, Ann Maury gave birth to their fifth child, Mary Herndon, whom the family called Tots. Such elegant quarters would delight the superintendent, but officers of higher rank on duty ashore began to ask themselves whether a lieutenant deserved such luxurious accommodations while so many of them lived on smelly supply ships anchored off a navy yard.

During his first two years at the observatory, Maury spent much of his time acting as the principal observer while training an astronomical staff composed of three lieutenants and six passed midshipmen. In May 1845, two navy professors of mathematics also joined the staff, followed later by a third. In December Maury put the professors to work systematically cataloging "every star, cluster, nebula or object that should pass through our field of view." For Maury's young astronomers, the task became enormous. Civilians had earlier declared that no officer in the navy possessed the training or academic credentials to function effectively as superintendent of the observatory. But when Maury published *Astronomical Observations Made during the Year 1845 at the National Observatory*, followed by like publications during each of the next six years, international praise silenced the critics, for it became evident that Maury's studies of the universe equaled or surpassed those of the finest observatories in Europe. There was a price for Maury's relentless pace, however. His brother-in-law, William Lewis Herndon, who had worked assiduously on Maury's whale charts, suffered a nervous breakdown and resigned from the observatory in 1845.

In 1846, war with Mexico threatened to interrupt Maury's work. On May 11, two days before Congress's official declaration of war, he offered his services and those of his staff to Secretary Bancroft for duty in the waters off Mexico or "wherever our services are most required." The Navy Department considered Maury's work too important to be disturbed, but Bancroft nonetheless detached some of the junior officers and created disruptions Maury found difficult to overcome. As the weeks passed, incoming logbooks began to stack up, unread, in the hydrographic wing.

Toward the end of 1846, hydrographers using data collected from the new abstract logs began to see trends emerging. Sufficient time had passed. Captains returning from long cruises had forwarded their logs to the observatory. Lieutenant William B. Whiting drew the first track chart of the North Atlantic Ocean. It would become the model for all others. Whiting had served as a midshipman on *Falmouth* and assisted Maury in coastal surveys on the west coast of South America. There, back in 1831, he predicted that Maury would some day achieve great prominence. At the time, his shipmates had laughed at the thought.

With the first wind and current track charts for the North Atlantic coming off the drawing board, Maury's objective to provide charts that would "generalize the experience of navigators in such a manner that each may have before him, at a glance, the experience of all" was taking shape. The chart tracked a vessel's course, and along that track Maury used the symbol of a brush to graphically summarize a day's observation. The rounded head of the brush was centered on the track and pointed to the direction from which the wind blew (see illustration page 130). The trailing hairs of the brush flared out to show the variance of wind directions during the day. When the hairs were tightly bunched, the winds had been steady; when the hairs diverged widely, the winds had varied, sometimes from one quarter to another. Rather than show recorded wind velocities directly, Maury let the spacing of the daily symbols speak to the distance covered by a specific vessel each day, from which wind strength could be inferred. A small arrow showed the strength and direction of local current, its flow designated in knots. Maury's charts depicted the track of vessels "showing the time of the year, the prevailing winds and currents encountered," and all other information helpful to the navigator. A careful sailing master could scan a track sheet for any section of the Atlantic and chart his course using the best experience of those who had passed before him.

The more Maury studied the logbooks, the more convinced he became that even the most roving winds could be tracked and charted. The paths of winds and the currents of the sea could not be changed, but the paths of ships could be redirected, speeding them on their way by other routes. In terms an uneducated sailor could understand, Maury wrote:

> The direction in which a wind blows is so constantly changing that we often speak of the winds as fickle, inconstant, and uncertain. There is, however, order in the movements of the atmosphere. The fickle winds are obedient to laws.
>
> Certain of the winds blow without interruption in the same direction, and at nearly the same rate. So constant are they that vessels often sail in them for days and days without, as sailors say, "changing a stitch of canvas." It was the steady blowing of these winds that so alarmed the crew of Columbus on his first

voyage to America, and led them to fear that they should never get back to Europe. From their always pursuing one trade, or from their importance to navigators, these winds have been called the trade winds or trades. They are currents of air ceaselessly but consistently winging their flight from the polar and temperate regions toward the equator.

The periodical winds are those which blow for a certain time in one direction, and then for an equal, or nearly equal time, in the opposite direction. They are the land and sea breezes and the monsoons.

Because the war had filled the Gulf of Mexico with naval vessels on blockade duty, Maury's staff expedited the completion of charts for Mexican waters. The study had been of much interest to Maury because he discovered that "the general currents of the Gulf of Mexico are almost as regular in their courses and as sharp in their outlines as is the Mississippi River itself." If the navigator used the chart as a guide, Maury believed that a vessel, "by turning a little to the right, or a little to the left, according to its indications, may convert an unfavorable into a favorable current, and the reverse." The chart also displayed all hazards—rocks, reefs, and shoals—which, "by reason of their uncertainty as to their existence, disfigure the best general charts, harass navigators, and stand in the way of commerce."

The route to Rio de Janeiro had baffled mariners for years, the chief obstacle being the great bulge on the South American continent at Cape São Roque, located on the eastern tip of Brazil about 6 degrees below the equator and reaching far into the Atlantic. A skipper leaving New York usually set a course across the Atlantic nearly to Africa so as to safely weather Cape São Roque before turning south to Rio. Skippers took this roundabout course because they could not find another. They used the northeasterly trades of the North Atlantic to work down to the southeasterly trades below the equator, but the two trades were separated by bands of calms. Once in the doldrums, a vessel could drift about for weeks before finding enough wind to break through the calms and pick up the southeasterlies.

A twentieth-century sailor in a four-masted bark bound from Australia to France remembered his experience crossing the doldrums, writing:

We were two months from the Equator to the Bay of Biscay—a longish passage. Day after day in the burning doldrums the sun beat down and the wind, when it came at all, played useless tricks, like coming at the ship from ahead to blow her backward and then, by the time we had all the yards hauled round and the sails properly trimmed, dying at once, so suddenly and thoroughly that it was hard to believe it had ever blown. All the while, the Equatorial Current bore us westward, away from our destination, and I began to understand all too well the fears of the ancient mariners who, drifting into these windless zones and observing the current's stealthy, silent thwarting of their every effort to gain ground, held that their ships never could return to the ports whence they had sailed, never could progress again but in one way and that way hopeless.

Three calm belts had puzzled navigators for centuries. Maury compared them to "mountains on the land [that] stand mightily in the way of the voyager, but, like mountains, they have their passes and their gaps."

The calms of the doldrums occurred at the equator, and the other two belts occurred along the horse latitudes around the Tropics of Cancer and Capricorn. Barometric pressure readings were high on average in the horse latitudes and low in the doldrums, a configuration Maury described as a "barometric valley, between . . . two barometric ridges." From those two ridges the trade winds originated, blowing equatorward—from the northeast in the Northern Hemisphere and the southeast in the Southern Hemisphere—to disappear when striking that barometric valley.

Seeking an explanation for these observations, Maury suggested that the northeast and southeast trades collided in the equatorial region, pressed against each other, and created a band of light airs, calms, and baffling winds that extended entirely around the Earth. Where the winds met, the stronger of the two would push against the band, causing it to stretch and diminish in thickness until reaching a point of equilibrium with the opposing winds, thereby falling off and creating the calms. Maury had no way of elevating himself above the planet, but if he could have done so and added different colors to the northeast and the southeast trades flowing into the equatorial calm belts, he would have observed belt shifts of several degrees with each season of the year. The entire system of belts, including the trade winds, moved north during May through August and then remained stationary until December, after which the belts began moving south. As the shifting occurred, the thickness of the belts diminished seasonally by several degrees along specific sectors of longitude. But what might be detected from aloft could not be seen at the level of the ocean. Maury figured all this out not from observations in space but from data collected from more than one hundred thousand observations made by sailors at sea level. "The changes that are continually going on in the strength of the winds keep the calm belt in a trembling state," Maury concluded, "moving now to the north, now to the south, and always shifting its breadth or its place under the restless conditions of our atmosphere."

Today we know that Maury's observations were more accurate than the mechanisms he postulated to explain them. We know, for example, that heated air rises at the equator—creating the barometric trough there— then flows poleward in the upper atmosphere, cooling as it goes. Some of it subsides again near 30 degrees North and South, forming the barometric ridges of the horse latitudes typified by the persistent Bermuda–Azores High. Lacking knowledge of such upper-atmosphere circulation patterns, Maury made the most of what he could see. The northeast and southeast trades do not contend with one another; rather, they are warmed and drawn aloft as they near the equator. But mechanisms mattered less to Maury's mariners than his empirical predictions—and on these he was rarely wrong.

He also discovered that the southeast trades were colder than the northeast trades, though both were dry, while air flowing off the poleward sides of the horse latitude belts—the prevailing westerlies of the middle latitudes—formed rain winds, which took up vapor from the seas, conveyed it to other parts of the Earth, and let it back down as snow, sleet, or rain. Maury referred to these bands of wind as being "as steady and as constant as the currents of the Mississippi River" until falling upon a mass of land.

Maury further observed that because the ocean south of the equator tended to be cooler than the water north of the equator, the winds of the Southern Hemisphere were stronger. The Roaring Forties in particular were stronger than the Northern Hemisphere's prevailing westerlies, mainly because there was no landmass to slow them down between Cape Horn and Australia. They swept unimpeded under the Cape of Good

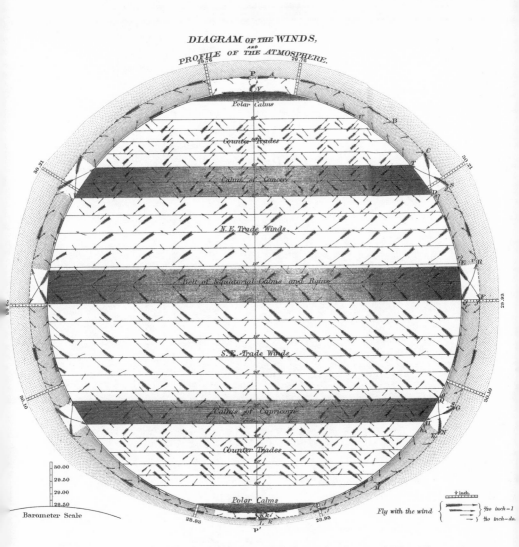

This Diagram of the Winds from the eighth (1860) edition of The Physical Geography of the Sea shows the northeast and southeast trades, the prevailing westerlies of the temperate latitudes in both hemispheres (Maury called them "counter trades"), and the calms of the equatorial doldrums and the horse latitudes around 30 degrees North and South (which Maury called the "calms of Cancer and Capricorn," respectively). Maury correctly deduced from barometric observations that air rises at the equator and sinks in the horse latitudes, but he confused cause and effect, suggesting that the meeting of the northeast and southeast trades drives air aloft, when in fact it is the rising of heated air that helps create the trades.

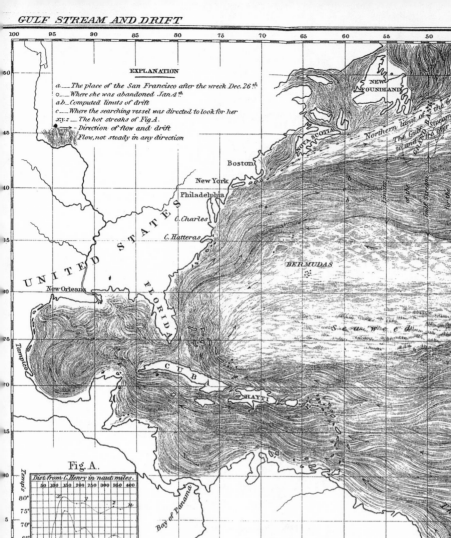

Gulf Stream and Drift, a map from The Physical Geography of the Sea, showing a seasonal shift in the northern boundary and retaining the sailor's traditional perception of the Sargasso Sea as a vast trap for the unwary.

Hope, joined by northwesterlies flowing down from the South Atlantic. Maury said that for one "to appreciate the force and volume of these polar-bound winds . . . it is necessary [to] . . . 'run them down' in that waste of waters beyond the parallel of 40° S., where 'the winds howl and the seas roar.' The billows there lift themselves up in long ridges with deep hollows between them. They run high and fast, tossing their white caps high in the air, looking like the green hills of a rolling prairie capped with snow, and chasing each other in sport." Away from Cape Horn with its fickle gales, the winds in the Roaring Forties blew steady from one direction only. Maury discovered that a voyage from any port in the Atlantic to Australia returned home faster by rounding Cape Horn than by bucking the "brave west winds" upwind to the Cape of Good Hope. Had Captain Bligh understood the Roaring Forties during the time he sailed *Bounty* into the South Pacific, he might never have tried to round Cape Horn on the outbound passage.

However, American and European sailors returning home by way of the Cape of Good Hope found favorable winds along the north side of the Capricorn calm belt and again along the east coast of Africa. But by using that route, a sailing vessel had to cross the calm belt three times instead of once. Once around the Cape of Good Hope and into the South Atlantic, southerly winds blew directly up the west coast of Africa to the equatorial doldrums. These southerlies were so constant and remarkable that Maury called them a "Gulf Stream in the air."

From Australia to England or New York, the voyage is more distant in miles going east around Cape Horn, but in terms of sailing days, it is much shorter than going west around the Cape of Good Hope. Maury discovered the swift Cape Horn route seven years before doubting navigators began to adopt it.

Five years had passed since Maury became the superintendent of the Depot of Charts and Instruments, where he first uncovered the dusty crates of forgotten logbooks, and he was ready to apply his developing picture of the globe-girdling belts of winds and calms to the route between New York and Rio de Janeiro. For more than a hundred years skippers had believed that a vessel would encounter hazardous currents on a straight course south to Rio. Therefore, generations of navigators had fallen into the habit of zigzagging their way down the Atlantic. They bore southeasterly into the North Atlantic, headed for the vicinity of the Cape Verde Islands, and finally steered southerly to cross the equator near 20 degrees West longitude. From there they stood west for the Brazilian coast below Cape São Roque, so that reaching Rio de Janeiro required two nearly complete crossings of the Atlantic. Maury computed the accepted course on a track sheet and found that many vessels actually traveled in miles the equivalent of three crossings of the Atlantic. Decades of word-of-mouth advice had put mariners on the wrong tracks, driven them into calms, and sent them against contrary winds and currents.

The difference between a swift or slow passage often depended upon the time lost passing through the horse latitudes and the doldrums. After Maury discovered that calm belts varied in width, and that those widths varied with the season, he plotted them month by month. Where the bands were narrowest, Maury created new tracks, finding ample wind for a vessel to take and hold a great circle course from New York to an equatorial crossing in the vicinity of 30 degrees West, and he lost no time drawing attention to his discovery.

Conventional wisdom misled mariners when navigating Cape São Roque. Old salts claimed that if a vessel fell to leeward of the cape, she would not be able to beat around it because prevailing winds blew from the southeast. Hence, every vessel approaching the cape tacked far to the east to avoid the possibility of being blown ashore. When comparing log entries from the area, Maury discovered that the São Roque Current, which comes from the South Equatorial Current, split at the cape, with one branch going south and the other flowing north and westward to become an obstacle to southbound vessels. But Maury found that, contrary to popular belief, a narrow band of favorable westerlies ran right down the coastline. So long as a skipper held his ship close to the hitherto dreaded cape, he would make better time, and if he fell into the western current, he could escape by sailing inshore to pick up the westerlies. Certain of his discovery, Maury's *Sailing Directions* advised navigators to "Stand boldly on, and if need be, tack, and work by under the land."

After so many years of following the old route, few mariners were quick to adopt Maury's revolutionary and unconventional instructions for faster and safer sailing. Doubters began to disappear after one courageous shipmaster, Captain Jackson of Baltimore, decided to take the bark *W.H.D.C. Wright* over the exact track laid out by Maury's charts and *Sailing Directions*. Having regularly sailed to Rio laden with flour in exchange for Brazilian coffee, Jackson knew the old way by heart. Using Maury's route to Rio, he shaved seventeen days off his normal voyage of fifty-five days. Feeling more optimistic with his unexpected good fortune, he decided to follow Maury's instructions when sailing home. He made the voyage in thirty-seven days and arrived in Baltimore thirty-five days ahead of his expected return. After the entire shipping community recovered from the shock of seeing Jackson back in Baltimore more than a month early, every shipowner and countinghouse up and down the waterfront suddenly discovered Maury's work. The gimpy lieutenant sequestered in the Naval Observatory actually knew what he was talking about. If someone any longer had doubts, all they had to do was to talk with Jackson. *W.H.D.C. Wright*'s voyage was not a piece of marvelous luck but the advent of a new and magnificent science.

But could a landbound lieutenant in the navy with less than ten years of sailing, and a man without a single academic credit, convince the maritime nations of the world, much less the old salts of his own profession, that he had plucked from their logbooks a better way of sailing?

By sea, following Maury's more direct route, the voyage to Rio de Janeiro spanned 4,093 miles. Years later, after hundreds of trips had been made, Maury tallied the results and found that the distance sailed between New York and Rio averaged 4,099 miles, only six miles more than his computed average. In the 1840s, six miles equaled about an hour's sailing time. Not only did sailors follow his route, they barely wavered from it. As Maury later discovered, "the best-navigated steamships [could] not sail closer than this."

Chapter Seven

SAILORS AND WHALERS

ON May 18, 1848, the editorial page of the *Baltimore American* publicized the speedy voyage of *W.H.D.C. Wright*, giving full credit to Maury's *Wind and Current Charts*. Within days, word spread across the eastern seaboard, into the chandleries of Salem, the alehouses of Boston, the shipyards of New York, the wharves of Charleston, and the merchant houses of Philadelphia. Some asked, "Who is this Lieutenant Maury?" and those who replied probably mispronounced his unfamiliar name.

Shippers knew that every day saved at sea cut costs and lessened the danger of losing ships, cargoes, and crews. Everywhere, competition had become brisk, both in the states and abroad. Thirty years earlier foreign bottoms carried most of the ocean trade. Now, the faster American vessels touting cheaper rates were making headway in European markets.

Within weeks, Maury distributed five thousand copies of his *Wind and Current Charts* free of charge but with a condition of exchange. Knowing that he needed to collect far more data, the wily lieutenant required every navigator who took the charts to complete a standardized recording form and at the end of the voyage send it to the observatory.

With every set of charts went a new ten-page *Abstract Log for the Use of American Navigators*, which was the successor to Maury's *Abstract Log for the Merchant Service*. The pamphlet explained how to interpret the symbols used on the charts, and inside were twelve different blank forms to be filled out by the navigator who used the charts during his next voyage. The booklet contained instructions for making observations at sea and for recording them in the log. At the completion of the voyage, the log was to be returned to Maury at the observatory, where the data could be compared with existing charts or applied to future charts. To applicants for charts, Maury's terms read:

> Notice to Mariners
> Navigators who are disposed to try these routes should have the "Pilot Charts" on board, which "Pilot Charts" will be furnished to them on application either at the National Observatory, at Washington, or to George Manning, No. 142 Pearl Street, New York, provided the applicant will agree to furnish this office an abstract of his log according to the form with which he will also be gratuitously supplied.

The *Baltimore American* editorial started an avalanche of requests that virtually swamped the observatory. Some shipmasters were simply curious about the program, but most were dead serious about shortening their voyages and increasing their profits. By September, the logs began flowing into the observatory, and Maury and his staff were busy trying to handle the volume.

Some vessels sent in logs showing no improvement, but after a thorough examination Maury discovered that some old salts stuck stubbornly to their former routes, still zigzagging about the ocean and paying no attention to the charts. These bullheaded skippers actually did Maury a favor because they validated the charts by not using them. Those who followed the charts, on the other hand, saved enormous amounts of time. The average passage to Rio de Janeiro once took fifty-five days. Maury's charts cut it in half. In May and June 1852, *Grey Eagle* made the trip from Rio to Philadelphia in twenty-three days. In January 1853, *Phantom* sailed from New York to Rio in twenty-three days. As those reports made their way around the shipping community, the zigzagging stopped.

By the end of 1849, Maury's staff had produced six track charts on the North Atlantic and one for the North Pacific. Meanwhile, Maury developed a new kind of wind and current chart and published a prototype pilot chart for the North Atlantic and one for Brazil. After experimenting for several years with track charts, he had devised a way of further simplifying navigation for the sailing master.

His pilot charts (see illustration page 129) divided the oceans into quadrangles, each representing five degrees of latitude and five degrees of longitude. The quadrangle contained the full figure of a compass, sectioned into sixteen equal parts or compass points. Starting with a blank diagram, Maury's staff plotted the frequency of calms and the direction and speed of the winds and currents for each month of the year, placing the values in subsections of each of the sixteen compass points. The charts also showed the number of observations obtained for each square and the percentage of calm days. The pilot chart enabled a navigator to choose the fastest route based upon the experiences of hundreds of navigators who came before him. Maury simplified the use of the pilot chart by providing the navigator with a template that could be fitted over the fastest route and girdle the most favorable winds.

To reduce the work of the navigator, Maury's staff calculated the percentage of winds blowing from each quarter. They placed at the extremity of each compass point the percentage of miles a vessel would lose if she attempted to sail one hundred miles through a particular quadrangle on a particular course. Maury calculated that if the wind did not allow a vessel to sail within six points of her desired course (each point equaling 11¼ degrees of arc), she would lose sixty-two miles in every one hundred she sailed, making good only thirty-eight miles in the direction headed. Maury showed that if the vessel could sail within four points, she would lose only twenty-nine miles, and within two points, she would lose only eight miles. Using this information, a navigator could make faster time by taking a detour when the chart indicated the presence of more favorable winds several miles to port or starboard.

Maury discovered that winds, currents, and calms changed month by month in every latitude, so he created a pilot chart for each month, giving each five-degree sector twelve box diagrams. In this way the navigator of a vessel leaving the Cape of Good Hope for New York could plot his course box by box before sailing, and by following the best wind and current percentages given for the months involved, complete the voyage in the shortest possible time.

After Maury produced a pilot chart, he did not stop taking observations. The work continued as more logbooks arrived at the observatory, and as the staff collected more data, the charts became more accurate. Maury issued the first pilot charts for the North Atlantic and for Brazil in 1849, and by 1854 each had been published in a third edition.

⚛

DURING the year of 1848 Maury attempted to shorten the passage of packets between New York and the major ports of England and France. He set a goal to shave a day from the voyage to Liverpool and a week off the trip to Le Havre. He believed that all vessels, coming and going, crossed too far to the south. In his eagerness to complete the analysis, he wrote Sarah Mytton Maury, a cousin in Liverpool, and asked for her help in convincing English shipowners to contribute to the study. His concept of international cooperation had merit, but Sarah Maury, though an established English author, was not the right person to promote the scheme.

In 1848, Maury still struggled to make ends meet, even though he now lived in the spacious superintendent's house on observatory grounds. Congress recognized his worth by authorizing the newly created Superintendent of the Marine to be paid a salary of $3,000, replacing his lieutenant's pay of $1,500 a year. Due to a congressman's honest error, however, treasury auditors refused to pay the increase because neither Maury, a naval officer, nor anyone else had ever held such a title. Many months passed before Congress clarified that by "Superintendent of the Marine" they meant Maury, the Superintendent of the U.S. Naval Observatory. On August 25, 1848, Congress made his pay retroactive to March 3, 1847—the time when Maury's scientific work first received international recognition as a product of the United States hydrographic staff. Though still a mere lieutenant after twenty-three years in the navy, Maury finally drew enough pay to care for his family and provide an education for his children. Matthew Fontaine Maury Jr., the next addition to the family, was born

January 9, 1849. His parents would nickname him Brave. In the troubling days that lay in the future, Brave would become one of his father's closest companions.

❧

MAURY'S plans for navigation charts continued to expand. As more pilot and track charts became available, European shippers grasped them with the same eagerness as Americans. But to realize his personal objective—plotting the paths of the seas—Maury needed more funding for oceanographic research, and for that, he needed more staff. Merchants understood Maury's financial needs better than the navy, and in June 1848 a group of Boston shipowners offered to raise $50,000 to buy a vessel and put it at the observatory's disposal. Their motive: to verify new routes suggested by the charts. So enthused had Boston merchant Robert B. Forbes become that he copied and restructured several logbooks of vessels returning from the Orient and sent them to the observatory. Maury rejected the offer of a ship on the premise that such work should be carried out by a navy vessel.

Toward the end of 1848 the incoming volume of abstract logs dramatically increased. Navy captains and merchants such as Forbes of Boston and Robert C. Wright of Baltimore demanded that their skippers fill out the forms and follow the charts. Not every shipmaster complied with the request. Nonetheless, Maury wrote with enthusiasm, "The *Wind and Current Charts* come on famously, as rich as famous. I find that tracks of vessels at sea are full of meaning." The pathways of the oceans were beginning to reveal themselves.

Then, at the newly organized American Association for the Advancement of Science, Maury gave a full report on the *Wind and Current Charts*. After informing the assemblage that hundreds of navigators had been sending their logs to the observatory, he said, "Never before was such a corps of observers known," but, he cautioned, the research required many more simultaneous observations from every sector of the seas. "The work," he added, "is not exclusively for the benefit of any nation or age," and his statement prompted the association to suggest that all "the states of Christendom . . . be induced to co-operate with their Navies in the undertaking; at least so far as to cause abstracts of their log-books and sea journals to be furnished to Lieutenant Maury at the National Observatory." The association formed a committee of five members to ask the secretary of the navy to use his influence in obtaining "for Lieutenant Maury the use of observations of European and other foreign navigators, for the extension and perfecting of his charts of winds and currents." Members of the five-man committee included Joseph Henry, who in 1846 had become secretary of the Smithsonian Institution, which was then under construction. In time, Henry, who had cast his lot with Alexander Dallas Bache, would not be so willing to help Maury.

In 1849 Maury settled on developing five different types of charts, most of which he printed on sheets roughly 35.3 inches by 24.1 inches and then sent to an engraver in Washington to be produced in volume. Series A were the original Track Charts covering the North and South Atlantic, the North and South Pacific, and the Indian Ocean. They depicted the frequented sectors of the ocean, the general character of the wind and weather, and the force and direction of winds during different seasons of the year.

The more specialized series B charts included a Trade Wind Chart for the Atlantic and a Monsoon and Trade Wind Chart for the Indian Ocean. Series B charts showed the limits, extent, and general characteristics of the trade wind regions, together with their neighboring zones of calms.

Series C contained the important Pilot Charts on which quadrangulated sections of the ocean recorded prevailing winds, currents, and calms and guided the navigator along the swiftest route.

Series D contained Thermal Sheets of the North and South Atlantic, and Maury used colors, symbols, and isothermal lines to distinguish between the surface temperatures of water during different seasons.

Series E provided Storm and Rain Charts containing the same arrangement of five-degree squares, charting the number of observations by month and showing the number of days of rain, fog, calm, lightning and thunder, or storms, as well as the quarter from which storms had blown.

In 1852 Maury developed Whale Charts, which he titled series F. They

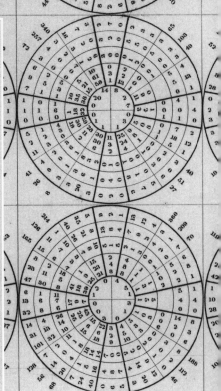

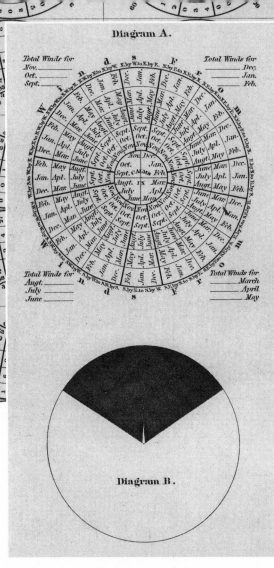

A section of an 1853 Pilot Chart (series C) for the South Indian Ocean. Each square represented a 5- by 5-degree patch of ocean, and the compass rose within each square was an ingenious graphic representation of the frequency of recorded winds from various directions in various months. Comparing the topmost complete square with diagram A, we see that for this patch of ocean there were 340 wind observations in November, and of these only one was from the north and very few were from the east, while there were fourteen instances of calm. The navigator was directed to create a paper pattern similar to diagram B with the black sector cut away. Laying this pattern over any of the squares in the Pilot Chart, with the missing sector centered on the ship's desired course, would enable the navigator to gauge at a glance the chances of a contrary wind.

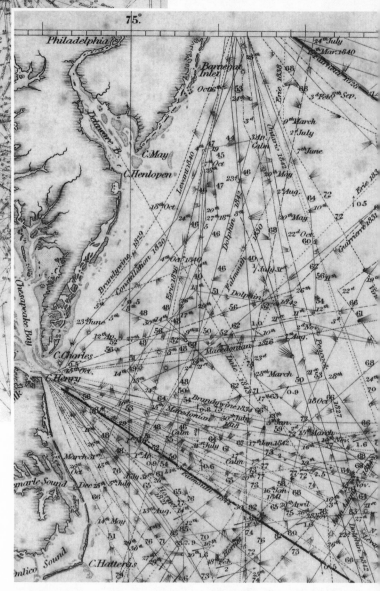

Enlarged section of Maury's first (1848) edition of the Wind and Current Chart of the North Atlantic, Series A. Given the almost overwhelming detail included, eight large sheets were required to cover the Atlantic. After one shipmaster used Maury's charts in February 1848 to save 35 days on a round-trip voyage between Baltimore and Rio de Janeiro, demand built quickly. Upper left: This section of sheet 1 shows U.S. coastal waters. "The winds are denoted by small brushes," read the key, "the head of the brush pointing to the direction from whence the wind blows, the length of the brush showing the comparative force [gale, fresh breeze, moderate breeze, light breeze, light variable airs, moderate breeze with fresh squalls, or light breeze with fresh squalls]." Prevailing currents were denoted by arrows of a length proportionate to speed. Water temperature readings were also shown. Inset: This further enlarged section from the approaches to the Chesapeake Bay shows, among other ship tracks, the homeward-bound track of Brandywine in 1829, three years after Maury, as a young midshipman, had been transferred from that ship to Vincennes.

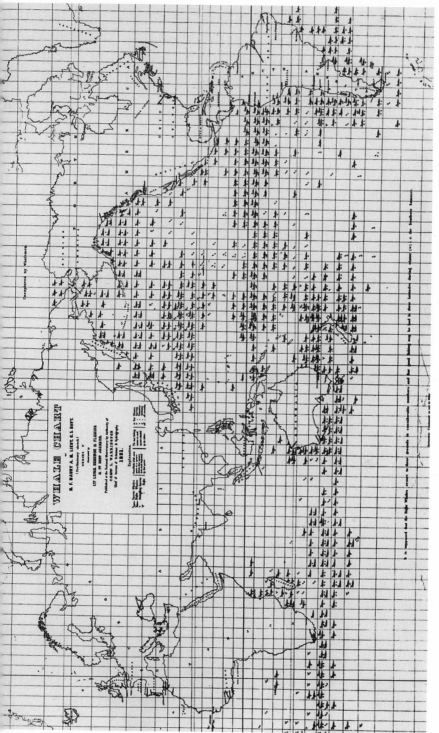

Maury's Series F Whale Charts, like this one published in 1851, offered a visual summary of the distribution of sperm and right whales through the world's oceans in each of the four seasons. Just as whalers used these charts to track whales, Confederate raiders used them to track Union whaling ships during the Civil War.

provided information on the breeding habits, migrations, and sections of the globe where whales had been found during certain seasons of the year. The whales seemed to know the mysteries of the Gulf Stream well, as they followed its drift and used its rich flow as a food source. As the analysis of logs progressed, Maury became acutely aware that new facts of nature were constantly appearing.

In tracking the voyages of whalers, Maury discovered a warm surface current flowing through the Bering Strait and into the Arctic Sea, while on the opposite side of North America a cold undercurrent flowed out of the Arctic and into the Atlantic. At the time, no explorer had measured the currents north of the North American continent, nor was the existence of a Northwest Passage yet confirmed. Only seven years previously, in 1845, Britain's ill-fated Franklin Expedition, with 129 men, disappeared into Baffin Bay in search of the passage and not to be seen again. But Maury's observations of currents gave him confidence that a great mass of open water lay between the Bering Strait to the west and the Davis Strait to the east. Whalers went places few others wanted to visit, and the information they sent to the observatory provided Maury with great insight into the circulation of winds and water around the poles.

Maury discovered that the winds of the upper Indian Ocean were much different from those of the North Atlantic. The monsoons caused changes by season, enabling a vessel to sail with a good northeaster in one season and return months later by a stiff southwester along the very same course, as Arab traders had been doing for centuries. Between Europe and America, however, the North Atlantic could blow gales in any season, and there were no seasonal winds obligingly changing direction twice a year as did the breezes of the Indian Ocean.

Maury's charts and sailing directions were gaining credibility, but nothing speeds acceptance like commerce and sport, and the age of the clipper ship provided both.

Chapter Eight

THE CALIFORNIA CLIPPERS

MAURY'S charts held special meaning to owners of a uniquely American class of vessels: the clipper ships. Built for speed, clippers sacrificed cargo space for narrower hulls that could slice through waves like a knife through soft butter. Prior to 1800, France built the fastest warships on the oceans. By 1812 American shipbuilders had copied the design, evolved it, and became famous for fast sailers of small tonnage, the best of which came first from the yards of Baltimore. During the War of 1812, many of these ships served as privateers. They outran England's frigates and sloops-of-war, exacting a huge toll on British commerce. When the war ended, privateers reverted to their peacetime enterprises. Vessels ranging from 100-ton topsail schooners to 350-ton ships returned to the overseas trade.

Using the best features of the fastest vessels built in Baltimore, Kennard & Williamson in 1833 built for Isaac McKim, a wealthy merchant of the city, *Ann McKim*, the first true clipper ship. At 494 tons, she entered the water with a length of 143 feet, a beam of 27 feet, 6 inches, and a hold amidships of 14 feet. Like the clippers to follow, her draft forward was only 11 feet, but she drew a full 17 feet aft. The builders raked both stem and sternpost at a slight angle and gave her a large deadrise and fine, slightly concave entrance and clearance lines. She had very little freeboard and very little sheer. When launched, she was the first of the brigs and schooners known throughout the world during the late 1830s and early

1840s as the Baltimore Clippers. By the time Maury produced his first chart in 1847, *Ann McKim* had seen better days, and the owners sold her to a merchant house in Chile. Not for twelve years were builders able to improve upon her design or performance, however, and by then, speed had become the name of the game.

The rapid evolution of clipper ships that followed *Ann McKim* astonished European builders. In design and overall performance they eclipsed the best sailing vessels of England, France, the Netherlands, and Spain.

In 1844 New York shipbuilders began work on clippers to outmatch *Ann McKim*. They improved the design and enlarged the vessels. The 752-ton *Rainbow*, launched January 22, 1845, from the yard of Smith & Dimon in New York, was longer (159 feet) and broader (31 feet), but her depth forward had been reduced to 10 feet and her depth aft increased to 18 feet, 4 inches. She became the prototype of the vessels characterized as China clippers. Though she resembled *Ann McKim*, she had long, hollow lines and carried sky sails set above the topgallants. A cloud of extra canvas and over-sparring made her a wet ship but a fast one.

One event more than any other married Maury's scientific work to the expanding growth of the clipper industry: James Marshall's discovery of gold in January 1848 while cleaning out a sluice at Sutter's Mill in California. Soon, prospectors from all over the world made their way to the rich watershed along the tributaries of the American River, which flowed out of the Sierra Nevadas and into the Sacramento River.

Enormous trade opportunities on the West Coast placed new demands on builders to produce faster ships. Almost simultaneously, the discovery of gold in Australia during 1852 added an extra incentive. One trip could pay for the vessel and still return a profit to the owner. Shipyards such as Ewell & Jackson's of East Boston—which laid *John Bertram*'s keel on October 8, 1850, and launched her in sixty-one days—rushed to fill the demand for clippers. A month after launching, fully laden, *Bertram* sailed from Boston for San Francisco.

Rather quickly, Maury put his staff to work on the best routes to San Francisco, a voyage that he called among "the longest in the world—longest both as to time and distance." And since many clippers, after reaching San Francisco, sailed to the Orient, the men at the observatory bent their backs to the task of charting routes across the Pacific and then back again around the southern capes. As Maury had once hoped, his work suddenly turned global.

Publication of the *Wind and Current Charts* and *Explanations and Sailing Directions to Accompany Wind and Current Charts* began about the same time as the mad rush in 1849 to get to California. The stampede of fortune hunters demanded speed in getting to the West Coast. Shipowners answered the call, their vessels being the fastest means for transporting and supplying the mob of prospectors demanding passage to San Francisco and prospectors' tools to use when they got there. The California gold rush resulted in legislative action bearing directly on Maury's work. Congress passed an appropriation for three small navy vessels—though Maury got only one—to assist in the further study of winds and currents and for finding shorter and safer sea routes. The men who sailed the clippers on the fifteen-thousand-mile passage from the East Coast, around Cape Horn and up the West Coast to California, soon discovered that the fastest way to get there was to diligently follow Maury's charts and sailing directions.

Clippers, however, seldom carried more than five passengers, so shippers hastily fitted with bunks the motley collection of laid-up brigs, barks, ships, and schooners languishing for lack of trade and pressed them into the gold rush fleet. Old converted whalers still carried the smells of their former profession, and when these vessels were used for passenger service, skippers converted their huge cast-iron try-pots into soup kitchens, giving new meaning to the term "greasy spoon." For some vessels, it was the last roundup before the boneyard.

These voyages often took six months, and to escape the drudgery, the time lost on long cruises, and the horrors of Cape Horn, gold seekers began hacking their way through jungles to cross the Isthmus of Panama, hoping to catch a charter to San Francisco. Maury suggested that a railroad be built from Aspinwall (Colón) on the Caribbean side to the Gulf of Panama on the Pacific side, thereby eliminating the long, arduous voyage around Cape Horn. He believed that a canal could be built across the isthmus, but at much greater cost. He also supported a national railroad from the Mississippi River to the Pacific, knowing that such matters were projects for the future and not likely to happen for many years. For the 1850s, it would be clipper ships that carried the merchandise, and old tubs or steamers that carried the passengers.

California's gold brought more than wealth to the horde of prospectors who struck it rich in the watershed of the Sacramento River. The enormous opportunity for profit brought about by the demand for goods on the West Coast also accelerated the building of clippers and led to some of the most exciting races the nation ever witnessed. If Maury had not yet convinced the world that his charts and sailing directions had revolutionized navigation, the clipper ships would. A new age of speed had begun. Ship design played an important role, but without Maury's charts the fleetest clipper afloat could sail wayward courses and lose time in fickle winds and unfriendly currents—and there were those who did.

Prior to 1850, the first clipper ship to round Cape Horn and make the voyage to San Francisco had been *Memnon*, with George Gordon as shipmaster. She made the passage in 120 days and arrived on August 28, 1849, setting a record for vessels sailing from New York. In that year, 775 vessels cleared for California, including 12 steamers, together carrying more than 90,000 passengers from all over the world.

In 1850 the first contest between clippers took place. *Houqua*, *Sea Witch*, *Samuel Russell*, and *Memnon* were all rivals from the China trade, and the four of them jumped into a race with three new clippers, *Celestial* from the shipyard of William H. Webb, *Mandarin* from the shipyard of Smith & Dimon, and the clipper bark *Race Horse*. *Houqua* had been built for the Chinese government to be used as a warship and still wore the scars of having eight gunports cut in her sides. China rejected her as too small, so the builders reconfigured her for the merchant trade. *Sea Witch* had a reputation for speed, but the other three vessels in her class were several years older and slower. The three new clippers sailed as outsiders, but this did not prevent large sums of money from being wagered on all seven vessels.

The competitors did not leave port at the same time because the race was not head-to-head competition but rather sailing time; the ship that took the least time to get to San Francisco won. The seven clippers sailed at slightly different times of the year and stumbled into different conditions of wind and weather. *Samuel Russell*, commanded by Captain Charles Low, departed from New York first and arrived at San Francisco on May 6, 1850, in 109 days, beating *Memnon's* old record by eleven days. When word of the record run reached New York, *Samuel Russell's* backers rejoiced, confident that no other vessel could beat her. *Houqua* confirmed their predictions when she arrived on July 23, 120 days out of New York. But *Sea Witch* came romping up the bay the following day, setting a new record of 97 days from Sandy Hook, beating *Samuel Russell's* record, not seventy-eight days old, by twelve days. The passage astonished everyone because *Sea Witch* had skirted Cape Horn in winter storms.

Though the first charts on Cape Horn and the South Pacific would not be available from the observatory until 1852, Maury was not so surprised at *Sea Witch's* performance because he knew, though others did not, that winter storms in that region were less severe than summer storms. An old log from *Helena* showed that she had made a fair run during the winter of 1843. Her skipper, Deliverance Benjamin, reported on May 19 not the usual westerlies but several days of southeasterlies blowing for as many as four days at a time. With a name such as Deliverance, one might not be surprised at Benjamin's closing log entry, which read, "The Lord be praised."

The remainder of the competitors arrived in due course; *Memnon* on September 27, 123 days; *Celestial* on November 1, 104 days; *Race Horse* from Boston on November 24, 109 days; and *Mandarin* from New York on November 29, 126 days. Every vessel made a fine passage for ships under 1,100 tons register. During the same period of time, seventeen vessels arrived at San Francisco from New York and sixteen from Boston—their average passage was 159 days, twenty-eight days shy of the overall average of 187½ days figured by Maury. Even *Mandarin's* dead-last performance of 126 days was fast by comparison. The race presumably occurred during an unusually favorable period of weather.

None of the vessels involved in the race, or those that arrived in between, had the advantage of Maury's collective wisdom because no chart had been prepared for sailing conditions beyond Brazil. The spread between the fastest and slowest ships—twenty-nine days—must have had much to do with sailing speeds, but also with winds and currents and the navigators' abilities to choose the most propitious courses relative to the wind and weather.

Though Maury had not finished charts for Cape Horn, he had provided instructions for rounding the cape and traveling up the west coast of South America in his *Sailing Directions*. Based upon 1,432 observations, the barometer at the Horn ranged between 29.37 and 29.28 inches, lower than some hurricanes. Maury found no place on Earth where more rain fell than on the polar side of the cape, other than a remote mountain station in India that acted as a condenser for monsoons fresh from the sea. Heat flowing off the southern Patagonian peninsula of Argentina mixed with colder polar air and during the summer months created brutal storms containing fierce winds, rain, sleet, and hail. Storms were fewer and less harsh during Patagonia's winter. During the summer months, a sailing vessel standing for the cape encountered less severe weather conditions by "standing boldly south." During the winter months, a sailor could round the Cape farther to the north. The only problem of "standing boldly south" during the summer was the dangerous presence of icebergs carried by northerly currents into alarmingly thick banks of intense fog. Maury laid out *Sailing Directions* for rounding Cape Horn during every season of the year, and most of the early California clippers carried a copy.

By 1851, clipper watching had become a popular sport, and no event captured the interest of the public more than the launching of Donald McKay's extreme clipper *Flying Cloud* from his yard at East Boston (extreme clippers were long and narrow, with little deadrise but with sharp, concave entrance lines and clouds of sail). Grinnell, Minturn & Company bought the vessel for $90,000 and sent her to New York, where Captain Josiah P. Creesy took command. Born in 1814 at Marblehead, Massachusetts, Creesy had made a great name for fast passages to China and the East Indies in *Oneida*, and New York merchants considered him "a most competent navigator and a great driver" of sailing ships. The competent navigator, however, was not Josiah Creesy but his wife Eleanor, who sailed with him.

Flying Cloud wore the lines of a winner. From knightheads to taffrail the massive 1,782-ton vessel stood 235 feet in length with a beam of 41 feet, a hold averaging 21 feet, 6 inches, being deeper aft, with 20 feet of deadrise at half floor. Her entrance lines were slightly concave and very sharp, and she carried a figurehead of an angel pressing a trumpet to her lips. The clipper's three towering masts were raked at 1¼ inches to the foot and were rigged and sparred to carry every square inch of canvas possible. She carried a main yard 82 feet long and a mainmast 88 feet tall, and like all large clippers of her day, she wore three standing sky sail yards: royal, topgallant, and topmast studding sails at the fore and main; square lower studding sails with swinging booms at the fore; single topsail yards, with four reef bands in the topsails, single reefs in the topgallant sails, and topsail and topgallant bowlines.

Flying Cloud arrived in New York on April 28, 1851, under tow of the tug *Ajax*. Four weeks later the clipper watchers along New York's Battery Park spied another new ship standing in the harbor looking like a swan among ducks. Merchants of the well-known firm of N. L. & G. Griswold had gone to William H. Webb and asked him to build the fastest and largest clipper in the world, regardless of cost. On May 24, 1851, Webb's shipyard launched the clipper *Challenge* with a length of 224 feet, beam of 43 feet, depth of hold of 25 feet, and tonnage of 2,006, making her the largest American vessel afloat—27 feet longer than the nation's largest ship-of-war, USS *Pennsylvania*. (Though not quite as long as *Flying Cloud*, she was considerably heavier.) *Challenge* drew 20 feet of water when loaded, had 42 inches deadrise and 36 inches sheer, and was thought to be the most extreme clipper ever built. Her masts were raked more sharply and ranged about 9 feet higher than those of *Flying Cloud*, and she carried 12,700 yards of specially woven cotton duck for extra drawing area and durability. The owners boasted that she would make a record-breaking voyage to California and another to China. After *Challenge* returned, the owners planned to send the clipper to England with an offer to race any distance with any vessel put up by the British, winner take all.

As captain the Griswolds hired Robert H. Waterman, a physically powerful man who among many able captains of the day was not only the most fearless but also one of the worst to sail under. "Bully" Waterman had skippered *Sea Witch* and taken her on record-smashing voyages to China and the East Indies. In 1849 he had brought her home from Hong Kong in seventy-four days, breaking all previous records. He did so by shaving a thousand miles off the normal passage, and his log suggests that he had followed a route laid out by Maury. One historian claimed that Waterman "could take a coal barge to sea and bring her home in creditable condition looking, aloft, at least, like a clipper." For the first voyage to California he signed a crew of sixty, all but two of whom were foreigners and thus ignorant of his reputation as a hard and ruthless driver, "wholly reckless of life and limb." The owners promised him a bonus of $10,000 if he reached San Francisco in ninety days, and Waterman intended to collect.

The so-called hard drivers, like Creesy and Waterman, had earned their reputations in the China trade. The souls of the clippers were her masters. They drove their mates and the mates drove the men, making nerve-shattering and record-breaking runs around the world. From the time the anchor rose until it fell again, these men pressed relentlessly to get the utmost out of spars and canvas. In freezing winter gales or white summer squalls, sailors went cursing and clawing into the tops to strain every inch of sail, and if a few men toppled overboard, it was all part of the job.

With two other extreme clippers in New York's harbor, *Flying Cloud* and *Telegraph*, both from Boston, frantic betting ensued among the clipper watchers. They waged money that *Challenge* would beat them both. *Telegraph*, a smaller clipper, would never get in the game, and the contest would center around *Flying Cloud* and *Challenge*, or more accurately around their skippers, Creesy and Waterman.

Flying Cloud sailed from New York on June 2, 1851. When three days out, "Good breezes, fine weather" increased from strong to gale-force winds. The ship's towering rigging thrummed and beat as the wind roared out of the northwest, skimming the giant clipper through immense combers that pounded against the bow and swept the deck with salt spray. Two men clutched the huge spoked helm to keep the vessel from swinging about when riding down from the crests of mountainous waves. In a sudden series of loud, crackling reports, ropes parted, and the main topgallant mast canted, snapped, and carried with it the royal and sky sail masts. Wood split, sails ripped, and the topgallant mast crashed to the deck, severing the rigging of the upper mizzenmast as it fell. With its support gone, the mizzen topgallant cracked and fell into the tangle of shrouds below. Creesy ordered the helmsmen to ease off the wind while crews cleaned up the mess. As one chronicler wrote, "Even a partial dismasting of a clipper ship in a gale at sea could make a veteran's blood run cold," but Creesy calmly put the vessel back in order and sped away, noting nothing more in his log than "Lost Main & Mizzen Topgallant mast & Main Topsail Yard" as if the misfortune was no more than a routine occurrence. Two days later he had the clipper back in trim and plowing south. His best day's run covered 374 nautical miles, and for four consecutive days *Flying Cloud* averaged 314 nautical miles. On August 31 she arrived at San Francisco, 89 days and 21 hours out of New York.

Challenge departed from New York on July 13, 1851, seven weeks before *Flying Cloud* entered San Francisco Bay. Captain Waterman did not hear until he reached the western harbor 108 days later that his vessel had been beaten by nineteen days. He had more than the usual run of trouble when fifty of his crew mutinied off Rio de Janeiro. Waterman restored order and flogged eight of the ringleaders. Off Cape Horn three men died when they fell from the mizzen topsail during a storm, and another four died of dysentery. Waterman's only consolation was that *Challenge* beat *Telegraph*, which fell into several days of calms and reached San Francisco in 125 days. Waterman could complain about bad weather and a recalcitrant crew, but the reason *Flying Cloud* beat *Challenge* so decisively had more to do with preparations made before the race by Captain Creesy's wife. Eleanor Creesy ran the ship's chart table aboard *Flying Cloud*, and on it were all of Bowditch's five-place logarithm tables, Maury's *Wind and Current Charts* and *Sailing Directions*, and pads of foolscap for her calculations.

By 1851 Maury had published only a few track charts on the Atlantic and three on the North Pacific, but as he had done for Cape Horn, he covered most of the gaps with advice in his *Sailing Directions*. There were three pilot charts on the Atlantic, one on Brazil, and one on the South Pacific. When Creesy reached the millpond of the doldrums, he complained to his wife about the delay, but she got him through the mariner's slough in the remarkable time of four days. Maury had not released his chart on Cape Horn, but Eleanor Creesy studied the charts on the South Atlantic and the South Pacific and told her husband when approaching Cape Horn to drive directly south and, if weather moderated, to slip through the Strait of Le Maire. The storms let up just long enough for Creesy to follow his wife's advice, and *Flying Cloud* passed between Cape San Diego and Staten Island with all sails set. For every difficult phase of navigation, Eleanor Creesy had the answers, and she attributed every move of the clipper to Maury's charts and sailing directions.

With *Flying Cloud* and *Challenge* the clipper design reached perfection. In 1852, shipbuilder Donald McKay attempted to eclipse the 1,793-ton *Flying Cloud* with the enormous 2,421-ton *Sovereign of the Seas*. When he could find no shipping house to buy her, he financed her himself. What looked like a mistake proved to be profitable. He paid for the clipper in nine months, but her best time to San Francisco fell short of *Flying Cloud*'s record by fourteen days.

The marvelous performance of clippers stifled the arguments of those who promoted steam. Adherents divided into two camps: those who advocated sail for long cruises and steam for short, and those who supported exclusively steam. Without coaling stations around the world, steam would have to wait, and for the next few years clippers would enjoy their most glorious days at sea.

In 1851, there were still skippers who did not embrace Maury's charts, but when *Flying Cloud* whipped *Challenge*, everyone took notice. A year later, fourteen clippers made the voyage to San Francisco in no more than 110 days. All but two would have beaten or tied *Challenge*, but none of their times eclipsed *Flying Cloud*'s record. Old habits were hard to break, and in 1851, only one clipper had Eleanor Creesy, Bowditch's logarithm tables, and Maury's charts. But all this would change.

Maury took as much interest in the records being set by clippers as the merchants who owned them, the shipyards that built them, and the wagering public who bet money on them. Some gambling merchants, such as the Griswolds who owned *Challenge*, bet their ship. Maury understood that no event in the maritime industry could put more emphasis on the value of his charts and sailing directions than the publicity emanating from

races between the stunningly beautiful clipper ships. Merchants also recognized that when pitting their fastest vessels against competitors, they
needed more than a vessel—they needed Maury. The arrangement worked
to the benefit of both. Maury got more information, and the clippers made
faster voyages. The lieutenant in the observatory also got something else—
enormous recognition at home and abroad.

On the heels of *Flying Cloud*'s record-setting victory over *Challenge*,
three more clippers entered the competition: the 711-ton *Raven*, an extreme clipper launched on July 1, 1851; the five-year-old 908-ton *Sea
Witch*, already a sailing legend; and the 1,611-ton extreme clipper *Typhoon*,
launched on February 18, 1851, from the yard of Fernald & Pettigrew in
Portsmouth, New Hampshire. All three vessels carried the latest *Wind
and Current Charts* and *Sailing Directions*. While *Flying Cloud* and *Challenge* enjoyed the most recent publicity, the real race involved the new
contenders, none of which were anything alike in size. For once, all three
ships sailed only a day or two apart during the first week of August—*Raven*
from Boston, *Sea Witch* and *Typhoon* from New York. Experienced captains commanded each clipper: William W. Henry, *Raven*; George W.
Fraser, *Sea Witch*; and Charles H. Salter, *Typhoon*. Each skipper carried a
carrot on a stick: a fat bonus if his vessel came in first. If size mattered, *Typhoon* had the advantage, with more than twice the displacement of *Raven*.
She also had the advantage of design improvements when compared with
the older *Sea Witch*. By all accounts, oddsmakers gave *Typhoon* the edge in
the race to San Francisco.

August, a month of light and baffling breezes, portended a bad start for
all three vessels. But using Maury's charts, the clippers threaded their way
across the calm belt of Cancer, ran down the northeast trades, and drifted
through the doldrums with surprising speed. *Sea Witch*, the first to sail,
still held the lead at the equator, crossing on August 30. *Raven*, though
departing from Boston two days after *Typhoon* had sailed from New York,
caught up with the big clipper on August 31, and both crossed the equator together, a day behind *Sea Witch*. The close proximity of all three vessels demonstrated that their skippers were following Maury's charts and
leaving little to chance. Four weeks into the race, *Sea Witch* had lost four
days to *Raven* and two days to *Typhoon*.

After rounding Cape São Roque, all three vessels picked up the southeast trades exactly where Maury predicted. Running down the three-thousand-mile course to Cape Horn, they found strong westerlies farther south, exactly where the charts indicated. All three vessels prepared for the swing around Cape Horn exactly where Maury prescribed—50 degrees South by 64 degrees West—at which point *Raven* pulled abeam of *Sea Witch* and left *Typhoon* two days astern.

Maury had published sailing directions for rounding Cape Horn, but his first chart lay on the drafting table back at the observatory. So all three skippers followed Maury's advice in *Sailing Directions*, standing southward. From aloft, the crews sent down studding sail booms and sky sail yards and then set to work adding extra lashings to boats, spare spars, and skylights. As the clippers bowled southward, the weather worsened, and all hands steeled themselves for a thrashing to windward as they attacked the Horn. Late winter winds whipped across a tumultuous ocean, and all three clippers were in the grip of strong westerly gales. They slanted down mountainous head seas and pounded into the next frothing comber. For fourteen nerve-racking days and nights, *Raven* and *Sea Witch*, constantly in sight of each other, battled the elements, making slow headway while single-reefing, double-reefing, and close-reefing the topsails and then shaking them out during every lull, trying to take every advantage of lulls and slight changes in wind direction to drive their vessels westward. *Typhoon*, in hot pursuit, closed slowly, her greater length and power flouting the storms with a distinct superiority. All three skippers fought for small advantages, each knowing whoever brought his ship around the Horn first might gain a day or two on the final run to San Francisco. As friendly competitors, every skipper piled on as much sail as prudence permitted, pressing the long, sharp bows of their vessels into the wild, surging seas and sending a rushing wall of water flying down the decks and out through the scuppers. By the skillful sailing of all three captains, not one spar was carried away or a rope parted.

Fourteen days later *Raven* and *Sea Witch* were running side by side, and crossed into the Pacific together. Both vessels remained in good sailing trim, but neither skipper knew that *Typhoon* had recovered lost days and entered the Pacific hard on their heels. The start for the final leg of the race was as close as three ships, having sailed eight thousand miles, could get to being dead even.

Maury's charts were not as advanced for the Pacific as for the Atlantic, but by using *Sailing Directions*, *Raven* and *Sea Witch* found favorable winds exactly where Maury predicted. Once clear of Cape Horn, they sped away fast to the northward, bounding through the southeast trades with studding sails, sky sails, water sails, and ringtails, using every set of canvas that could snatch a wisp of wind.

On the stretch to the equator, *Sea Witch* fairly flew through the water, crossing the meridian in twenty-two days, leading *Raven* by two days and *Typhoon* by four. Now they stood to the northward, close-hauled on the starboard tack for the final run. Once again, *Typhoon*'s length and power gave her an edge, and during the final leg she came up first with *Raven* and then *Sea Witch*, passing each to the cheers of her crew. Off California's coast *Raven* overhauled *Sea Witch*, but she could not gain on *Typhoon*. *Typhoon* glided through the Golden Gate on November 18, 1851, 106 days from Sandy Hook; *Raven* followed a day later on November 19, 105 days from the Boston lighthouse; and *Sea Witch* on November 20, 110 days from Sandy Hook. *Typhoon* reached San Francisco first, but *Raven* won the race by a day.

Abstract Log Records

Course	Days		
	Raven	Typhoon	Sea Witch
To equator in the Atlantic	25	27	29
From the equator to 50° S	21	23	22
From 50° S in the Atlantic to 50° S in the Pacific	14	13	14
From 50° S to the equator	24	25	22
From the equator to Golden Gate	21	18	23
Total Days	105	106	110

Though sixteen days slower than the record established by *Flying Cloud* on August 31, it was a great victory for *Raven*. By outsailing *Sea Witch* she became the only ship of her tonnage to do so, and she vanquished *Typhoon*, a ship more than double her size. Because of her age, *Sea Witch* had lost some of her speed, but during her prime when under the command of Waterman, she was probably the fastest sailing ship of her class ever built.

Raven, *Sea Witch*, and *Typhoon* all zealously adhered to Maury's charts and sailing directions. So diligently did they follow his track that time and time again, though leaving from different ports on different days, they sailed in sight of each other and entered San Francisco Bay, after a voyage of fifteen thousand miles, within a few days of each other.

To appreciate in 1851 what a passage of a hundred days meant requires an examination of the logs of other vessels, whose trials and tribulations testify to the long, weary days and nights of exasperating calms and the backbreaking pain and constant anxiety from fighting the tempests off Cape Horn:

> *Arthur*, from New York, 200 days
> *Austerlitz*, from Boston, 185 days
> *Barrington*, from Boston, 180 days
> *Bengal*, from Philadelphia, 185 days
> *Capitol*, from Boston, 300 days
> *Cornwallis*, from New York, 204 days
> *Franconia*, from Boston, 180 days
> *Henry Allen*, from New York, 225 days

Although clipper ships captured national attention, skippers of lesser vessels also grasped the significance of Maury's new science. Of the many voyages to San Francisco in 1851, one of the most remarkable passages involved a schooner only 71 feet in length, 18 feet, 4 inches in breadth, and 7 feet, 2 inches in depth. The 84-ton *Fanny*, commanded by William Kelly, had been a Boston pilot boat (not the clipper bark *Fanny*) whose owner wanted to profit from the San Francisco trade. Kelly sailed from East Boston in 1850 and on February 18, 1851, arrived at San Francisco 108 days later. In that year, he matched or outsailed all but nine clippers. Unlike the larger vessels that sailed to the southward when rounding Cape Horn, Kelly took the nimble schooner through the narrow and dangerous

Strait of Magellan, thereby shortening the voyage by hundreds of miles. The feat did not go unnoticed by Maury, whose staff had begun to compile data for rounding the Horn.

Maury took special interest in abstract logs covering voyages to California. After a laborious calculation of data, he concluded in 1851 that his charts and sailing directions, though still incomplete, shortened the passage between New York and San Francisco by roughly forty-three days. The average ship using his charts made the voyage in 144½ days, while those not using his charts took 187½ days. With this fact in mind, he set about to refine the course and make further reductions to the average sailing days. In doing this, he did not expect to change the sailing capabilities of any ship, only the sailing time. But he admired the great accomplishments of the greyhounds of the sea, later writing: "Some of the most glorious trails of speed and prowess that the world ever witnessed, among ships that 'walked the waters,' have taken place over it. Here the modern clipper ship—the noblest work that has ever come from the hands of man—has been sent, guided by the lights of science, to contend with the elements, to outstrip steam, and astonish the world."

Guided by Maury, the staff of hydrographers went to work on the flood of abstract logs flowing into the observatory from California voyages. During 1852, the men at the observatory published eight track charts on the North Atlantic, six on the South Atlantic, ten on the North Pacific, and five on the South Pacific. Pilot charts now numbered three for the Atlantic, one for Brazil, two for Cape Horn, five for the North Pacific, and one for the South Pacific. Work had also been started on charts for the Indian Ocean. By the close of the year, Maury had barely reached the midpoint of the work he had laid before his hard-pressed staff.

By 1853, competition between the clippers sailing to California reached its peak. No vessel had yet eclipsed the 89-day record set by *Flying Cloud*, though *Swordfish*, built by William H. Webb of New York, missed tying the record by one day. Clippers now garnered so much notoriety, and the racing was so closely matched and exciting, that passengers on their way to California would often find themselves a part of a race when two or three vessels would meet at sea and strive to outsail each other.

For shipbuilders, shipowners, and gamblers, the game had taken the shape of a horse race. They all colluded, and in 1852 matched fifteen clippers, ranked among the swiftest vessels afloat, all with masters of comparable merit, for the deep-sea derby of the decade. Nine of the vessels stood little chance against the four front-runners, but oddsmakers enjoyed a brisk business handling bets. All sailed during a favorable season of the year where one could find fair winds in the North Atlantic, though more storms around Cape Horn, and, when arriving in the North Pacific, good runs to the coast. Though not a betting man, Maury picked the four to watch. He knew the builders as well as the skippers.

The focus of the race pitted the shipyard of Donald McKay (*Flying Fish*) of East Boston against those of Samuel Hall (*John Gilpin*) of Boston, George Raynes (*Wild Pigeon*) of Portsmouth, and Jacob Bell (*Trade Wind*) of New York. Oddly enough, Maury did not pick the famous *Flying Dutchman*, an extreme clipper built in 1852 and added to the race by William H. Webb, the great shipbuilder who had created *Challenge*. Nor did he take any special interest in *Contest*, which came from the yard of another distinguished builder, Jacob A. Westervelt. Both vessels were commanded by experienced shipmasters, *Flying Dutchman* by Ashbel Hubbard and *Contest* by William E. Brewster, and both men sailed by Maury's charts. Why he excluded them from closer analysis could only have been a matter of personal preference.

From Maury's perspective, the race would test the mettle of four accomplished skippers. Captain Edward Nickels, an old packet master and expert navigator, commanded the 1,505-ton *Flying Fish*. She had already made one voyage to San Francisco, having sailed from Boston in November 1851, and reached the Golden Gate in 100 days. Justin Doane also had mastered the course, but not in the sharp-ended 1,089-ton *John Gilpin*, a masterpiece of refined craftsmanship. Captain Nathaniel Webber commanded the largest clipper yet built, the 2,030-ton *Trade Wind*. She had been once to California but took 121 days to get there. By all rights, she could do much better. George W. Putnam commanded the 996-ton *Wild Pigeon*, the smallest of the racing quartet. Putnam had taken *Wild Pigeon* over the course in 1851–52, during which he fought long stretches of light winds but still strode into San Francisco in 107 days.

The race about to commence, however, would be as much about ship-builders and shipmasters as the clippers themselves. And the fact that all fifteen clippers sailed within a thirty-seven-day period between October 11 and November 17 of 1852 made the race especially interesting to Maury and even more interesting to the gambling public and their bookies.

Unlike the 1851 race between *Raven, Typhoon,* and *Sea Witch,* the four principal competitors started down the course at different times, but they all had one objective in mind: to beat the 89-day record set by *Flying Cloud* in 1851. *Wild Pigeon* sailed on October 12, *John Gilpin* on October 29, *Flying Fish* on November 1, and *Trade Wind* on November 14. Each carried a complete set of Maury's charts and sailing directions, but differences in seasonal conditions created inequalities in any contest. *Wild Pigeon* got off first, but for thirteen of her first nineteen days she encountered variable winds and gales as she stumbled south. *Flying Fish* and *John Gilpin* flew down the same course, though on slightly different tracks, each gaining several days on *Wild Pigeon.* Maury took exceptional interest in the contest, and behaving much like a sportscaster at a racetrack, he announced (in retrospect, after the race was completed) the action as each vessel followed the charts.

Wild Pigeon continued to struggle through the horse latitudes, after which she made a fine run to the equator, crossing it in excellent position for a fast passage down to Cape Horn. The four-hundred-ton bark *Hazard,* rigged like an extreme clipper, fell in with *Pigeon* after crossing the equator, and her skipper, Captain Pollard, who Maury described as "an old hand with the Charts," reported that *Pigeon* "had accomplished all that skill could do and the chances against her would permit." Once clear of Cape São Roque, the clipper bowled quickly out of sight, leaving *Hazard* nearly standing on her heels.

Despite the skill displayed by Putnam as *Pigeon's* navigator, *Flying Fish* and *John Gilpin* came roaring down the coast, "not under better management," stated Maury, "but with a better run of luck and fairer courses before them." In the same stretch of sea, *Flying Fish* picked up ten days and *John Gilpin* seven, so that now the logs showed *Wild Pigeon* ten calendar days ahead but more than seven sailing days behind.

Convinced he had shown his heels to his competitors, Captain Nickels placed enormous confidence in *Flying Fish's* strength. Maury agreed. "She felt her speed," he observed, "and was proud of it. She was most anxious for a quick run, and eager withal for a trial. She dashed down southwardly . . . looking occasionally at her Charts; but, feeling strong in her sweep of wing, she kept, on the average, 200 miles to leeward of the right track. Rejoicing in her many noble and fine qualities, she crowded on her canvas to its utmost stretch, trusting quite as much to her heels as to the Charts, and performed the extraordinary feat of crossing, the 16th day out from New York, the parallel of 5 degrees north."

On the seventeenth day out she paid the price for being west of the right track. "Now her heels became paralyzed," noted Maury, "for Fortune seems to have deserted her for a while—at least her master, as the winds failed him, feared so." Nickels seemed to be hopelessly baffled by light winds, and, said Maury, "The bugbear of a northwest current off St. Roque began to loom up in his imagination, and to look alarming. Then the dread of falling to leeward came upon him. Chances and luck seemed to conspire against him, and the mere possibility of finding his fine ship backstrapped filled the mind of Nickels with evil forebodings, and shook his faith in the guides. He doubted the Charts, and committed the mistake of the passage." Maury analyzed the error, writing:

> The *Sailing Directions* had cautioned the navigator, again and again, not to attempt to fan along the eastward in the equatorial doldrums; for, by so doing, he would himself engage in a fruitless strife with baffling airs, sometimes re-inforced in their weakness by westerly currents. But the winds had failed, and so too, the smart captain of the *Flying Fish* evidently thought, had the *Sailing Directions*. They advise the navigator, in all such cases, to dash right across this calm streak, stand boldly on, take advantage of slants in the wind, and, by this device, make easting enough to clear the land. So, forgetting that the Charts are founded on the experience of great numbers who had gone before him, Nickels, being tempted, turned a deaf ear to caution, and flung away three whole days and more of precious time, dallying in the doldrums.

Nickels actually spent four days meandering along the latitude of 3 degrees North without making any headway, and after wasting time running back and forth, *Flying Fish* finally crossed the doldrums at nearly the same meridian as she had entered them.

Because Nickels sailed the clipper too far to the west of Maury's route, when he reversed course he struck a strong current running from the east. Nickels now realized his error, though a little late to be of help. Leaving the spellbinding calms behind him, he penned in his log, "I now regret that, after making so fine a run to 5 degrees north, I did not dash on, and work my way to windward to the northward of St. Roque, as I have experienced little or no westerly set since passing the equator, while three or four days have been lost in working to the eastward, between the latitude of 5 degrees and 3 degrees north, against a strong westerly set." And he might have added, wrote Maury, "with little or no wind." Nickels's mistake became crystal clear when Maury, comparing the log of the swift *Flying Fish* with that of the lazy bark *Hazard*, observed that *Hazard* outsailed *Flying Fish* by two days merely by following the *Sailing Directions*.

Trade Wind sailed from the New York harbor last, leaving Sandy Hook on November 13, 1852, and crossed the equator on December 6, twenty-two days out. Captain Webber lost two days when fire broke out between decks. To extinguish it, he had to face into the wind and force water through holes chopped in the upper deck. This slid *Trade Wind* to the leeward, taking her off track and compelling Webber to fall too far to the west of the position specified by Maury. After clearing São Roque, *Trade Wind* put on her best heels to Cape Horn and in twelve days reached the latitude of 50 degrees South. At this point, *Trade Wind* and *Flying Fish* were dead even at forty-eight sailing days, *John Gilpin* had an edge of just one day, and *Wild Pigeon*, because of an unlucky start, lagged far behind all.

On the leg from São Roque to 50 degrees South, Nickels made a remarkable recovery. On November 24 he came even with *John Gilpin*, the ship he acknowledged as his principal competitor, though neither could see the other because they stood thirty-seven miles apart. *John Gilpin*, being to the eastward, had the advantage of position according to the charts, for *Flying Fish* had yet to take advantage of the slants and stand offshore to clear the land.

For the preferred and safest course to round Cape Horn, the charts called for a run down to 53 degrees South before sweeping southward under the Strait of Le Maire to begin westing into the Pacific. *John Gilpin* took the route and gained two days on *Wild Pigeon* and one on *Flying Fish*. Though Nickels could not predict what misfortunes his competitors may have encountered, he knew he must make up time. Instead of taking Maury's safe route, he went to the charts and decided to risk a run through the Strait of Le Maire, which would take him into a narrow passage between the tip of Cape San Diego and Staten Island, Argentina. Because of better-than-average weather, Nickels made a lucky decision. *Flying Fish* dashed through the straits and gained three days on *John Gilpin*. In an effort to gain time, *Wild Pigeon* also tried the strait, got hammered by a gale, almost drifted into a reef, twirled about in whirlpools, and sailed into a blinding snowstorm. A change in tide helped *Pigeon* pass through the strait, but there ensued another ten-day struggle clawing against westerly gales and inching through befuddling calms. *Trade Wind* had not reached Cape Horn when her three competitors rounded into the Pacific, but she had followed the charts, picked up favorable winds, and could not be forgotten.

At 51 degrees South off the coast of Chile, *Flying Fish* and *Wild Pigeon* came on swiftly, each standing one day ahead of *John Gilpin*. According to the charts, *Pigeon* had moved into the best position with *John Gilpin* next and *Flying Fish* last, but all three vessels worked north in fine winds. Maury liked *Pigeon's* position because of the time of year. Winds blew from the northwest before giving way to the southeast trades, and *Flying Fish* had taken a position that allowed too little sea room should a stubborn northwester come on. But once again, Nickels enjoyed a piece of luck. The fair winds held; *Flying Fish* picked up the southeast trades and, when crossing the parallel of 35 degrees South, overtook *Wild Pigeon*. Captain Putnam of *Wild Pigeon* saw only a clipper ship. He could not believe that the ship in sight could possibly be *Flying Fish*, as she was not to have sailed from New York until three weeks after *Wild Pigeon*. At the same time, *John Gilpin* lay no more than forty miles behind both vessels.

For the three clippers, now bunching together, the clear stretch of 2,500 miles to the equator became an exciting head-to-head competition. *Flying Fish* led the way, with *Wild Pigeon* pressing hard and both easing further ahead of *John Gilpin*, which had strayed too far to westward. The two leading clippers reached the equator first, the *Flying Fish* leading *Wild Pigeon* by only 25 miles. *John Gilpin* had dropped 260 miles astern, unaccountably sagging off several degrees to the westward.

When Putnam reached the equator, he saw an opportunity to outsail Nickels and gain back time lost in the Atlantic. A belt of northeast trades still had to be passed, and by crossing where he planned, Putnam intended to make a fair wind of them without getting so far to the west as to lose their force. It had been exactly one year since *Wild Pigeon* had passed this way before, after which she had made a capital run to San Francisco in seventeen days. Putnam studied the fourth edition of *Sailing Directions* and noted that Maury did not "discountenance it," and his previous year's experience justified the attempt. Putnam could not imagine that by a difference of forty miles in crossing the equator, and by being two hours behind *Flying Fish*, he would fall into a weak streak of wind that would enable Nickels to blow through the equator and leave *Wild Pigeon* in her wake. Maury, having studied the logs, lamented that *Wild Pigeon* simply encountered "nothing but what sailors call 'a streak of ill luck.' "

At the equator Justin Doane pulled the *John Gilpin* together, crossed the line two days behind *Flying Fish*, and in fifteen days made a remarkable run to the pilot grounds of San Francisco. Along the way they passed Nickels and *Flying Fish*, but neither reported seeing the other. *Flying Fish* sailed the final leg in eighteen days, completing the voyage from New York to San Francisco in 92 days and four hours. If Nickels had paid more attention to Maury's charts on the Atlantic side of the equator, *Flying Fish* might have broken the record. In 1854 *Flying Cloud* broke her own record by a mere thirteen hours, and only four other ships ever came close: *Sword Fish* in 1852, *Flying Fish* in 1853, and the medium clipper *Andrew Jackson* in 1860.

John Gilpin, though entering San Francisco Bay first, lost to *Flying Fish* by a day and sixteen hours. One might wonder why Doane could not have applied the same sailing skills to the entire voyage that he demonstrated on the final leg from the equator. *Trade Wind* finished third in 102 days, and the two days lost because of fire would not have changed her placement.

Wild Pigeon, with her "streak of ill luck," luffed in at 118 days; Putnam could have done better, for earlier in 1852 he sailed the same course in 107 days. The overlooked *Flying Dutchman* came in fourth at 104 days, and *Contest* ran the course in 108 days.

The public generally ignored the remarkable records set by clippers on return voyages from the West Coast. For those records, one must turn to markers in the cemetery. Carved on a gravestone in Eastham, Massachusetts, are the words: "Freeman Hatch, 1820–1889. He became famous making the astonishing passage in clipper ship *Northern Light*, from San Francisco to Boston in 76 days, 8 hours—an achievement won by no mortal before or since." Hatch sailed by Maury's charts. He would not have been without them.

After studying the logs of the four clippers, Maury made the observation that "The result of this race may be taken as an illustration as to how well navigators are now brought to understand the winds and currents of the seas." His charts were accomplishing their purpose. He intended them to enable a navigator "to blaze his way among the winds and currents of the sea, and so mark his path that others, using his signs as fingerboards, may follow in the right track." He had come a long way from sailing master on *Falmouth*, where he began a search for knowledge that led him to a new science, one he happily shared with all mariners.

There were other remarkable runs made by clippers. Many of the vessels that sailed to San Francisco continued on to China and the East Indies, making an intermediate stop at the Sandwich (Hawaiian) Islands. Maury tracked every vessel with the same care as those celebrated voyages made to San Francisco. He did not care whether a vessel was a clipper, a brig, a bark, a small schooner, or a whaler on a four-year journey. They all made valuable observations. But Maury took special interest in an exceptionally large clipper, *Sovereign of the Seas*, because many predicted the 2,421-ton behemoth would become an elephant on the hands of her builder, Donald McKay of East Boston.

McKay gave *Sovereign of the Seas* the longest and sharpest ends of any vessel yet built. She combined the grace and beauty of smaller clippers, but no ship could match her strength and power. She carried twelve thousand

running yards of canvas, and her masts, counting from the foremast and including the sky sail pole, were 185, 210, and 166 feet in height from heel to
truck. When nobody wanted to purchase the vessel, Captain Lauchlan
McKay, Donald's younger brother, took command of the clipper. He
planned to sail from New York to San Francisco in early August 1852—a
poor month of the year for a rapid voyage.

Maury provided McKay with a set of charts and *Sailing Directions*, pre-
dicting that if he adhered to them, *Sovereign* would reach San Francisco in
103 days. Twenty-five days later McKay crossed the equator in record time
for the month of August and boomed down to 50 degrees South twenty-
three days later. When rounding Cape Horn, a passenger on board wrote, "It
was fearful to see the topmasts bend and we hardly dared to look aloft lest
we should see the whole fabric blown away." Yet tremendous seas and strong
northwest gales did not prevent *Sovereign* from crossing into the Pacific in
nine days. Storms and headwinds greeted the ship along the Chilean coast,
and a sudden gale struck the ship off Valparaíso, snapping off her main
topmast, knocking it over the side, and tearing away the fore topsail yard,
mizzen topgallant mast, and ripping every stitch of canvas off the foremast.
It took Herculean efforts to keep the dangling spars from pounding the
ship full of holes, let alone getting the ponderous weight of top-hamper
and backstays on board again. McKay ignored the dictates of prudence and
chose not to pull into Valparaíso. For twelve days the clipper limped north
while the crew made repairs. By the time she reached the equator, McKay
had *Sovereign* in top shape and for the month of November made a record
run of seventeen days to San Francisco. He never strayed from the charts
and made the voyage in 103 days, exactly as Maury predicted. Had the
ship not suffered damage to her tops, McKay may have shaved a few more
days, but no clipper ever beat his record for completing the course from
New York to San Francisco during the months of August to November.

Sovereign had not yet seen her best days, however. McKay obtained a
contract for carrying a cargo of whale oil from Honolulu to New York. With
half a crew, he set sail from San Francisco on December 22, 1852, for the
Hawaiian Islands. "We started out with 45 men," one of the officers wrote.
"On the third day out down went the barometer and up went the wind.

We were flying light and she heeled over until the lee rail was under water and we finally had to run before the wind; how she did fly; I have seen her sail away at a rate of 20 miles an hour when drawing 21 feet, but flying light, as she was, she must have been going at the rate of twenty-five."

Most of the crew left the ship at Honolulu, and McKay encountered much difficulty rounding up thirty-four men to take her home. On February 12, 1853, *Sovereign* sailed from the islands laden with eight thousand barrels of whale oil and a small amount of bone. With a crew much too small for her tonnage and "the fore and main topmasts crippled; the fore topmast sprung in two places and the main topmast tender," it did not seem possible for the clipper to make a fast passage. But McKay had Maury's *Sailing Directions*, and on March 9 he got a fair wind from the northwest. *Sovereign* made the most famous run of any clipper ever built, sailing 472.92 statute miles in 23 hours and 18 minutes. During the long voyage home, one officer wrote, "She ran about as fast as the sea and when struck by a squall would send the spray masthead high. Now and then she would fly up a point and heeling over skim along between the deep valleys of the waves, and then, brought to her course again, righten with majestic ease and as if taking a fresh start would seem to bound from wave to wave."

Maury tracked the voyage with immense interest because McKay followed the charts the entire distance from Honolulu to New York. *Sovereign* made the passage in an astounding time of 82 days, setting new records during every leg of the journey.

Over time, *Sovereign of the Seas* sailed under different skippers, but they all shared one attribute—they lived by Maury's charts and sailing directions. In June 1853, she sailed from Boston to Liverpool on the same day as the Cunard steamer *Canada*, and in five days had outsailed the coal burner by 325 miles. Then, during a voyage from Liverpool to Melbourne, *Sovereign* outdistanced every vessel on the same track, including the British clipper *Gauntlet*. From Melbourne she returned to Liverpool in sixty-eight days, beating the steamer *Harbinger* by four days and every other vessel by fifteen to twenty days. She was a powerful vessel whose captains used every advantage to speed her from one port to another, and Maury's charts gave them the edge.

So fast and able were the clipper ships that some said steam was "fin-ished," that it had "reached the limit of its possibilities," but events would prove otherwise. By 1851, fifty steam vessels were under construction in or near New York, many to carry passengers to land routes to the Pacific through Central America. The great age of the clippers—the culmination of the Golden Age of Sail, would be over in a brief ten years.

❧

FROM the early 1850s on, Maury had little trouble getting shipmasters to buy into his program, nor did he any longer have trouble persuading them to submit the abstract logs furnished by the observatory. Some cap-tains wrote Maury that by avoiding storm areas indicated on the charts they had completed voyages without reefing topsails more than once or twice. By the end of 1851, he had heard from more than a thousand cap-tains. By 1854 he had accumulated more than a million observations on the prevailing directions and velocities of the ocean's winds and currents. Clippers such as *Sea Serpent*, laden with merchandise for San Francisco, followed Maury's charts from New York to the West Coast, crossed from there to Hong Kong, loaded at Shanghai, and returned to New York, never veering from the course outlined in the *Sailing Directions* and adding their voyage to the research piling up at the observatory. Though some of the in-formation requested on the abstract logs may have seemed trivial to the navigator, Maury had his reasons for wanting it. There was more to the sci-ence of the seas than daily computations of latitude and longitude, and some of Maury's best work still lay ahead.

By 1855 the average voyage for all vessels from New York to California had been cut from 187½ days to 136 days, but scores of clippers made the passage in no more than 110 days. Using Maury's charts and sailing direc-tions, merchants estimated savings of more that two million dollars annu-ally on outward voyages to the East Indies, China, and South America, with comparable savings achieved when sailing to other destinations. So appreciative were merchants and insurance underwriters of Maury's work that in 1853 they presented him with an expensive silver service and a purse of $5,000—an amount almost twice his annual salary.

Other honors followed. On July 15, 1853, Columbian College (now George Washington University) awarded Maury an honorary LL.D. This, coupled with an LL.D. received from the University of North Carolina in 1852, "strengthened his hand" when in the presence of men of achievement. In the years to come, there would be many admirers. But fame begets envy, and Maury had collected competitors in the game of science. Battles lay ahead, not solely because of his achievements as a meteorologist and oceanographer, but because his accomplishments had only begun to edge out his competitors. A mind so inquisitive and fertile could not be prevented from nibbling on the edges of other fields of science where self-appointed incumbents looked sourly upon intruders. Maury's life had been a series of ups and downs, and there would be more to come.

Chapter Nine

DISASTERS AND DISCOVERIES

ON November 19, 1851, Maury advised his superior, Commodore Crane, that a thousand ships sailing the high seas were now faithfully forwarding their abstract logs to the observatory. With the logs came comments from shipmasters, with one writing, "I am happy to contribute my mite towards furnishing you with material to work out still farther towards perfection your great and glorious task, not only pointing out the most speedy route for ships to follow over the ocean, but also teaching us sailors to look about us and recognize the wonderful manifestations of the wisdom and goodness of the great God. . . . For myself I am free to confess that for [the] many years I commanded a ship . . . I yet feel that until I took up your work I had been traversing the ocean blindfold[ed]." Such were the appreciative comments of those who followed Maury's charts.

By 1853 Maury's knowledge of the ocean's winds and currents had become so sharply honed that he could sit at his desk and predict the outcome of sailing problems brought to his attention. In late December the ship *San Francisco* sailed from New York with a regiment of soldiers bound for California. On Christmas Eve she stumbled into a late season storm three hundred miles off Sandy Hook. Hurricane-strength winds struck suddenly, ripped off her sails, tore down her masts, swept away her deckhouses, and cast 179 passengers into the sea. Ravaged and without a single usable lifeboat, the ship lay on the outer edge of the Gulf Stream with monstrous waves crashing over her decks. The skipper of the small brig *Napoleon* sighted the crippled ship wallowing in heavy seas. He could not fasten to her or put his boats in the water, so he sailed to New York to get help. Other ships passed *San Francisco*, unable to offer aid. Only *Three Bells* from Scotland stood by, and for seven days and nights her captain hung doggedly to windward of the wreck, thinking of neither his own ship nor himself. When word reached Washington, the naval secretary ordered out two fast revenue cutters, but before dispatching them, he asked Maury to work out the position of the drifting vessel.

Having studied the Gulf Stream for more than a dozen years, Maury went to his pilot and thermal charts for December and January, which by 1854 consisted of 380,284 observations. Making careful computations of prevailing winds and currents, he plotted *San Francisco's* drift and estimated the length of time it would take the cutters to reach her. With a blue pencil he placed an X on a chart and said, "Just here, she will likely be found." Leaving nothing to chance, he prepared a hurried set of detailed sailing instructions to show the cutters the fastest route for intercepting the drifting hulk and dispatched the documents to Commodore Charles Morris, the new head of the Bureau of Ordnance and Hydrography.

The cutters followed Maury's route and located the dismasted vessel almost exactly where shown on the chart. The seas having calmed, *Three Bells*, a six-hundred-ton square rigger, had removed five hundred survivors, helped by two other vessels that came to the rescue of the sinking hulk. Any old salts who still doubted Maury's mastery of the seas, including those in the navy, had their skepticism trimmed. And the feat did not go unnoticed by British shippers, who were already beginning to enjoy the benefits of Maury's scientific work.

Maury did not publish his first pilot chart of the Indian Ocean until 1853 and his first Indian Ocean track chart until 1854. Even before the data became available, merchants in Bombay predicted that the British would save between one and two million dollars a year by following Maury's routes. The estimate proved conservative. As more charts became available with revised sailing directions, the British Association for the Advancement of Science credited Maury with reducing the nation's shipping costs by ten million dollars a year. Such enormous savings came cheaply to those who followed Maury's tracks. He shared his science with every sailor, and often the smallest changes in routes made the greatest difference between a fast voyage and a slow and circuitous one.

For many decades the standard British Admiralty route to Australia and New Zealand followed the coasts of Spain, Portugal, and Africa, turned eastward close around the Cape of Good Hope, and then ranged straight across the broad South Indian Ocean. When homeward bound, they returned by the same route, fighting against the strong and constant westerlies or sailing north through the Capricorn calm belt to find the easterlies that would speed them to Africa, but such a track as the latter forced them to cross the calms a second time before reaching the Cape of Good Hope. The voyage averaged 120 days each way.

Maury's track down the Atlantic took a vessel farther to the westward, away from Africa, and then south into the Roaring Forties and Furious Fifties. For the homeward voyage, he sent them eastward around Cape Horn running before the strong westerlies of the higher latitudes, whipping the ships around Cape Horn and into the trades that sped the ships back up the Atlantic. The new route reduced the passage for American vessels by one-third and for British vessels by one-fifth, saving a thousand-ton vessel from London about forty-eight sailing days, or $6,500 one way and twice as much on a round trip. Using his new route, and calculating the effect of winds and currents, he estimated that Liverpool was ten days closer to Melbourne than was New York, owing to the presence of more favorable winds on the early part of the voyage from England. The *Melbourne Argus* tracked all arrivals between the dates of December 31, 1853, and July 7, 1864, and reported that "the average passage of all vessels without charts was one hundred and twenty-four days, while the average of those (from the same ports) using the charts was ninety-seven days."

In 1854 Maury received the abstract log of the clipper *Flying Scud*, Captain Warren H. Bearse, whose 1853 voyage to Australia began as a navigator's nightmare. When leaving New York, Bearse believed his chronometers were out of order because he felt the ship could not have sailed so far in one day, but she did. On the outer edge of the Gulf Stream *Scud* ran into a storm. A bolt of lightning struck the ship forward and knocked down sev-eral men, all of whom recovered. A second bolt struck the ship aft, knock-ing more men senseless. The pilot noticed that the ship's compass began to spin erratically, and after it finally stabilized, days passed before the nav-igator realized that the compass varied five points to the east. Captain Bearse surmised that the bolts had traveled down the mast and descended by the lightning rod to the channels, where it blew the copper wire off the rod and against chains, which in turn conducted the electricity through the ship and magnetized a large quantity of iron in the afterhold. When several days later the compass returned to normal, Bearse discovered that his ship had sailed too far to the south. After reconciling his position, he struck a new course using Maury's tracks to Australia—the strong westerlies south of the Cape of Good Hope—and sailed 6,420 miles in sixteen days, aver-aging close to 400 miles a day. Richard McKay, who chronicled the cruise of the clipper, wrote, "Taken as a whole, this voyage of the *Flying Scud* ap-pears to have been one of the most successful attempts at speedy navigation accomplished by any vessel out of New York going eastward, since a due ap-preciation has been had of circular sailing, so beautifully and elaborately detailed by Lieutenant Maury, United States Hydrographer."

The experiences recorded by shipmasters fascinated Maury, and he lived them again in vicarious ways. To capitalize on the opportunity to collect their experiences, he continued to expand the staff at the observatory—and not solely because of the increased flow of abstract logs. Maury's in-quisitive nature drew his attention to the unexplored regions of the globe, to investigate their climate and weather. Unlike many Americans, who in the 1850s espoused isolationism, Maury grasped the globe as his per-sonal playground. Using the observatory as a vehicle for other enterprises, he intended to broaden the study of hydrography, astronomy, and espe-cially meteorology into an all-encompassing physical science of the world. Winds, currents, weather, and the universe knew no national boundaries, nor did hurricanes and other meteorological phenomena. Maury knew that much of the Earth, including vast landmasses, had never been scien-tifically explored, yet they all shared a role in the Earth's weather pump. To capture new data required international cooperation, and some countries, such as Japan, which had shut its doors to Westerners, and Brazil, whose emperor did not want foreigners exploring the country's interior, barred scientific inquiry.

Maury had more than a simple scientific interest in Brazil. As early as 1850 he viewed with foreboding the rising wave of irreconcilable sectional differences that threatened to split the Union asunder. Opening the Amazon Basin would give the United States a place to relocate its slaves, thereby averting a national crisis. In 1850 he wrote, "The Southern states may emancipate just as New York and Massachusetts [have done]. But large numbers of slaves were not set free. They, after the emancipation acts [of Northern states] became laws, were sold to the South, and so the South may sell to the Amazon. The slaves of the South are worth 15 hundred million. Their value is increasing at the rate of 30 to 40 million a year. It is the industrial capital of the South." From Maury's perspective, one way to curb slavery was to open the Amazon, develop new plantations, and transplant the slaves to Brazil where the practice of slavery still operated with little adverse interference. In response to a query from his cousin, Jacquelin Ambler Caskie, Maury replied, "No, my dear cousin, I am not seeking to make slave territory out of free, or to introduce slavery where there is none. Brazil is as much a slave country as Virginia, and the valley of the Amazon is Brazilian. I am sure you would rejoice to see the people of Virginia rise up tomorrow and say, from and after a future day—there shall be neither slavery nor involuntary servitude in Virginia."

❧

WHEN Maury wanted information, he found ways to obtain it, sometimes using unconventional methods. After resigning from the observatory in 1845, Maury's brother-in-law, Lieutenant William Lewis Herndon, had gone to sea during the Mexican War in 1846, commanding the steamer *Isis*. While spending an uneventful eighteen months in the Gulf, Herndon recovered from the nervous breakdown he suffered while working at the observatory. When the war ended in 1848, he returned to the observatory for another year of arduous labor under the gentle lash of his brother-in-law. In 1850, the navy transferred him to *Vandalia* and sent him around Cape Horn for a cruise in the Pacific off the Peruvian coast. Though Herndon found Maury to be a demanding supervisor, they were great friends and enjoyed a partnership of mutual interests.

As soon as Maury learned of Herndon's reassignment to the Pacific, he sought ways to alter it. If Dom Pedro II, emperor of Brazil, would not let an American exploring expedition go *up* the Amazon, perhaps Maury could obtain permission from Secretary of the Navy William Alexander Graham for an expedition to go *down* it from its Andean tributaries. Graham approved the plan, which included Herndon and Passed Midshipman Lardner Gibbon, and dispatched orders through Gibbon to have Herndon detached from *Vandalia* and transferred to Maury's Amazon project.

On May 21, 1851, thirty-eight-year-old Lieutenant Herndon and twenty-year-old Passed Midshipman Gibbon departed from Lima, Peru. They traversed the continental divide—16,044 feet high but only sixty miles from the shores of the Pacific—and into the headwaters of the Amazon. With pack mules, guides, and canoes, the two men separated, descending the Amazon by different routes. Herndon followed a Peruvian tributary while Gibbon crossed into Bolivia and took another. As part of his equipment Herndon carried a sextant and a pocket chronometer to mark his position and a barometer as a weather indicator. Matthew Maury had become especially interested in barometric readings; he believed that winds blew from a high-pressure area into a low-pressure area, and that the low pressure around the poles and the low pressure at the equator each operated like a vacuum, pulling the winds toward them, thereby creating the prevailing winds. He had observed this phenomenon at sea, and the exploration of the Amazon might help validate his theory through readings taken by Herndon over a large, tropical landmass.

Both Herndon and Gibbon worked their way to the mouth of the river, making precisely the type of observations Maury needed to understand the geographic nature of South America's vast tropical interior, its weather, and immense rain forests. During the yearlong expedition, Herndon compiled extensive data, keeping timetables, measuring boiling points, and recording barometer and weather phenomena. He studied flora, geology, anthropology, the natural history of the Amazon, and the tribes who inhabited its watershed. From Maury's perspective, the Amazon offered vast opportunities for capitalizing on the skills of slaves for cotton and tobacco cultivation.

Herndon, a balding redhead, was physically slight in stature and never a robust individual, and as such he may not have been the ideal candidate to send on so exhausting a journey. But he had been trained by Maury and shared some of his brother-in-law's unique qualities—a fine investigative mind, a marvelous talent for observation, and a facile pen. Maury trusted Herndon more than any other officer on duty in the South Pacific, and he knew the man's capabilities. After Herndon and Gibbon separated at the headwaters of the Amazon, each kept journals, and Gibbon enhanced his with dozens of fascinating sketches. Instead of submitting to the department a typical dry report on observations, Herndon wrote in a delightful narrative style. Struck by the explorer's marvelous travelogue, Congress published it and released ten thousand copies to the public. In 1854 they added a second volume of Gibbon's narrative and sketches, but Gibbon's account proved to be disappointingly boyish. So fascinated did young Samuel Clemens become when reading Herndon's narrative at home in Missouri that he quit his job to go to the headwaters of the Amazon and make a fortune trading in coca. Had he succeeded, young Clemens might have become the nation's first drug dealer, as the leaves of the coca plant make cocaine. Unable to raise the cash to book passage or find a ship to take him there, he instead got stuck on the Mississippi and became "Mark Twain."

Maury, however, became one of the first readers of Herndon's unedited journal, as both explorers came to the observatory to prepare their reports. Herndon's account amazed him. The scientific details, combined with his brother-in-law's literary style, surpassed his expectations. Maury fleshed out the data he wanted from the journal and used it to publish an assessment of Herndon's exploration of the Amazon. Dom Pedro II read Maury's version and publicly complained of unwanted American interlopers nosing into the affairs of Brazil. From Herndon and Gibbon, Maury got what he wanted: a better understanding of the effect of the Andes range and the Amazon River on equatorial weather. But Herndon and

Gibbon had made other discoveries, finding evidence of mineral wealth—gold, silver, and copper—hidden in the upper stretches of the valley. Maury advocated the opening of the Amazon to free navigation, believing it would bring wealth to Brazil, improve the country's international standing, and make a new home for southern slaves. No wonder Dom Pedro accused Americans of interfering in his domestic policy. Once again, the navy lieutenant in the observatory had made a statement that was heard around much of the Western world, but not until 1867 would Dom Pedro open the upper river to the steam vessels of foreign nations.

In 1855 William Lewis Herndon took leave of the navy and became the captain of the U.S. mail steamer *Central America*, one of the largest side-wheelers in the service. Like most steamers of the day, the vessel also carried three short masts, and on days with a favorable breeze she could be seen breasting the waves under both steam and sail. Christened in 1853, *Central America* made monthly runs, leaving from New York on the twentieth of each month for Aspinwall (Colón), Panama, where she disembarked five to six hundred passengers on their way to California in exchange for roughly the same number returning east. By the summer of 1857, *Central America* had transported to New York one-third of all the consigned gold crossing Panama's isthmus for delivery from California. Forty-niners returning home carried another lode in vests, chests, money belts, and sacks, along with tons of personal articles in trunks and crates. On the morning of September 8, 1857, having made a regular homeward-bound stop at Havana, Herndon ordered the vessel under steam and wove his way out of Cuba's most congested harbor, carrying 575 passengers, $1,230,000 in gold, and a hold stuffed with mail and baggage. Like the captains of gold-bearing galleons of Spain, he passed the rocky crest of El Morro and set a course for the Florida Keys.

During the previous thirty years, advances in steam technology had sharply reduced passenger service on sailing ships. Steamers were far more expensive to operate and needed access to coaling stations, which was one of the reasons, besides mechanical failure, why steamships still carried sail. Because steamers generated their own power, skippers became less concerned about the vagaries of the winds. They could plow through a headwind and give little thought to tacking. When cruising near shore, they could use power to avoid navigational hazards that would fret the captain of a sailing ship. So when Herndon departed from Havana, he took the inner edge of the Gulf Stream, which flowed within sight of the Keys, and steamed northeast across the Straits of Florida. His route could not have been laid out better had Captain-General Don Juan Estaban de Ubilla, sailing from Havana with a fleet of treasure ships on July 24, 1715, prepared the course himself. Unlike the captain-general, Herndon also carried a set of Maury's pilot charts and sailing directions, but for steamers, the charts had lost much of their importance.

On the morning of September 9, *Central America* steamed into the Gulf Stream and headed north, tracking between the coast of Florida and Grand Bahama Island. During the night, a twenty-knot headwind had whipped up the Straits of Florida. Heavy seas tumbled into the ship, causing her bow to lift and crash as she plowed northward. Throughout the day the eastern sky thickened ominously as each hour passed. The gale had strengthened, and by nightfall a fury of seawater and rain swept the decks. Sailors called it a storm, but Herndon read the signs and, knowing the season, predicted the approach of a hurricane. He steered away from the mainland and by the next morning stood two hundred miles off St. Augustine. Running through the valleys of giant waves, the vessel sometimes rolled so far over as to bury a paddlewheel completely under the water. Unable to predict the movement or direction of the hurricane, Herndon plodded north. Rocked by winds of fifty knots and blinded by torrents of rain streaming horizontally against the wheelhouse, he set a course for Cape Hatteras.

At daybreak on September 10, winds out of the northeast began building to sixty knots, sending even stronger gusts and heavier seas crashing against the ship's bow and pouring waves of froth down the decks. Herndon's best estimate of the ship's position put her 175 miles east of Savannah and making little headway. He had not been able to shoot the meridian to fix his position. A screen of rain mixed with spray that leapt high over the ship's bow made observation from the wheelhouse impossible. Water washed down the deck and flowed into the staterooms. That was small concern, however, compared with worrisome news from the engine room. Chief Engineer George Ashby reported all the steam pumps at work but water rising in the bilge.

Unlike sailing ships, steamers used coal for ballast. When leaving New York, Herndon had filled *Central America* with more than enough fuel to complete the round trip. Having burned more than half of it, however, the ship began to lose her ballast, and standing in the face of a hurricane, she burned it even faster. Three thousand pounds of California gold loaded at Panama could not offset the loss of ballast. Now the ship rode high in the water, careening back and forth, and at times her paddlewheels barely brushed the surface of the water. Under normal conditions, steam-powered bilge pumps worked like the modern-day electric sump pump. When water reached a certain level, a float tripped a switch that activated the pump, and the pump sucked up the water. But ships tilt, and the storm canted *Central America*, trapped all the water on the starboard side, and held it there. The list rendered the portside pump useless and lifted the blades of her portside paddlewheel clear out of the water.

To feed the furnaces, coal heavers faced the problem of wheeling the fuel from bunkers a hundred feet away. Because of the ship's list, they could not get the coal to the furnaces fast enough. Herndon sent down stewards and porters and set up a bucket brigade, but steam pressure began to drop. To keep the vessel headed into the wind, he ordered the storm spencer (a trapezoidal gaff sail) set without a boom on the mizzenmast, hoping it would blow the stern to port. When the vessel dipped into a trough, the crew shot the storm spencer, but when the vessel rose on the next crest, a savage gust struck the sail and ripped it to shreds. Herndon then tried other sails, lower down on the masts, but none could withstand the force of the winds. By noon the helmsman could no longer manage the wheel, and two hours later the engines all but stopped. When passenger Addie Easton heard beams cracking, she cried to her husband, "Ansel, we're sinking!"

Addie Easton sensed what all 575 passengers had come to fear: Herndon had lost control of the ship. *Central America* now drifted to the southeast, listing more heavily than before, and each giant comber that struck her broadside threatened to capsize her. Passengers struggled to the central dining saloon, waiting for word from the captain. When Herndon finally entered the saloon, he merely ordered, "All men to prepare for bailing the ship. The engines have stopped." He explained his plan—to remove enough water to restart the engines. Hundreds of volunteers formed into three gigantic bailing brigades. The men were tough and muscular miners. They bent to the work with stubborn determination while others worked the manual pumps. Herndon seemed to be everywhere, giving comfort to the women and children and encouragement to the bailing brigade. Men remembered him saying, "Work on, m'boys, we have hope yet." And in a short space of time the water level dropped, coal heavers stoked the fires, and the wheels again turned—but only a few revolutions, and once again the engines stopped, this time for good.

Herndon tried to set a drag device to bring the bow into the wind, but because of the ship's list, no men could get forward to reach the heavy anchors. The crew located a smaller anchor, tied it to a yard, pushed it over the side, and paid out forty fathoms of cable. With masts now angled over the water from the ship's list, Herndon ordered the foremast chopped down. Everything went well until the mast snapped, snagging as it fell. It somersaulted, became entangled in the rigging, shot under the side of the ship, and began pounding against the hull, straining planks and opening more leaks. No amount of effort could bring the vessel's head into the wind, and at nightfall the cable holding the sea anchor parted. The bailing brigade kept at their work, but muscles began to knot, and waves breaking over the ship gushed water into the hold faster than the bailers could remove it. Now in the darkness, without food or water, they fought on, but some, thinking the battle lost, slipped back to their rooms to lie quietly in the dark waiting for the end.

By Saturday morning, August 12, the passengers could hear the water swishing just below the central dining saloon, but dawn brought hope. The crests were not so high or the wind so strong, having dropped to forty knots. Clouds sweeping across the horizon were thinning, and to rally the bailing brigade, Herndon announced clearing weather ahead but kept his doubts to himself. He urged crew and passengers alike to keep bailing, at least until noon, filling them with hope while they bent their backs to filling the buckets. Privately, Herndon knew that no amount of effort could keep the vessel from sinking, but every hour she stayed afloat increased the chance of rescue by another vessel. With the wind dropping a few knots, he hoisted the Stars and Stripes upside down, and the banner flapped and clapped but held to the mizzenmast. When water began to seep through the portholes, he gave up all hope of saving the mail and millions in gold, but he did not give up hope of saving lives.

If passengers could choose whether to ride out a hurricane in a sailing vessel or a steamship, all would have chosen a steamer. By mere chance, on September 12 the two-masted brig *Marine* appeared on the horizon, and her captain, Hiram Burt, noticed flashes from *Central America*'s signal guns, so he bore off to investigate. Burt had been scudding along with bare poles on his 120-foot bark, and it took two hours to con the vessel over to the weather bow of *Central America*. He hove-to about a hundred feet off the steamer's lee. Herndon could see that the brig had been partially dismasted and the jibboom swept away. The steamer wallowed in the water like a ship carrying too many servings from the sea. Herndon knew *Central America* was sinking and coaxed Burt to remain alongside to take off passengers. Of the steamer's six lifeboats, only four remained serviceable. Each lifeboat could carry forty to fifty passengers, but with the seas running at so great a height, Herndon thought no more than fifteen or twenty persons could be removed at a time. Rather than wait for the inevitable, he began lowering boats to transfer women and children to *Marine*. As passenger Annie McNeill prepared to be lowered by rope into a boat, she spoke with Herndon, who told her that he would not try to save himself but would go down with the ship.

Men left the bailing brigade just long enough to bid their wives farewell. Neither expected to see the other again, but the men coaxed their wives into the boats by promising to join them shortly. During the transfer, a crest hurled one of the boats against the side of the steamer and smashed it to bits, leaving just three boats. Herndon shouted to the helmsman of one of the boats, "Tell the captain of the brig, for Heaven's sake, to lay by us all night." By the time the lifeboats pushed off, *Marine* had drifted off three miles, and Burt was frantically trying to make enough sail to intercept the three approaching lifeboats. By late afternoon he had the women and children on board and sent the lifeboats back to *Central America*, but his drift had pushed him farther away. For his part, Herndon knew he must keep in sight of *Marine* and ran up another spencer sail. It held, and he worked the steamer back to meet the returning boats. This time he loaded them with men. When the lifeboats again cast off, Herndon did not know whether they would be able to return, as *Marine* could not make headway and continued to fall farther astern. So to save the rest of the passengers, he ordered the cabins ripped apart and the wood made ready for use as flotation devices.

At 4:00 P.M. Captain Samuel Stone, in the old square-built schooner *El Dorado*, sighted the steamer off his windward bow. Having been tossed about in the same storm, *El Dorado* had lost her foresail, her bowsprit carried away, and sections of her bulwarks crushed, but she could still make way. As Stone closed slowly on the steamer, he noticed her foremast gone, a distress flag flapping from her mizzenmast, her sails in tatters, and her lifeboats gone. At 6:30 P.M. he came alongside the sinking steamer and hailed the captain. Herndon asked him to lie to until daylight. Stone said he would, and to make room for survivors, he put his crew to work jettisoning the schooner's cargo of cotton.

Passengers on *Central America* did not like the idea of waiting until morning to be rescued, but Herndon promised that the weather would clear, making the transfer of passengers to the schooner faster and safer. In truth, he needed the bailing brigade to keep the steamer afloat. He knew the schooner could not hold all the remaining passengers, and he hoped that by firing distress rockets through the night other passing vessels might come to his aid.

Of the three leaky lifeboats that reached *Marine*, only one attempted to return to *Central America*, the other two having no men physically capable to pull the five miles back to the steamer. The lone boat came in sight of the steamer and lay off to leeward. When a rocket came off the ship, it skimmed along the water instead of going upward. The oarsmen recognized the slant as an omen of disaster. They returned to *Marine* and told Captain Burt, "The steamer has gone down and every soul on board of her lost."

During the final moments a flash of lightning illuminated the decks, and a survivor spotted Herndon standing atop the wheelhouse, trumpet in hand, and dressed in his finest uniform. Three enormous seas swept over the steamer, filled the hold, and sent her to the bottom. *Marine* and *El Dorado*, joined in the morning by other vessels, circulated through the area picking up survivors clinging to boards, but Maury's brother-in-law was not among them.

When news of the disaster reached Washington, Matthew and Ann Maury were devastated; she had lost a brother and he a loyal colleague. Matthew and Ann invited Herndon's widow, Francis, and daughter, Ellen, to live with them.

The public's howls of rage created a second storm, and this one inundated the owners after reporters learned that *Central America* had been unseaworthy, having rotten frames, leaky planking, and a sprung bottom. Her owners had sent her out knowing her defects rather than stand the cost of repairs. In San Francisco the press joined the public in castigating the United States mail service for nearly a decade because the government continued to use unsafe steamers that caused a series of maritime disasters.

Maury studied the events leading to the loss of *Central America*, mainly because two old sailing vessels withstood the tempest better than what he believed, at least in design and appearance, to be one of the finest steamers afloat. He also observed that paddle wheelers manifested a weakness that could only be corrected by ships designed with screw propellers. On October 19, 1857, he published his findings, focusing mainly on Herndon's role. One hundred and fifty-two passengers and members of the crew had been saved, and Maury, in praise of his brother-in-law, concluded:

> Everything that could be done by the best sea-captain to save his ship was done by this one. . . . There was no lack of skill or courage. Order and discipline were preserved to the last: and she went down under conduct that fills the heart with unutterable admiration.
>
> Affectionate in disposition, soft and gentle in his manners, he won the love and esteem of his associates, and became a favorite throughout the service. None knew him better or loved him more than, Respectfully, M. F. Maury, Lieutenant, U.S.N.

Hurricanes were not new to Maury, but they were even more of a meteorological mystery in the nineteenth century than they remain in the twenty-first. Searching back in time, he discovered a Florida hurricane so violent "that it forced the Gulf Stream back to its sources, and piled up the water in the Gulf to the height of thirty feet. The *Ledbury Snow*," wrote Maury, "tried to ride it out. When it abated, she found herself high up on dry land, and discovered that she had let go her anchor among the tree-tops on Elliott's Key." Another hurricane, which he believed commenced at Barbados, blew bark from trees, uprooted the depths of the seas, created waves that washed away forts and castles, and carried "their great guns . . . about in the air like chaff . . . and [lifted up] the bodies of men and beasts . . . and dashed [them] to pieces in the storm." Both hurricanes probably originated as tropical depressions flowing off the coast of western Africa, but Maury's work had not led him into the origin of hurricanes, and he still blamed the Gulf of Mexico or the West Indies for spawning them.

Maury tended to lump hurricanes, typhoons, cyclonic winds, and tornadoes into the same category because they were all rotating storms. With the exception of tornadoes, he believed that the other three types of storms spanned as many as a thousand miles, rotated around a vortex much like a whirlpool in a river, and contained a near-calm eye having very low pressure, around which furious winds whipped. The Coriolis effect on the circulation of winds and currents would not be described for another fifty years; lacking this knowledge, Maury could not explain why hurricanes in the Northern Hemisphere rotated counterclockwise whereas storms in the Southern Hemisphere turned with the clock. He blamed the difference in rotation on a combination of the flow of trade winds coupled with the diurnal rotation of the Earth and the tendency of all storms to eventually move toward the poles. He also believed that the equatorial edge of a storm carried the strongest winds, though in a westward-tracking Northern Hemisphere hurricane the opposite is true. He advised navigators "to avoid the heavy side" when passing into a hurricane, which was good advice but in most cases too late to be practical. Most sailors could not be certain of the size of the storm, its direction, the location of its eye, or its intensity, and under such circumstances they found themselves in the storm before any preventive action could be taken to avoid it.

What Maury did publish were Storm and Rain Charts, which gave the navigator clues about where and when tropical depressions, cyclonic storms, and hurricanes most frequently occurred. This information became far more helpful to the navigator than the dynamics of the hurricane itself.

Nobody, however, comprehended the importance of connecting to-gether winds, currents, and weather better than Maury. Despite the storm-ravaged seas off Cape Horn, he believed that "storms along the Gulf Stream are more to be dreaded than those encountered anywhere else in the world." This statement seemed to have emanated from his embedded belief that most hurricanes were hatched in the vicinity of the Gulf of Mexico. Whether a comprehensive study of meteorology in the early 1850s would have led to an ability to predict the creation, force, and tracks of hurricanes is questionable, but Maury was looking in the right places for answers. He might not have been able to save the life of his brother-in-law and four hundred others, but he understood the importance of induct-ing the nations of Europe and South America into a study much broader than the one initiated at the observatory.

Maury's instincts about the weather led him to many predictions, one being that somewhere in the high arctic regions—north even of the arc-tic islands among which explorers were seeking the fabled Northwest Pas-sage—lay an open sea, uncovered by ice and unobstructed by landmass. Few believed him. No scientific expedition had yet ventured into the arc-tic wastes north of Baffin Bay and Devon Island, and many believed that under the polar ice cap lay another vast landform.

But Maury's investigations of whaling voyages had provided him with clues. Whales killed in the Bering Strait had been found with harpoons embedded in their hides bearing the markings of vessels that hunted only in the waters of Baffin Bay, on the other side of the North American con-tinent. Maury suspected that whales could only have crossed to the Bering Strait by passing through open waters in the high Arctic. He suspected and thought he saw evidence for a warm surface current through the Davis Strait and into the Arctic Ocean, pushing icebergs north instead of south. He also discovered a cold undercurrent flowing out of the polar regions and into the Labrador Sea through the strait.

In 1850, Lieutenant Edwin J. De Haven, who had been working with

Maury at the Naval Observatory since 1848, commanded an expedition into the Arctic ostensibly to search for the Franklin party, which had been missing since 1845, but also to thrust America into the search for a Northwest Passage. The following year De Haven brought back a report of a wide, westward-trending channel north of Cornwallis Island at 76 degrees North. Sea smoke in the distance convinced him that open water had lain in that direction, just as Maury had predicted. There had been other reports of a water sky—a dark, moisture-laden sky and not the bright sky reflected by ice—to the north of the ice fields, and because the pack ice shifted in a barely perceptible but continuous motion and slowly drifted westward, Maury believed it remained perpetually afloat, with no polar landmass on which to settle. But he could not prove it, nor would it be proven until 1896, when Fridtjof Nansen of Norway locked the specially constructed *Fram* into the icepack off New Siberia and proved Maury's theory by letting the ice drift the vessel from 140 degrees East longitude to 10 degrees East longitude, crossing more than a thousand miles of the Arctic Ocean by drifting north and west with the ice.

In 1853, Maury spoke with navy doctor Elisha Kent Kane before the latter departed in command of a second expedition to the Arctic—again ostensibly to search for the Franklin Expedition, but in fact to reach the farthest point north. Kane had been the medical officer on the first expedition and was familiar with Maury's open-water theory and De Haven's support of it. Now the two men discussed where and how the open water might be reached. (Kane impressed Maury's daughter Diana as "an interesting looking but silent little man with dark hair and keen black eyes.") Later that year Kane pushed his ship, *Advance*, as far north as the ice would permit, then intentionally beset himself in the winter ice of what is now known as the Kane Basin, between Greenland and Ellesmere Island, Canada, at 79 degrees North. From there he sent a sledge party headed by William Morton north to prove or disprove Maury's theory. After crossing a barrier of ice about a hundred miles broad, Morton reached a point five hundred miles from the pole (83 degrees North) and encountered a vast sweep of open water—despite nighttime temperatures of minus 60 degrees Fahrenheit—in the notch between Ellesmere Island and northern Greenland. Without a boat, he could go no farther, but before him extended "an unbroken sheet of water as far as the eye could reach [at least forty miles, Kane estimated in his report] toward the pole." Morton had reached what is now known as the Lincoln Sea. "Its waves were dashing on the beach," wrote Maury, "with the swell of a boundless ocean. The tides ebbed and flowed in it." The area teemed with seals and waterfowl, but what impressed Maury were the tides and the warmth of the water that, he assumed, could only have been brought there by currents flowing from the south. What he learned from Kane's exploration convinced him that the arctic ice cap floated and circled the pole with no landmass to stop it. Kane's expedition also found large quantities of drift material along arctic shores that could only have come from lands more than a thousand miles away, either from the south or from the east.

The *Advance* was trapped for two years by the ice and then crushed. Kane and his crew made a desperate eighty-three-day sledge journey through Greenland and were finally rescued, returning to New York in 1855. Back in Washington, Kane confirmed that Maury had been right. He attempted to name the newly discovered body of water north of Greenland after Maury, but the lieutenant declined the honor, and it was eventually named after America's sixteenth president.

Chapter Ten

ORGANIZING THE NATIONS

WHAT began in 1851 as an opportunity for international scientific co-operation lost its luster in the details. Britain's Royal Engineers asked the United States to join them in making uniform meteorological land observations at a number of foreign stations around the world. Secretary of the Navy William Alexander Graham sent a copy of the British offer through Commodore Charles Morris to Maury, who in his quest for a better understanding of global weather at once recognized the possibilities inherent in the Royal Engineers' proposal, but he also anticipated a problem from a fellow scientist.

In 1847, Joseph Henry, the secretary of the recently established Smithsonian Institution, had stationed volunteers at fifty points across the nation to make meteorological observations on the nature of storms. Also in 1847, Maury, through the abstract log program, had more than a thousand ships at sea sending similar data to the Naval Observatory. The two organizations collected information for different reasons and therefore in a different form, yet they competed as scientists for recognition. In his reply to Commodore Morris, Maury commented little on Henry's use of the Army Signal Corps as volunteers except to say that changes were needed because the work at the Smithsonian differed from the role of the foreign stations established by the Royal Engineers.

Maury planned to push forward his own plan for international participation. Though he admitted that any cooperation would be better than none, he reminded Morris that most of the Earth was covered by water, and that any study must "look to the sea for the rule, to the land for the exceptions." He made the point that "no general system of meteorological observations can be considered complete unless it embrace[s] the sea as well as the land." Knowing that a central collection center would be required to analyze, condense, and utilize the data, Maury informed Morris that "The value of the researches conducted at this office with regard to the meteorology of the sea would be greatly enhanced by co-operation from the observatories on land." He did not want outsiders modifying his collection methods, and instead of adopting the suggestions made by Joseph Henry, he spoke of amending the plan of the Royal Engineers and asked that "England, France, Russia and other nations be invited to cooperate with their ships by causing them to keep an abstract log according to the form to be agreed upon and that authority be given to confer with the most distinguished navigators and meteorologists both at home and abroad, for the purpose of devising, adopting and establishing a universal system of meteorological observations for the sea as well as for the land." Maury looked beyond the present. He wanted an international forum as a platform to promote his ideas.

Maury's appeal for a "universal system" made so much sense that Secretary of State Daniel Webster, on the recommendation of Secretary of the Navy Graham, authorized Maury to open negotiations with the Royal Engineers "and others of proper jurisdiction at home and abroad" to agree on a system that would unify observations for both sea and land. Maury jumped to the task. He did not want the conference limited to the British or by the British, so he launched a two-prong campaign—one through friendly scientists and astronomers in Europe and the other through foreign attachés assigned to Washington. To draw in the French, he suggested the meeting be held during August 1852 in Paris. He then contacted every minister in Washington from the great sailing nations of Spain, Russia, the Netherlands, and Denmark to the German state of Hamburg and the Italian city-states of Sardinia, Two Sicilies, and Parma. Nor did he neglect South and Central America, inviting Argentina, Chile, Peru, Mexico, and several other countries, including from abroad minor participants as Turkey, China, and the Hawaiian Islands. He knew the names of most countries' foremost scientists and invited them directly. The one stumbling block, the brilliant and equally assertive Joseph Henry, had been at work on his own agenda and was not at all receptive to Maury's plan.

Joseph Henry had become first secretary of the new Smithsonian Institution in 1846. Earlier in his career he had tinkered with electricity, working on such devices as a practical electromagnet, the electrical relay, the telegraph, and the electric motor, but he never took any of his work beyond the experimental stage. What he discovered about electromagnetic self-induction at the age of thirty-four, however, he failed to publish as his findings, with the consequence that in April 1832 British scientist Michael Faraday received the credit for discovering the principle of magnetoelectricity. Henry's failure to announce his discovery emanated from a personal uncertainty of its real value. Faraday had no such doubt and became famous. The disappointment irked Henry to such a degree that it produced a "nervous twitch in his upper lip." The twitch eventually disappeared after he joined the College of New Jersey at Princeton in November 1832 as a professor of natural philosophy, where he declared that "My whole ambition is to establish for myself and to deserve the reputation of a man of science." Having missed one opportunity to achieve his ambition, he intended not to waste a second chance by playing second fiddle to Maury, who had become the recognized authority on marine meteorology.

During his years at Princeton, Henry met Alexander Dallas Bache, great-grandson of Benjamin Franklin. In 1843 Bache had become superintendent of the United States Coast Survey. As biographer Patricia Jahns observed, when Henry and Bache first met, "it was as if both had suddenly found some hitherto-missing part of themselves [to] become in each other's company a complete person." Because of their close relationship, Bache wanted Henry in Washington and in 1846 successfully used his influence to get his spiritual double appointed to the new Smithsonian Institution.

Though Bache had once praised Maury's *Navigation*, the admiration ended after he failed to secure for Lieutenant Gilliss the superintendency of the Naval Observatory in 1844. Maury excused Bache's efforts to promote one of his cronies, and when Bache became head of the Coast Survey, Maury extended genuine professional courtesies, knowing that the two departments had common interests. Maury even expressed hope that he and Bache could work together. Bache, however, continued to grumble secretly to Henry and other personal admirers that Maury should never have been given the appointment. To Henry, Bache complained that Maury was infringing on his research of the Gulf Stream, which Bache considered a matter for the U.S. Coast Survey. Bache supported men who returned personal and professional allegiance, and although Maury was not of that character, Henry was. It did not take Bache long to realize that his distinguished credentials and personal charm were not enough to control Maury, who had been hard at work on his oceanic research at the Depot of Charts and Instruments a year before Bache took command of the U.S. Coast Survey.

In 1852, Bache worried that Maury's rising reputation as a hydrographer and his constant nibbling into other areas of science might induce the navy to place the U.S. Coast Survey under the control of the Naval Observatory. This fear, coupled with Bache's own ambitions, induced him to recruit Henry, Senator Jefferson Davis of Mississippi (later president of the Confederate States of America), naval scientist Lieutenant Charles Henry Davis of Boston (another Maury detractor), and Sears C. Walker (a former astronomer with the observatory) in a joint effort to impede the expansion of Maury's enterprises. Maury and Charles Henry Davis had been good friends through the early 1850s, and Jefferson Davis had stayed away from the business of the Coast Survey, but all this began to change. When Walker worked at the observatory he openly deprecated Maury's astronomical knowledge and would not follow orders. Such behavior led to his termination in 1847. This thrust Walker into the cabal being formed by Bache, who hired him and then sent him to the Smithsonian to inform Henry of the astronomical work being performed at the observatory.

Back in the early 1840s, the government-published *Naval Almanac* was to have been the responsibility of the Naval Observatory. But when Congress finally funded it in 1849, the assignment went to Charles Henry Davis with the support of Maury as well as Bache and Henry. With Bache on his

Matthew Fontaine Maury around 1853, the year he convened the first international marine meteorology conference in Brussels with the blessing of Navy Secretary James Dobbin and despite the determined opposition of his rival Joseph Henry, the director of the Smithsonian Institution. The conference was a complete success. "Every ship that navigates the high seas with these charts and blank abstract logs on board, may henceforth be regarded as a floating observatory, a temple of science," Maury exulted.

Alexander Dallas Bache, who became superintendent of the United States Coast Survey in 1843 and recruited Joseph Henry from Princeton to the directorship of the Smithsonian in 1846. When Henry and Bache met, "it was as if both had suddenly found some hitherto-missing part of themselves." A political animal, Bache valued allegiance and deference. Fellow members of the Scientific Lazzaroni, a group he organized, addressed him in correspondence as "Most Darling Chief," "Most Potent Chief," etc. In Washington he hosted a group of political intimates called The Club, whose members included Jefferson Davis. Fearing that Maury's ever-enlarging scope of oceanographic inquiry would encroach on the Coast Survey, Bache, like Henry, repeatedly opposed and undermined Maury's work.

A Mathew Brady photograph of Joseph Henry, about 1862. Bitterly disappointed over losing to Michael Faraday the recognition for discovering the relationship between electricity and magnetism, Henry spent the rest of his life seeking "to establish for myself and to deserve the reputation of a man of science." As the first secretary of the new Smithsonian Institution, in 1847 he instituted the systematic collection of meteorological observations over land, using Army Signal Corps volunteers, even as Maury was launching a parallel program at sea. Henry became a jealous rival of Maury, declaring in 1855, "I will out-meteorology him, or know why not."

side, Davis conspired to have the almanac prepared in Cambridge, Massachusetts, where he could work with Harvard professor Benjamin Peirce, another of Bache's friends. Davis had studied under Peirce, had married Peirce's sister-in-law, and had worked for Bache on the Coast Survey, during which time he became one of the latter's disciples.

Jefferson Davis had met and admired Bache when both were cadets at West Point. Soon after becoming a senator from Mississippi in 1847, the Senate named Davis as a regent of the Smithsonian Institution, where he, Joseph Henry, and Alexander Dallas Bache became inseparable friends until the outbreak of the Civil War. Maury formed no such close alliances, and for many years he remained unaware of the secret plot to diminish his work.

Maury's first trouble with Henry had occurred shortly after Sears Walker's visit to the Smithsonian in 1847. Walker deposited with Henry an abstract of his astronomical work on the planet Neptune, researched while at the Naval Observatory, and suggested it be published. Henry jumped at the opportunity and sent it to a German journal, stating that he intended to include the same article in the forthcoming *Transactions of the Smithsonian Institution.* When Maury learned the pirated information contained Joseph Henry's endorsement, he at first believed that Henry's signature had been forged. He doubted that a person of Henry's stature could have transmitted official government work done by the observatory to a foreign publisher, much less included it in the Smithsonian's own publication. He still regarded Henry with great respect, for in early 1847 they had exchanged "mutual pledges of good will and promises of kind offices which each made the other in behalf of the two noble institutions." After privately exonerating Henry from committing such an unprofessional act, he nonetheless discussed it with Commodore Crane, who considered the matter serious enough to investigate. On October 20, 1847, Maury wrote Henry a polite letter asking for an explanation. Henry skirted the issue, claiming to have done no wrong. He would not admit to making so careless a mistake as to offer the results of U.S. government research to a foreign publication, but his thin denials did not go unnoticed. For Maury, the incident translated into a storm signal that put him on watch, and neither he nor Henry forgot the matter.

So on March 2, 1852, after writing Henry in January on the subject of coordinating land observations with sea observations and receiving no reply, Maury took a carriage to the Smithsonian Institution to strike an arrangement that would enable each to share equally in the proposed weather project. After nearly five years, he also wanted to reestablish friendly working relationships with a man he once respected. To salve old wounds, Maury agreed to withdraw his request to participate in collecting data from land operations. He would confine his work to the sea, but he politely asked Henry to perform a cooperative role in the enterprise. Henry, however, had already begun his study of storms, working in league with the British in Canada. He saw no need to disrupt his program and even less reason to adopt Maury's expansion of the Smithsonian's data collection methods. But when meeting with Maury, Henry said nothing about his opposition to the lieutenant's proposed international conference. Instead, he quietly rallied Bache's support and the latter's arsenal of cohorts in an effort to block it. He also recruited the support of Colonel Edward Sabine of the British Royal Engineers, with whom he was already working.

Secretary of State Webster never anticipated any personal rivalries when he asked the secretary of the navy to reply to an invitation from the Royal Engineers. But Webster had also sent the same request to the secretary of war, who passed it on to Joseph Henry at the Smithsonian because of the involvement of the Army Signal Corps. When Maury responded with a proposal that Webster found acceptable, Henry took a narrower view and independently teamed up with the Royal Engineers, thereby acting with Bache to reduce the scope of Maury's program. When Maury discovered Henry's surreptitious actions, he considered them underhanded. This created a deeper breach between the two men, who could have accomplished more for science had they worked together.

As a consequence of Henry's actions and Bache's influence, the British Royal Society reviewed Maury's proposal, listened to arguments from the Royal Engineers, and decided to limit the international conference to a program giving "greater extension and a more systematic direction to the meteorological observations at sea," thereby quashing Maury's hope of including land observations. Had they sought advice from their own British

Meteorological Society, the Academy of Sciences in France, or the Royal Danish Society, they would have learned that all other scientific organizations agreed with Maury that land and sea observations should be combined. So with deep regret, Maury advised the secretary of the navy on November 6, 1852, that the segment of the "universal system" involving land observations be tabled in view of the importance of "the rich harvest to be gathered" by focusing on the sea. The secretary agreed, so once again Maury began setting the groundwork for an international conference, as he would rather have two-thirds of the pie than none of it.

Because the Royal Engineers had asked the United States for cooperation in making only land observations, and because Joseph Henry had already done so, the British now hesitated to attend the first Meteorological International Congress on the sea as proposed by Maury. The navy's new secretary, James C. Dobbin, told Maury to hold the conference whether or not the British attended, so on June 25 the lieutenant in the U.S. Naval Observatory sent invitations, this time to attend a conference beginning on August 23, 1853, in Brussels, Belgium. He believed once the conference became a reality that Britain, the most powerful maritime nation in the world, would participate.

On July 23 Maury departed on a steamer for Brussels by way of Liverpool. With him went four young ladies: his daughters, Elizabeth (Betty) and Diana; his niece, blonde, blue-eyed Ellen Herndon, the daughter of his brother-in-law, William Lewis Herndon (whose tragic death was then four years in the future); and Ellen Maury, the brunette beauty of the foursome and the daughter of Maury's cousin John Walker Maury, mayor of Washington, D.C. Maury thoroughly enjoyed the lively and vivacious company of the girls and thought it a great joke when passengers named them the Magpie Club. Little did he know that among his four charges, Ellen Herndon would one day marry Chester A. Arthur, the twentieth vice-president of the United States and president after the death of President Garfield. Diana, who later became Mrs. Spotswood W. Corbin, many years afterward recalled her childhood years: "I don't think I ever went to school more than three months altogether. [My father] was my loving and tender teacher always; and when Betty and I grew to be fifteen or thereabouts we had to take care of one or two of the younger ones and teach them to read, write, and cypher, yet without allowing this duty to interfere with our own lessons." Maury believed in travel as a great educator and took his sons and daughters with him as frequently as possible.

Although Great Britain made no commitment to attend the conference, Liverpool merchants invited Maury to speak at Town Hall. After hearing his proposals, dozens of shipowners and underwriters wired Parliament the following day urging them to adopt Maury's program.

On August 18 Maury traveled to London, where he spoke before a much larger group at Lloyd's, Britain's primary maritime insurance carrier. He told them of new charts being prepared at the observatory that would enable merchants to sail from England to Australia in the unheard-of time of sixty to sixty-five days. While he was in England, Maury's speeches and public statements on meteorology were reported in both the British and U.S. press.

Parliament could no longer stave off pressure from the public, and on the day Maury crossed the English Channel to Calais, Britain joined the Brussels conference, sending Captain Frederick W. Beechey of the Royal Navy and Captain Henry James of the Royal Engineers to represent the queen's interests.

Already aware of Maury's charts, in 1851 the British Admiralty began producing their own. What is interesting is that the Admiralty had partially copied Maury's charting methods but limited their data to the tracks of too few vessels, such as the Blackwell ships belonging to Messrs. R. & H. Green. Britain's most distinguished hydrographer, Rear Admiral Sir Francis Beaufort, produced more than 1,200 track charts between 1829 and 1855, but they lacked the comprehensiveness and systematic usefulness of Maury's charts. Instead of Beaufort becoming known as another pathfinder of the seas, posterity remembered him best for developing a scale for visually estimating the wind velocity; the Beaufort Scale.

Eleven men from nine European nations attended the Brussels Marine Meteorology Conference in 1853, including Captain Henry James of the British Royal Engineers, the sole expert on land meteorology. The members asked Maury to serve as president, but he declined and nominated L.

Adolphe J. Quetelet, the director of Belgium's Royal Observatory. Maury did make the opening address, explaining the purpose of his charts and sailing directions and encouraging all nations of the world to adopt them. He strongly recommended that the navies of Europe make mandatory the use of his charts and abstract logs, but he asked that the documents be offered voluntarily rather than imposed on merchant vessels. He informed the delegates that the United States would extend to cooperating nations charts and sailing directions at no cost, as long as navigators kept an abstract log and sent it to the U.S. Naval Observatory as a contribution to research. This generous offer on the part of the United States Navy led to an endorsement of Maury's proposals, especially on the part of the British, whose vote Maury sought like no other.

The most vocal support for Maury's proposals came from Lieutenant Marin H. Jansen of the Netherlands Royal Navy, who encouraged the delegates to accept the offer without change. A lengthier discussion involved the uniformity of instruments used, because all believed in the importance of taking observations off the same or similar devices. They were particularly interested in the systematic use of the hydrometer at sea. Maury believed a relationship existed between trade winds and their influence on the specific gravity of seawater, especially in different climates. He could not be certain of his assumptions without collecting data, and with such studies as these, he hoped to advance the world's knowledge of the seas.

Once in accord on how to standardize instrument readings, the delegates worked small changes into the abstract log. They simplified the document for merchantmen, and by the end of the second week, they were ready to make a final decision on the entire system.

For two weeks Maury had quietly and persuasively nursed his program through the conference. The final vote, including that of Captain James, was unanimous. This established the groundwork for a universal system of marine observations. Every country that wished to could participate. Revised abstract logs would be used uniformly by all nations and forwarded to the U.S. Naval Observatory in Washington for the ongoing perfection of charts and sailing directions. When the conference closed on September 8, the delegates expressed their enthusiasm for the agreement by stating their wish to continue the meteorological program even if the participants should enter into war with each other, which they often did. The unprecedented international agreement preserved for later generations a precious heritage. The conference eventually led in 1921 to the modern International Hydrographic Organization, established under the League of Nations, which ensured the free interchange of hydrographic information and charts among participating members. Maury moved in directions well ahead of his time.

This meeting was historic: never before had there been a U.S.-inspired meeting that so successfully achieved an understanding among the leading nations of the Western world. That a lieutenant in the U.S. Navy provided the catalyst made the agreement even more remarkable. In Europe and America the press hailed the success of the conference as a monumental diplomatic and scientific achievement. Maury summarized the essence of the accord, writing: "Rarely before has there been such a sublime spectacle presented to the scientific world. All nations agreeing to unite and co-operate in carrying out one system of philosophical research with regard to the sea. Though they may be enemies in all else, here they are to be friends." Though it had taken the better part of ten years, Maury now had what he wanted from the very beginning. "Every ship that navigates the high seas," he added, "with these charts and blank abstract logs on board, may henceforth be regarded as a floating observatory, a temple of science."

On October 21 Maury's traveling entourage returned to Washington, where they celebrated with family and friends. On the following day he dispatched his report to the secretary of the navy. Without delay, Dobbin committed the United States to full participation in the Brussels agreement and ordered the navy to begin using, as soon as they became available, the revised abstract logs designed at the conference. To show that the United States intended to back Maury's commitments to the conferees, Dobbin also distributed copies of his order to the nations represented at Brussels. Within weeks, European countries ratified the agreement. When nations not in attendance, such as Prussia and Spain, learned of the agreement, they joined the consortium, followed by Portugal, the city of Hamburg, the republics of Bremen and Chile, and the empire of Brazil. By 1854, Maury observed that "nations owning more than nine-tenths of all the shipping in the world have come to this plan."

Maury's presentation at the Brussels conference convinced all members, including Captain James of the Royal Engineers, that meteorological observations should not be confined to the sea. No one on Earth understood the mixture of winds and currents better than Maury, nor the impact of warm or cold currents upon the weather in different climates. Discovery of aberrations in the Pacific, like El Niño and La Niña, lay far in the future, but even in the mid-nineteenth century Maury understood enough about the stirrings in the oceans to know they affected the weather on land far removed, and that depressions coming off the heated zones of the tropics seeded devastating storms that reached the higher latitudes. When the delegates returned home, they began a concerted effort to convince their governments that a second conference was needed to include observations on land. Even the U.S. Army agreed, thereby leaving Joseph Henry of the Smithsonian Institution as the sole director of a major meteorological effort still opposed to the program established by the 1853 Brussels conference.

Maury believed the next meteorological conference should be called an international congress and organized by a sovereign nation, not by a lieutenant in the United States Navy. A hundred scientists should be invited, not a mere dozen. His efforts to promote the scheme were impeded by unexpected laurels from Europe. Four European countries knighted him, eight nations awarded him gold medals, Russia and Austria sent jeweled pins to Maury's wife, and Napoleon III made him commander of the Legion of Honor. According to U.S. law, however, Maury could not accept decorations or gifts without the consent of Congress. Such recognition led to an excess of publicity, especially in Washington, and stirred further animosities from such rivals as Henry and Bache, and from those in the navy who had enviously watched Maury's rise to fame while they tinkered away their careers on lackluster assignments.

Maury could have soothed a professional conflict with Henry had he not continued to insist on combining land meteorology with marine meteorology. But having grown up on a farm, he thought constantly of a farmer's dependence upon the weather. His study of the ocean exposed so strong a relationship with weather flowing across the land that he could not separate the two. Each affected the other, and he suspected a connection between the two in the breeding of storms, tornadoes, and hurricanes. Even had he wanted to leave land meteorology to Henry, he no longer could, because after the Brussels conference, he now occupied a position of international leadership in a science that had captured the interest of the world.

Maury's grand vision of an international congress for scientific study never materialized. Henry and Bache did what they could to prevent the convention from being organized, and the twosome had many powerful friends. Maury tried to entice European colleagues to sponsor the affair, but they never did. Not until 1870—twelve years later—did the government extend meteorological cooperation and research to the land. If Maury had a rank more befitting his age than mere lieutenant in the United States Navy, men such as Henry and Bache would have been less likely to have gotten their way. Indeed, Maury believed he should be promoted to captain, but that he was not yet a commander presented a natural obstacle to such aspirations.

Maury firmly believed that both marine and agricultural interests would benefit from a centralized United States weather bureau. Many scientists agreed with him, but the stumbling block continued to be Henry. When Henry entered into the field of land meteorology, the U.S. Army Signal Corps had been awkwardly at work on it for thirty years—so the concept was neither new nor scientifically well organized. In 1855 Maury wrote an open letter published in the *New York Daily Tribune*, explaining that the very limited purpose of the Smithsonian's system of meteorological observations was to "question as to the origin, progress and character of winter storms of our country." Maury wanted more: "The great object I have in view, is to extend to the land for the benefit of agriculture and other great interests the system of observations that have done so much for commerce and navigation. . . . The object I have in view is to co-operate with, not to work in opposition to the Smithsonian Institution . . . or any establishment whatsoever."

Henry did not appreciate Maury's explanation to the public. Using the

U.S. Agricultural Society's forum to reply, he declared less than truthfully that Maury had "not treated the Institution with due courtesy on this occasion; that in his communication to the public he had ignored what the Institution had done, and the first information it received that Lieut. Maury contemplated a system of meteorology for the land, was obtained from the newspapers." Henry stumbled into unexpected criticism for his remarks. In the view of many participants, Maury had been able to map the oceans using common sailors, so why, they asked, could plain farmers not make observations on land? The Agricultural Society's conference ended badly. Henry foolishly suggested that Maury was neither a scientist—a claim aired by Bache among his inner sanctum—nor capable of devising a meteorological plan for the land. He advocated a commission of scientific men as arbiters, leaving friends such as Bache to determine who was a "scientist" and who was not. In the end, the president of the society, a man by the name of Medler, indeed created a committee of three to determine a system for cooperation—but he selected neither Bache nor Henry as members.

After the conference, Maury and Henry each returned to their respective offices. Whereas Henry had held Maury in small regard before, he now felt an active animosity toward him and vowed, according to biographer Patricia Jahns, to "out-meteorology him, or know why not." Maury returned to the observatory with mixed feelings, writing: "I had a regular scientific fight, and though the result was all I could have desired, yet it was utterly disgusting to encounter such miserable signs of jealousy and small feeling." He continued to fight for a central weather bureau, and for the next five years both Henry and Bache used all their considerable influence to prevent it. When in 1870 the government established the National Weather Bureau and Signal Service, it embodied all of Maury's 1856 and 1857 proposals for unifying land and sea observations. In 1880 Representative George G. Vest of Missouri spoke before the Forty-Sixth Congress and said, "The whole signal-service of this country originated with the Navy, not with the Army. The man who commenced it, in whose brain it first had existence, was M. F. Maury."

A man is known by his enemies, and Maury was becoming very well known. Those who pitted themselves against him were competent, distinguished, and articulate men of the times. He resented their efforts to prevent him from achieving scientific advances that he believed would benefit mankind. At times he became quite angry when confronted with injustice or interference, or when a scientific rival appropriated one of his ideas. The more successful he became, the more enemies he accumulated. Henry and Bache referred to Maury as a man of practical science, not pure science, and a pretender to knowledge—a category into which Bache liked to lump Maury along with other American scientists outside the coterie led by himself and Henry. Oddly enough, Bache, as superintendent of the Coast Survey, spent the majority of his time engaged in practical science, as did Henry at the Smithsonian, as neither had time to devote to pure science. These allusions did not go unnoticed by Maury, whose usually thick skin was growing thinner.

But the dirty little work of jealous associates had just begun.

Chapter Eleven

THE "INDEFATIGABLE INVESTIGATOR"

EXACTLY when Maury began work on his *Physical Geography of the Sea* is unclear, but for this established author, the notion of writing such a book must have been percolating in his thoughts for quite some time. Though immensely busy, he needed a stimulus. The thousands of abstract logs flowing into the observatory contained a wealth of information extending far beyond winds, currents, and weather. Each page of the daily log contained a Remarks section, and many skippers used it to record geographic observations of personal interest. Those with a flair for drawing sketched what they saw. When in 1853 Maury produced a manuscript for the sixth edition of *Explanations and Sailing Directions to Accompany the Wind and Current Charts*, he had expanded the book to 772 pages. It contained a 90-page chapter on his investigation into the depths of the oceans. He titled it "The Physical Geography of the Sea" and presented it in *Sailing Directions* as a new subject of scientific study. Thus, Maury had already formed the foundation for a book.

The Biddles of Philadelphia had become one of Maury's principal publishers, issuing both his first book, *Navigation*, and the most recent edition of *Sailing Directions*. They asked the lieutenant to come to Philadelphia for a meeting, but Maury declined, using his staggering workload as an excuse. Instead he asked a nephew, Army Lieutenant Dabney Herndon Maury, who happened to be in Philadelphia at the time, to call on the publisher.

Having reviewed the bulky chapter titled "The Physical Geography of the Sea," the Biddles suggested that readers other than navigators would be interested in the subject and proposed that Maury write a second, less technical book for the general public. So enthused did the Biddles become over the potential of the book that they warned Maury, through his nephew Dabney, that none of his publications on the sea or the atmosphere written under the auspices of the navy provided him with copyright protection. They suggested he get to work on the new book project before some other publisher could appropriate the idea and "reap a fortune" from it. The Biddles admitted to not being equipped to manage a large distribution and suggested that Maury try Harper & Brothers in New York. The latter promptly expressed interest and provided the incentive Maury needed to begin the task. Joseph Henry's theft more than six years earlier of astronomical data developed at the observatory by Sears Walker served as a sharp reminder that one man's work could be stolen by another, so in the early spring of 1854, Maury began work on *The Physical Geography of the Sea.*

From his charts and *Sailing Directions* Maury had earned international recognition but not a cent beyond his superintendent's navy pay. Those publications belonged to his employer, the United States Navy. The Harper project gave him an opportunity to make a few dollars, but only if he could write the book during off-duty hours. So every night he bent to the task of preparing the rough draft. That he finished it in the amazing time of three months, and that the manuscript included dozens of detailed charts and sketches, is the direct result of the book having been in progress—in one form or another—for a long period of time.

Six months later *The Physical Geography of the Sea* went to press, and early in 1855 Harper & Brothers released the first edition. For a man who dealt daily with the most complicated computations and whose casual vocabulary contained some of the most advanced technical terms of the day, Maury produced a wonderfully readable book. Through 1871, Harper & Brothers published eleven editions, many of them revised and expanded with redrawn and simplified maps of the world. The plate charting the winds of the sea came from 1,159,353 separate observations and more than 100,000 barometric readings. "The Drift of the Sea" chapter contained a chart of the world's currents. Other chapters illustrated the paths of storms, tidal flow, creatures of the sea, weather phenomena, and, in later revised editions, geographic characteristics of the land and sea.

Much of the material for the first edition actually came from the sixth edition of *Sailing Directions* and has the appearance of being a collection of previously published papers, augmented by some new material. This did not deter *De Bow's Review* from extolling the book as "occupying the first rank in its appropriate department, and Lieutenant Maury has erected for himself a statue that is imperishable." Another reviewer wrote: "Lieutenant Maury will be numbered among the great scientific men of the age and the benefactors of mankind." A third party, Sir Henry Holland of Great Britain, thought Maury had theorized "too largely and hazardously," not separating "the known from the unknown" while drawing airy conclusions without proof. Holland accused Maury of making questionable assumptions. Another reviewer wrote, "While the work contains much instruction, we cannot adopt some of its theories, believing them unsustained by facts." Maury had hurriedly written the book for commercial purposes, and where it may have lacked elements of scientific accuracy, it made a wonderful hit with the public.

In 1855, publishers in Great Britain and the Netherlands acquired secondary rights, followed by Germany, France, and Italy. Though many of Maury's conclusions attracted critics, some of the most advanced scientists in the world learned from Maury's simple geography, and those who read it offered effusive praise. Baron Alexander von Humboldt, a German scientist of great distinction who discovered the source of the Peru current that now bears his name, praised Maury's *Physical Geography* for inaugurating two new sciences: oceanography and marine meteorology. In his opinion, the work ranked as one of the most charming and instructive books in the English language. By 1861, Great Britain had published nineteen editions. Maury dedicated Harper's eighth American edition to William C. Hasbrouck, without whose help he may never have made the journey from Tennessee to begin his career in the navy.

While preparing *The Physical Geography of the Sea*, Maury remarked, "I set out with no theory and I have none to build up. I set out with the view of

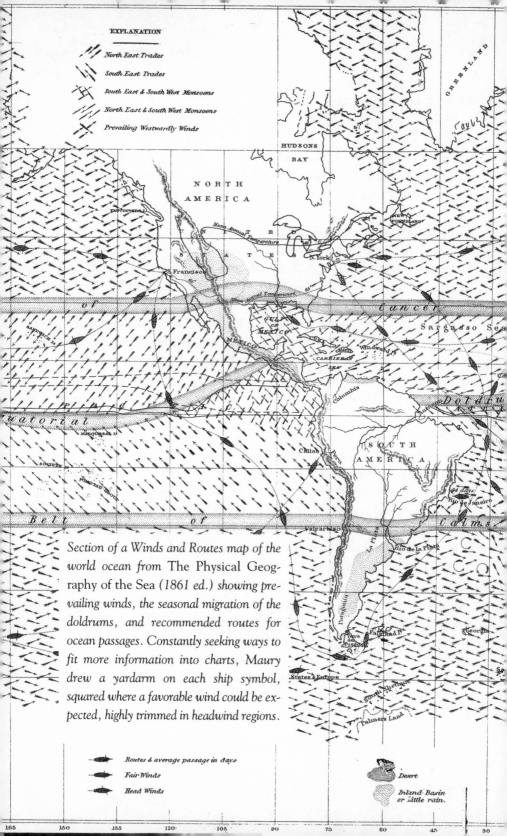

EXPLANATION

North East Trades

South East Trades

South East & South West Monsoons

North East & South West Monsoons

Prevailing Westwardly Winds

Section of a Winds and Routes map of the world ocean from The Physical Geography of the Sea (1861 ed.) showing prevailing winds, the seasonal migration of the doldrums, and recommended routes for ocean passages. Constantly seeking ways to fit more information into charts, Maury drew a yardarm on each ship symbol, squared where a favorable wind could be expected, highly trimmed in headwind regions.

Routes & average passage in days

Fair Winds

Head Winds

Desert

Inland Basin or Little rain.

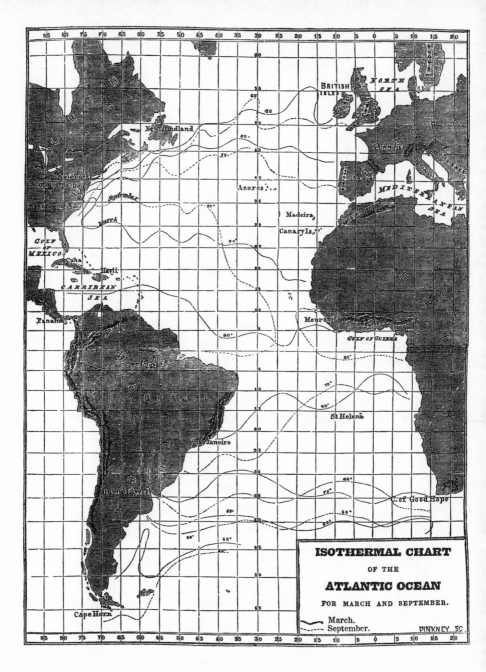

Plate 4 from the eighth edition of The Physical Geography of the Sea. Within
months of the publication of this edition, Maury left the Naval Observatory to join
the Confederacy.

collecting facts, of gathering and presenting side by side the experience of every navigator. . . . I have been governed altogether by the principles of inductive philosophy." Again, he says, "I only bring together the observations that others have made, and then leave it to the observations themselves to discover their own meaning in their own way. . . . As a student of physical geography, I regard the earth, sea, air, and water, as parts of a machine." Maury's statements about "bringing together the observations that others have made" and leaving "the observations themselves to discover their own meaning" fed into the deprecating remarks of Bache and Henry that Maury was not a scientist but merely a chronicler. Maury made the statement out of modesty, never suspecting it would be forensically examined by jealous derogators. But Maury had created his own problems by drawing whimsical conclusions and using obsolete and questionable sources to do so. He might also have saved for himself much energy and aggravation by enjoying his royalties and not trying to prove his critics wrong by writing rejoinders.

Had Bache and Henry not put so much effort into sabotaging Maury's efforts to include land meteorology in the work of the Brussels Marine Meteorology Conference, some of the shortcomings in *The Physical Geography of the Sea* might have become better understood and in later editions corrected. Years passed before the two sciences were merged into one. Maury understood that weather flowing off the sea affected weather on land, and vice versa, but he was not certain of how this worked. Consequently, forty years passed before Frank Waldo, at an International Meteorological Congress held in Chicago, declared, "Maury showed his strength by collecting and mapping the normal winds of the oceans; but shows his weakness in speculating on a philosophy of their origin." Waldo was correct in his conclusion, but perhaps a little harsh by putting all the blame on Maury.

Two chapters of the book—"The Depths of the Ocean" and "The Basin of the Atlantic"—caught special attention from a group of engineers attempting to lay the nation's first transatlantic cable. In 1849, Maury had used the schooner *Taney*, commanded by Lieutenant J. C. Walsh, to make soundings every two hundred miles across the Atlantic. Walsh took several reels of sounding twine, each containing ten thousand fathoms (sixty thousand feet), and marked every hundred fathoms. For a plummet, Walsh used a standard thirty-two-pound cannonball. From the ship, the crew lowered the plummet overboard and allowed the line to run off the reel. Walsh eventually discovered that the line, once started and dragged down into the depths of the ocean, would never cease to run, there being no precise way of determining when the plummet struck the bottom. Deep currents and surface drift drew off more line until it eventually broke. To complicate the soundings, *Taney* proved to be an unseaworthy vessel, and Maury lost much of his sounding equipment, though he salvaged enough data to keep the navy interested in the program.

He then went to work developing a thinner and stronger twine, one that could hold a sixty-pound weight suspended in air. After running more tests at sea, Maury discovered that deep water contained many currents, some of which ran in opposite directions. In order to minimize surface drift, he put the sounding equipment in a boat with instructions to oarsmen that they hold the boat in exactly the same position. Maury never completely solved the difficulties of deep-sea soundings, but through a series of experiments he developed "The law of the plummet's descent," which enabled the next sounding team to take more accurate readings.

In 1852–53, Lieutenant Otway H. Berryman in the brig *Dolphin* completed the soundings of the Atlantic. Maury now had enough data to begin his first orographic map (orography is a branch of physical geography that deals with mountains). He added two maps to the fifth edition of his *Sailing Directions* (1853): plate 14, showing a preliminary depth map of the North Atlantic basin, and plate 15, depicting a profile of the ocean bottom between the United States and Europe. These comprehensive outlines of the ocean's bottom were the first maps of their kind.

Knowing the depth and profile of the North Atlantic only made Maury more curious to know what was on the bottom: rock, mud, sand, or some other substance? No specimens of solid material had ever been brought up from deeper than three hundred fathoms. Maury discussed the problem with Passed Midshipman John M. Brooke, who took care of the instruments at the Naval Observatory.

Brooke worked up a sketch for a device that could be lowered to the ocean floor by a cannon ball. On touching the bottom, a rod running through the center of the ball retracted, releasing a pair of levers holding the ball. The weight of the ball, before being released, embedded the rod end in the ocean's bottom. A hollowed-out section in the bottom of the rod contained a soft wax that collected the samples. Brooke eventually improved the rod end by designing a small scoop that closed after collecting the sample. Once the ball detached, the crew rewound the wire and brought the rod with its sample to the surface. The apparatus worked successfully in depths up to fifteen thousand feet. Somewhat to everyone's surprise, Berryman's expedition discovered a relatively shallow plateau, smooth and regular, between Trinity Bay in Newfoundland and Valentia Island, in southwestern Ireland.

Maury labeled the ocean bed surveyed the Telegraphic Plateau, and the name stuck, even though the plateau reached a depth of two and a half miles and contained a rather sharp declivity about three hundred miles off the Irish coast. In 1855 the British survey ship *Cyclops* sounded the Atlantic slightly to the north of Berryman's route and confirmed the findings. The word *plateau* sprang from Maury's conception that a telegraphic cable, if laid across the Atlantic, would be in water deep enough to avoid icebergs and ship's anchors, and on a bottom smooth and regular enough not to injure the wire.

Berryman's samples from the ocean bed produced another surprise. The bottom consisted of neither sand nor mud, but of microscopic calcareous and siliceous shells showing no evidence of erosion. Even more surprising, not a particle of sand or gravel could be found among the many samples. This revelation led Maury to conclude that the bottom of the ocean contained no currents; otherwise the shells would have been abraded beyond recognition. As scientists later discovered, Maury's plateau fell between two major formations, both deep and mountainous, and both containing strong currents. Knowing that Samuel F. B. Morse, the inventor of the telegraph in the United States, had once spoken of the feasibility of a transatlantic cable, Maury wrote Secretary Dobbin that telegraphic wires could be placed on a plateau about two miles deep, which "seems to have been placed there especially for the purpose of holding the wires of a submarine

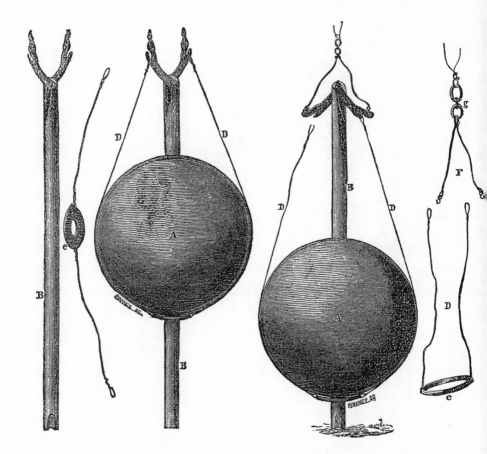

Passed Midshipman John Mercer Brooke invented this device for sounding and sampling the deep ocean floor while working under Maury at the Naval Observatory. A rod ran through a hole in the center of a cannonball. Once the seafloor absorbed the weight of the rod, the removal of tension from the cable permitted the levers at the top of the rod to trip, releasing the cannonball. The rod could then be recovered together with a sediment sample in its hollowed and waxed lower end.

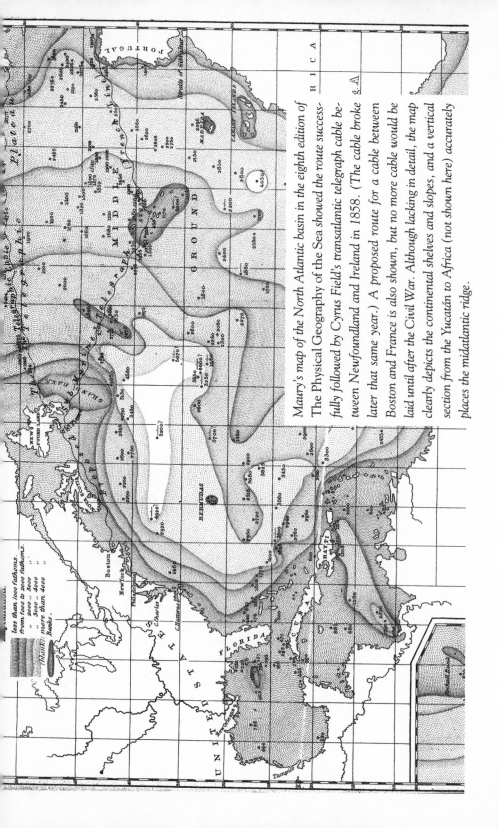

Maury's map of the North Atlantic basin in the eighth edition of *The Physical Geography of the Sea* showed the route successfully followed by Cyrus Field's transatlantic telegraph cable between Newfoundland and Ireland in 1858. (The cable broke later that same year.) A proposed route for a cable between Boston and France is also shown, but no more cable would be laid until after the Civil War. Although lacking in detail, the map clearly depicts the continental shelves and slopes, and a vertical section from the Yucatán to Africa (not shown here) accurately places the midatlantic ridge.

telegraph and of keeping them out of harm's way," and, he added, "once laid there . . . [the wire] would remain as completely beyond the reach of accident as it would if buried in airtight cases."

Maury had not finished his report to the secretary when a letter arrived at the observatory in November 1853 from Cyrus W. Field. The wealthy and retired American paper manufacturer had become curious about laying a transatlantic telegraph cable after a providential meeting with Frederick Gisborne, an English engineer who wanted to lay a telegraph cable across the Gulf of St. Lawrence to connect Newfoundland with Nova Scotia. After a crash course on cables from Gisborne, Field went to his globe, placed his finger on Newfoundland, and then traced it across the Atlantic to Ireland. That simple motion became the beginning of Field's twelve-year quest to make the transatlantic telegraph cable a reality.

Field knew Maury by reputation and went to him directly, asking the feasibility of such an endeavor. Maury confirmed the existence of the Telegraphic Plateau and stressed the importance of connecting Europe with North America by cable. He warned, however, that under the sea were mountains and plateaus, as well as low plains and little hills, and like tracks on the surface of the ocean, a track must be found on its bottom. Maury also sent Samuel F. B. Morse a full report of his findings, again urging that some thought be given to transatlantic telegraphy. In 1844, Morse had run the first telegraph line in America, connecting Washington and Baltimore, and since that time companies small and large, all using Morse's patents, had strung thousands of miles of wire from Maine to New Orleans.

Maury knew more about the sea than anyone in Great Britain, but the British knew more about laying submarine cables than anyone in America. Nonetheless, Maury's assurances that a cable could be laid, more than the opinions of others, motivated Cyrus Field to form a company and seek financial backing to lay a transatlantic cable. He wanted to involve Maury monetarily in the project so as to capture him as a consultant, but the lieutenant judiciously declined, replying, "of course it would be improper" though "I have the success of the enterprise much at heart and would be glad to do what I rightfully may to forward it."

Naval cooperation on the cable project almost got sidetracked when

Alexander Bache, acting in collusion with Commander Charles Henry Davis, attempted to insert the Coast Survey into the oceanographic work at the expense of Maury. The plot emanated from the ingenious mind of Davis, and to give it an aura of secrecy, he called it the "Steamer Plan," though it had nothing to do with steamers. When the navy hesitated to devote more vessels to the cable enterprise, the plan almost worked. Bache's intrusion made Maury so furious that he took his complaint directly to the secretary of the navy. When Dobbin learned of the conspiracy, he cleverly involved both men without taking from Maury or giving to Bache. He used the Coast Survey's vessels but told Bache to adhere to Maury's program. This rankled Bache, but he agreed to comply. He feared that if he complained too loudly, Dobbin might cause the Coast Survey to be transferred from the Treasury Department to Maury, a change in status that would be personally reprehensible. The arrangement, however, put two rivals into a combination of forced cooperation and head-to-head combat.

Ever since 1843, when Bache had obtained command of the Coast Survey, he and Maury had collided over professional matters, a rivalry exacerbated by their opposing personalities. Bache enjoyed the role of elitist, gathering around himself a coterie of highly educated potentates of scientific achievement. Maury also enjoyed friends, but he was too busy with his work to organize a group of followers who would pay him constant homage. Maury's axiom for most of his life had been "The only talent worth having . . . [is] the talent for hard work." He viewed Bache as someone who had sacrificed a marvelous talent for work by wasting time to recruit cronies who would pander to his schemes.

Much effort still needed to be expended on the Atlantic plateau. While drawing a bathymetric map of the North Atlantic using contour lines sketched at intervals of a thousand fathoms, Maury detected flaws in Berryman's soundings taken under Bache's guidance and in early 1857 dispatched a warning to Field, who received the letter in England. With the cable already in production, Field let the matter drop. He wanted nothing to interfere with plans to lay the cable during the summer of 1857. To investigate the most troublesome problems, Maury needed help from Bache, who had not bothered to check Berryman's work. Maury contacted both men and advised Field to wait for Bache. Unfortunately, in his eagerness to lay the cable, Field ignored Maury's warnings and pressed forward with the work.

The first effort to lay the cable during the summer of 1857 failed when the cable dispensing machinery became disabled and cut the wire. Maury had warned against using so heavy a cable, preferring one that would gently pay out and sink without any dependency on complicated machinery. Field fortunately ignored Maury's recommendations on cable design, deferring instead to the English engineers who understood the business better than Maury. Instead, Field made another expedition during the summer of 1858, this time bringing together two ships in the middle of the ocean, each to take half the cable and carry it to opposite shores of the Atlantic. Maury suggested sailing on July 20 and finishing by August 10, his charts showing those as being the calmest days on the North Atlantic. Field followed the advice of the British and chose the first week of June. The Wire Squadron, as the men called the four expedition ships, encountered ten days of storms with hurricane-strength gusts before reaching midocean. The cable, having been jostled about on the ships and damaged, then broke, spurring assertions from the croakers that laying a cable across the Atlantic would never succeed.

Field then listened more carefully to Maury's advice. On July 28 the Wire Squadron met again in the middle of the Atlantic, the USS *Niagara* heading for Newfoundland and the British HMS *Agamemnon* for the coast of Ireland. They connected the cable and sailed once more in opposite directions, paying out the wire as they traveled east and west. On August 5, 1858, *Niagara* dropped anchor in Trinity Bay, Newfoundland, and connected the cable to the telegraph station. *Agamemnon* anchored in Dowlas Bay, Valentia, Ireland, on the same day. For the first time in the history of the world, the code invented by Samuel F. B. Morse traveled from Ireland to Newfoundland, and from there to Washington, D.C.—a simple message of congratulations from Queen Victoria to President James Buchanan. The queen's 98-word message took sixteen hours of transmission time to reach Newfoundland. The president's 149-word reply took more than ten hours, but in each instance, the messages made history. Much remained to be learned about transoceanic cables, but had Maury not studied the science of the seas and set in motion an understanding of winds, currents, and the orography of the North Atlantic, more years might well have passed before telegraphic communications were established between the United States and Europe.

Maury and Alexander Bache both attended a banquet held in New York to honor those whose efforts led to the first successful laying of the cable, but Joseph Henry boycotted the affair. The two men relaxed to enjoy the temporary victory celebration at this joyous and friendly event. During a round of toasts, the party singled out Lieutenant Maury, extolling him as "The indefatigable investigator of the courses of winds and currents, and of the ocean depths," and a round of ringing cheers rent the banquet hall. Cyrus Field added, "Maury furnished the brains, England gave the money and I did the work."

The happy moment would not last. Maury wanted to use the cable to determine the exact difference in longitude between the Royal Observatory at Greenwich, England, and the observatory in Washington, and Bache, purely out of jealousy, attempted to block it. Before Maury could get his way, the cable went dead, destroyed through incompetence by a distinguished English electrician who falsely believed that by increasing the voltage on the line, the signals would be transmitted faster. Instead, he overcharged the conductor wires and destroyed the insulation. Another cable would not be laid across the Atlantic until the end of America's Civil War, eight years later, by the mighty thirty-two-thousand-ton British leviathan *Great Eastern*.

Because Maury had deftly used the Coast Survey in preparing the way for the cable, Bache continued to worry that his arch rival would gain control of his department. To ward off the threat, he invoked help from a close friend, former senator from Mississippi and then Secretary of War Jefferson Davis, who interceded on Bache's behalf to keep the departments separate. This did not ingratiate Maury to Davis. Three years later they would come together in a rebellion against the United States, though never as comrades in mutual harmony.

Men such as Maury, Bache, and Henry approached their scientific specialties separately and with equal zeal, but any possibility of the slightest infringement spawned a spirited fight for domain. Each published dozens of papers, though Henry lacked Maury's promptitude and motivation when sharing his research and inventions with the world. Bache disliked Maury because of the latter's enormous reputation for scientific research, especially from those abroad, where Bache's criticisms held little water. But what rankled Bache and Henry more was the astounding success of Maury's *Physical Geography of the Sea*, which neither of them had the knowledge nor the skill to write. Maury did nothing to curb the jealousies of Bache or Henry, but in his communications with others he usually kept his opinions of professional rivals to himself.

❧

WITH Maury's vast knowledge of the sea, he had yet to develop his greatest contribution to sailing—a divided highway in the sea with one-way traffic lanes. The incident pressing him toward this work occurred in October 1854, when on the fog-shrouded North Atlantic, the U.S. mail steamer *Arctic* rammed the French steamer *Vesta*. Steamers were rapidly replacing sailing ships for transatlantic travel. With few exceptions, they were faster, safer, and offered more comfort and amenities than the majestic sailing ships, and many shipyards that once turned out clippers now built steamers. The accident claimed more than three hundred lives and served as a reminder to the public of other close calls occurring in iceberg-infested waters. Looking for a solution, Robert B. Forbes, a Boston shipowner, turned to Maury and asked if some arrangement could be made for steamers traveling in opposite directions to do so by different routes. Maury studied the matter and a month later declared that a system for sea lanes could be devised without an appreciable reduction in travel time.

Forbes reported Maury's comments to his associates, and three weeks later a committee of Boston underwriters, shipowners, and merchants sent a formal request to the Naval Observatory asking the lieutenant to perfect his plan for steamer lanes and prepare a chart "lessening the liability of collision without materially lengthening the passage." The many petitioners included J. Ingersoll Bowditch, son of the famous navigator.

Maury worked at remarkable speed. He established the position of the lanes by analyzing logs encompassing forty-six thousand days of observations of winds, currents, and weather conditions along the routes traveled in the North Atlantic. He developed two lanes for steamers, each about twenty-five miles wide. Ships bound from the United States to Europe would travel the northernmost route. Ships crossing to the west would travel a route from one to ten degrees to the south. Because of seasonal changes in the weather, the lanes were different in summer than in winter. Maury also kept sailing vessels in mind, writing, "These [steamer] lanes are narrow [and] sailing vessels are requested not to run along in them; but to shear off alongside of them. So that they are like a double track railway—everything on the same track and in the same lane, going one way." Maury completed the work in five weeks and sent the committee charts, tables of distance, and sailing instructions. In 1855, the New York Board of Underwriters published the information in a booklet entitled *Lanes for the Steamers Crossing the Atlantic*.

Some steamship captains chose to ignore Maury's lanes, preferring to follow routes they had sailed for years. A few years later *Ville de Havre* collided with another ship and sank in the North Atlantic. Investigators determined that "If she had followed Maury's steam lines, this terrible loss of life and ship would have been avoided." When in 1889 a marine conference convened in Washington to fix routes for steamers crossing the North Atlantic, they studied the matter for nine years before deciding in 1898 on a plan almost identical to the one outlined by Maury in 1855. In 1930, Philip Vyle wrote, "Lanes across the oceans? I never heard of any Lanes— what are they—who laid them out?" And then answering his own questions, he added, "There are well-defined Lanes across the oceans, and ships follow them, too. Each time you take [a] ship you traverse a Maury's Lane. A Lane for your ship to go, and a Lane for your ship to come," and so it was for more than a hundred years.

Maury had barely finished his work on steamer lanes when in early 1855 the Navy Department handed him another problem, one that naturally led to a new conflict with Bache. At that time, the number of wrecks off Sandy Hook involving inbound traffic had been causing great consternation in the Navy Department. Instead of going to Bache and the Coast Survey for a solution, Secretary Dobbin turned to the Bureau of Ordnance and Hydrography. Though the problem belonged to Bache, Maury got the assignment. Bache considered the decision an encroachment on his domain, but the navy took the view that since Bache had done little to curb the growing number of shipwrecks, the time had come to insert a problem solver. Maury knew, of course, that he had been charged with what was normally the work of the Coast Survey, and he probably relished the assignment. He acted with alacrity, identifying the hazards and marking the channels. On May 5, 1855, he wrote a government pamphlet containing a new set of sailing instructions and for six months monitored its effectiveness. Not a single wreck occurred, which no doubt gave him a modest amount of satisfaction and Bache a twinge of discomfort.

Though still a lieutenant after thirty years in the navy, Maury's unique status as superintendent of the U.S. Naval Observatory gave him credentials and pay that no other officer in the navy of his rank enjoyed. Underwriters, shipmasters, and merchants both at home and abroad considered his scientific work worth every penny, and at times they tried to acknowledge his worth in monetary ways. For his labors as a civil employee, Maury could not legally accept a cent from anyone except the navy, and certain types of gifts and gratuities from foreign and domestic admirers could not be accepted without the approval of Congress.

Maury looked forward to 1855 as a year of even greater accomplishment. New track and pilot charts were on the drawing board for the Indian Ocean and the South Pacific, and the idea of charting the lanes of the seas to reduce the time of travel and prevent disasters provided him with great impetus for more scientific study. Sailing Directions had to be revised and new charts prepared, and with the steady influx of abstract logs, time also had to be found to revise and enlarge The Physical Geography of the Sea. In addition to an immense workload, Maury directed work for a book on astronomical observations and supervised the preparation of a new abstract log for men o'war. And during the same months he had just begun to work with Cyrus Field on the time-consuming Atlantic cable project.

The enormous success of his efforts created great admirers but also an increasing number of sulking naval officers who personally disliked him, envied his fame, begrudged his superintendent's salary of $3,000, and complained that while they went to sea on lengthy voyages Maury dwelled comfortably ashore, enjoying free use of a home provided by the navy. Their unified jealousy contributed in stealthy ways to Maury's lack of promotion. As in all matters of a military nature, rank had its physical and psychological advantages, and if enemies could not suppress Maury's reputation any other way, they could ensure that he stayed a lieutenant. Some old sea dogs still salved old wounds emanating from Harry Bluff's "Scraps from the Lucky Bag." Others remembered issues where Maury proved to be right and themselves wrong. They waited for an opportunity to settle old scores. Though acutely aware of the snub, Maury remained silent on the subject.

Yet there were those in Congress who agreed with shipowners and underwriters, voicing opinions that Maury had never been adequately compensated for his great work on navigation. On January 29, 1855, Senator Stephen R. Mallory of Florida, chairman of the Naval Affairs Committee, brought before the floor of the upper chamber a motion to award Maury the sum of $25,000 in recognition of services rendered the country by his *Wind and Current Charts* and *Sailing Directions*. Though monetary awards for distinguished service in Europe were common, senators in Washington declared the motion without precedent and rejected it.

❧

SINCE the days of Harry Bluff's "Scraps from the Lucky Bag," Maury had been quietly, yet influentially, working to restore efficiency to the United States Navy. When Senator Mallory became chairman of the Naval Affairs Committee in 1855 and began work on a naval reform bill, he asked Maury's advice. Armed with the best counsel he could obtain, Mallory took his bill before the Senate, and on February 28, 1855, Congress passed "An Act to Promote the Efficiency of the Navy" with little opposition. The bill was designed to eliminate deadwood, thereby opening slots for promoting the navy's best men. Every officer from the rank of passed midshipman to captain was to be scrutinized by a board of examiners to determine whether the individual could perform "promptly and efficiently all their duty both ashore and afloat." Mallory would essentially rubber-stamp the board's evaluations and then submit its findings to the secretary of the navy, who would review the list and present his recommendations to the president for executive action.

The Navy Retiring Board—scoffingly referred to as the "plucking board"—met for the first time on June 20, 1855, and remained in closed session until July 26. After examining 684 officers, the five captains, five commanders, and five lieutenants constituting the board forwarded their recommendations to Secretary Dobbin. Knowing little about the mission of the newly created plucking board, Maury took a brief leave during late summer to escape the torrid weather of Washington. While on vacation he received a letter from the secretary advising that by the recommendation of the plucking board, he had been placed on the "Reserved List on leave-of-absence pay," and that the findings of the board had "been approved by the President." Though the board placed Maury on the reserve list, Dobbin did not detach him from the observatory, ordering him to "continue on your present duty."

If Maury had not been so shocked by his unexpected change in status, he might have noticed the irony of being ousted by the very reorganization he had for so many years advocated. The more he thought about it, the madder he got. Then again, there were a few men on the plucking board whom Harry Bluff had criticized. Tempering his anger enough to write a civil letter, he asked the secretary to explain the decision that had thrust him "under official disgrace. This is a severe blow," he declared, "and I feel it a grievous wrong. May I not therefore be permitted to know what is the accusation against me, and who my accusers were before the Board?" Dobbin replied that the Board had given no reason, and he knew of no accusations having been made by its members. The reply so infuriated Maury's sense of justice that he vowed to continue the fight until his questions were answered and his honor restored.

Maury's efforts to investigate the proceedings of the plucking board hit a brick wall when he discovered that every meeting had been held in secret. He knew enough about his rights as a naval officer to demand a hearing before a court of inquiry. He suspected that envious members on the board wanted to diminish his reputation and throw his success back in his face. He also knew that the board's action would reduce his pay to $1,200 a year—an amount that would not pay the family's bills and would leave him in the dubious position of running the observatory without the authority of an active-duty officer. He argued his case in a letter to the secretary, writing, "My complaint is that I have been tried and condemned by my peers without a hearing . . . yet they proceeded so secretly in my case, that they not only reported no reasons for their finding but I am given to understand that they preserved no minutes of the accusation against me, made no memorandum of the evidence, kept no record of their votes, nor returned a list of accusers or witnesses." It had taken a number of senior naval officers fifteen years to get even with Harry Bluff, and when the opportunity came, they hid behind their anonymity. Maury summed up the action of the board from a personal point of view, arguing: "Their sentence deprives me of valuable professional privileges; it casts a stigma upon my name, and it inflicts Naval death;—for being tried without a hearing I am found incompetent to do the duties of my profession, and pronounced to be now and forever unworthy of any naval preferment whatever."

Maury would not settle for merely voicing a complaint to the secretary. He demanded that his questions be answered and formally asked the secretary to issue orders "commanding the officers who composed the Board to make known the accusations against me with the names of the accuser and witnesses, that charges with proper specifications may thereupon be framed and I be brought to fair and open trial according to law." What annoyed him even more was the knowledge that William Lewis Maury, a distant cousin, sat on the plucking board and would not reply to his letters. Only later did he learn that the members of the board had pledged themselves to secrecy. This convinced him that the pluckers were all cowards. Maury prepared for battle.

Scientists can be just as indefatigable when investigating aspersions on their character as when tackling new fields of knowledge. When Dobbin refused to make known the official reasons for the plucking board's decisions, Maury wrote all fifteen officers asking why they had forced him out of active service and denied him eligibility for promotion. Most replies remained evasive or sympathetic, but Lieutenant James S. Biddle let the so-called cat out of the bag when he wrote, "However rare be the attainments of an officer or unrivalled his qualifications for some most important professional duty on shore, he must be broken out for sea in turn, because he owes it to his brother officers to perform his share of the 'most unpleasant service.' " Maury reread Biddle's statement, for there was the rub. He reviewed the law that had created the plucking board and found no authorization for its members to draw any distinction between duty ashore or duty afloat. Armed with Biddle's admission, Maury petitioned both houses of Congress, stressing that he was an officer of inferior rank and subject to the order of the Navy Department, which, he said, retained him on shore duty but could, at any time they wished, have ordered him to sea.

Dobbin not only underestimated Maury's determination to remove the stain cast upon his name, but he also miscalculated the outrage of the press, which condemned the action of the plucking board with unexpected viciousness. The *National Intelligencer*, after castigating the plucking board, wrote in October: "Let his sword be restored to him with all the honour and reparation due to injured merit. Let this be done and done quickly."

Dobbin's actions encountered more sharp criticism when medals began to flow from Europe honoring Maury's great achievements. While the Retiring Board plucked, Maury's latest contributions to navigation came off the press in new editions of the *Winds and Current Charts* and the *Sailing Directions* that always accompanied the charts. Each year, more nations of the world joined the program for the expansion of oceanographic knowledge, and the funnel Maury had created for capturing and utilizing that knowledge had expanded far beyond the comprehension of the Naval Affairs Committee or the envious officers of the Navy Retiring Board.

By November, Dobbin began to have second thoughts and sought ways to ameliorate the problem with Maury, intimating that promotion might salve wounds. Maury thought not. He would settle for nothing less than having the professional stain "wiped out." Of 684 officers scrutinized by the plucking board, 184 had been retired or put on half-pay. Of that number, no officer created more havoc among the House and Senate than Maury. Senator Mallory, who in January 1855 had attempted to vote Maury a gift of $25,000 and who had brought the naval reform bill before Congress in February, now turned against him by defending the actions of the plucking board. The debate became one of the longest and most heated since the congressional fight over the Kansas–Nebraska Act of 1854, which opened the door for state self-determination and initiated a mini–civil war between pro-slavery and free-soil factions in the 1850s.

On March 6, 1857, Secretary Dobbin, who admired the work of Maury, probably felt a degree of relief from the interminable plucking board problems after James Buchanan, inaugurated president on March 4, 1857, chose a new secretary of the navy. On March 7 Isaac Toucey took over the reins of the navy and all of the service's problems. One such problem stemmed back to July 15, 1856, when the Senate had passed a bill to amend the Act to Promote the Efficiency of the Navy, but the House had not yet put the issue on the floor for debate. In February, 1857, Dobbin had authorized the court to be organized and then left the troublesome matter in the hands of the new secretary. Toucey stepped into a mightily tangled web, and to expedite the judicial process he created two more courts to try the cases, each with three captains presiding and one judge advocate.

While Maury waited his turn, he remained active. He continued to press forward his scientific study of the ocean, though with somewhat less enthusiasm than before. He worked with Cyrus Field to lay the Atlantic cable, published new charts for the Atlantic, Pacific, and Indian Oceans, started work on the eighth edition of *Sailing Directions*, and in 1857 enlarged *The Physical Geography of the Sea*. His work, however, suffered constant interruptions from fellow officers who called him into court to testify as a witness on their behalf.

Letters from skippers sailing the seven seas continued to flow into the observatory, personally addressed to him and absorbing more of his time. Captain Daniel McLaughlin, writing from Liverpool, was about to leave for Bombay on the ship *Ætos*, fourteen hundred tons, built at Eastport, Maine, for a Boston consortium. McLaughlin knew that his ship was being matched against three British clippers, *Conflict*, *Tiger*, and *Kunjee Oadunjee*, so he plotted his course using the charts and asked Maury's confirmation. Maury, also interested in the outcome of the race, replied that the

James Dobbin, secretary of the navy under President Franklin Pierce from 1853 to 1857. Credited with enlarging the navy, improving the treatment of its sailors, and instituting a merit system for promotion, Dobbin supported Maury's Brussels conference in 1853 but removed Maury from active duty in 1855 on the advice of the Navy Retiring Board—the infamous "plucking board."

Isaac Toucey, lawyer and former U.S. senator from Connecticut. As secretary of the navy under President James Buchanan from 1857 to 1861, Toucey inherited Maury's appeal of the plucking board's decision to place him on inactive status at half-pay.

D.

NAVY DEPARTMENT, September 17, 1855.

SIR : The Board of Naval Officers, assembled under the " act to promote the efficiency of the navy," approved February 28, 1855, having reported you as one of the officers who, in their judgment, should be placed on the " reserved list," on " leave-of-absence pay," and the finding of the Board having been approved by the President, it becomes my duty to inform you that, from this date, you are accordingly removed from the " active service list," and placed on the " reserved list," on leave-of-absence pay.

You are, however, not detached from the naval observatory. I avail myself of the authority of the law to direct that you continue on your present duty.

I am, respectfully, your obedient servant,
J. C. DOBBIN.

Lieutenant M. F. MAURY,
    U. S. Navy, Washington, D. C.

E.

UNIVERSITY OF VIRGINIA, September 20, 1855.

SIR : I received yesterday your communication of the day before, informing me that the President, acting under the advice of " the Board of Naval Officers, assembled under the act to promote the efficiency of the navy, approved February 28, 1855," has commanded that I be removed from the active service list of the navy, and be " placed on the retired list, on leave-of-absence pay."

This announcement has taken me by surprise.

I have been in the navy upwards of thirty years. During this time, I have aimed, in every station to which I have been called, to serve my country truly and well ; with what success, the department and the public can judge better than I. Suffice it to say that I am not aware that any charges or accusations, or even any complaint of duty neglected or badly performed during this long period, has ever reached the Department against me ; nevertheless, in the judgment of the Board, I should be, and have been placed under official disgrace.

This is a severe blow ; and I feel it as a grievous wrong. May I not, therefore, be permitted to know what is the accusation against me, and who my accusers were before the Board ?

As soon as health and the miasma of the Observatory will permit, or sooner should you desire it, I propose to return to the Observatory, and to enter upon the discharge of duty there in the new relations to which your communication has consigned me.

Respectfully, &c..
M. F. MAURY.

HON. J. C. DOBBIN,
    Secretary of the Navy, Washington.

A copy of Secretary of the Navy James Dobbin's 1855 letter informing Maury of his removal from active duty, together with Maury's response, as contained in Maury's 1856 petition to Congress to have the action overturned.

"proposed route [is] . . . very well projected." The *Ætos* made the passage in 77½ days, *Conflict* in 80, and the ships' logs produced exactly the type of information Maury wanted to verify his latest charts.

A log came into the observatory from a bark named *Maury*, commanded by Charles E. Fletcher. The lieutenant took particular interest in the ship's voyage because Fletcher matched himself against the fast British clipper *Lord of the Isles*. Both vessels made a fine run down the Indian Ocean in late July and early August of that year, arriving at Gravesend in mid-October, 127 days out. In a stunning upset, the swift *Lord of the Isles* sailed into port several minutes behind the bark *Maury*. When Fletcher had taken command of the bark, he vowed to sail her exactly in accordance with Maury's charts, and during the next two years he made exceptionally fast runs between London and Foochow (now Fuzhou), China. Reports such as these provided Maury with a small amount of gratification while struggling to solve his problems with the navy.

On November 25, 1857, Maury finally presented his case before the court. Twenty-six months had elapsed since Dobbin removed him from active duty. By then, three former secretaries of the navy had vouched for Maury's fitness. But Secretary Toucey denied Maury the right to know what questions would be asked, thereby preventing him from preparing his testimony or selecting witnesses. For a court of inquiry, the denial was unprecedented. It disturbed Maury, along with all the others "plucked" from the service. No wonder the process was taking so long.

Maury believed the plucking board had capitalized on his lameness as an excuse to remove him from active duty. He suspected, and accurately, that the navy would build its case around doctors' reports issued in 1839 and 1840. He called as a witness Navy Surgeon W. S. W. Ruschenberger, who admitted examining Maury's leg in 1840 and diagnosing it as "irreparable." Another doctor followed. Both now admitted they may have been wrong, as Maury looked "eminently fit" to fulfill his duties. The prosecutor asked the doctors to reexamine Maury's leg, which they did in a separate room. Both returned and declared Maury fully able to carry out his orders at sea or on land. Not until January 18, 1858, did Maury learn the outcome of his trial, nor until January 29 did he receive official notification from Toucey that "The President of the United States, by and with the advice and consent of the Senate, has appointed you a Commander in the Navy from the 14th of September, 1855, on the Active List." Maury still believed he should be promoted to captain but settled for having the issue resolved in his favor.

Though fully vindicated, Maury's troubles continued. His friend and advocate, Senator Mallory of Florida, had become his enemy. Other powerful southern figures such as Senator Judah P. Benjamin from Louisiana and Captain Franklin Buchanan from Maryland, a member of the plucking board, were not the type of men to be made to look foolish by a navy lieutenant. Maury had led the charge to force the inquiries, resulting in 62 cases out of 188 being reversed by the court of inquiry. The Navy Retiring Board deserved the condemnation it received from the public because it left its task undone. As Maury observed long ago, the navy still needed to be reorganized and reconstructed along more efficient lines. He had made the plucking board appear inept in the eyes of the public, and its fifteen members, along with Senator Mallory, blamed Maury for its failure.

MAURY'S CHARTS GO TO WAR

BY 1860 Maury's charts and sailing directions had mapped the seas, though he never seemed wholly satisfied with his pilot charts. He looked for ways to streamline the highways, increase the speed of travel, and minimize the variations caused by aberrant weather, storms, and calms. With the increase in steamer traffic, he sought ways to prevent collisions by putting sailing ships on slightly different courses than coal burners. With scrupulous adherence to the charts, getting from one port to another was no longer as risky a business. After thousands of observations, Maury's tracks had become almost as easy to follow as a modern road map. Shipowners no longer allowed their captains to sail without the latest copy of Maury's charts and sailing directions, and underwriters offered lower insurance rates to merchants who agreed to sail by the charts. But his work on the oceans rapidly approached its end.

After dedicating his entire adult life to the United States Navy, Maury became immensely distressed over the inability of the northern and southern states to resolve their sectional differences. Even though he had made enemies in the navy, he loved the service with as much ardor as he loved his native Virginia. He believed that if the warring nations of Europe could come together and reach accord as they did during the 1853 Brussels Marine Meteorology Conference, then solutions could be found to resolve the economic and moral issues dividing the North and South. Threats of the

[219]

Union dividing unsettled him, and the fiery voices of abolitionists and se-
cessionists were creating an atmosphere in which no compromise could
be reached.

In November 1860, Maury arrived in England to secure a copyright for
his latest edition of *The Physical Geography of the Sea*. There he learned that
Abraham Lincoln had won the American presidential election. From
Maury's perspective, only Tennessean John Bell, the leader of southern
conservatives, offered the moderating voice needed to avert secession.

While in England, Maury renewed old acquaintances, among them
Marin H. Jansen of the Royal Dutch Navy. Jansen and Maury shared the
same scientific interests, and during the Brussels conference the two men
had become great friends. In the troubling years to come, they would meet
again, but for vastly different reasons.

Maury returned to the United States on the eve of South Carolina's December 20, 1860, declaration of secession. Six days later Major Robert Anderson, U.S. Army, evacuated Fort Moultrie on Sullivan's Island in
Charleston Harbor and moved the garrison to Fort Sumter, a more defen-
sible bastion surrounded by water. On December 27 the South Carolina
militia seized Fort Moultrie, Castle Pinckney, and the United States cus-
tomhouse and post office. Commissioners from South Carolina demanded
that Anderson abandon Fort Sumter. Maury waited with others in Washington to see what action lame-duck President James Buchanan would
take. He also watched to see if other southern states would follow South
Carolina. On January 9 Buchanan ordered the troopship *Star of the West*
to reinforce Fort Sumter, but the plan suffered a setback when the ship received fire from shore batteries as she attempted to enter Charleston Harbor. The sound of artillery reverberated across the South. Mississippi seceded that day, Florida the next, and Alabama on January 11.

During the nation's portentous disruptions, Maury worked frantically
but ineffectually to find ways to reunify the states. He wrote the northern
governors, urging them to step forward and act as mediators. He appealed
to relatives in Virginia who had connections in the state capital. He even
urged friends in Great Britain to apply pressure on Parliament to "offer
resolutions that would lead to a solution." When the governor of Virginia,

John Letcher, called the General Assembly into session, Maury began to worry. If Virginia seceded, he knew there would be no chance for reunification. But Letcher asked for a peace conference, restoring hope that some form of reconciliation might yet be negotiated. Believing he could help map a way through the problems of secession as he had mapped the lanes of the oceans, he wrote to friends in Tennessee, volunteering to serve as their delegate to a peace conference scheduled to convene on February 4 at Willard's Hotel in Washington. But when Georgia seceded on January 19, Louisiana on January 26, and Texas on February 1, all hope for a settlement of differences vanished. One hundred and thirty-one delegates attended Letcher's peace conference, but none came from the Deep South. Maury predicted the conference would fail, and it did, but he nursed one last hope: that Tennessee and Virginia would stay faithful to the Union.

On February 4, 1861, delegates from the secession states met in Montgomery, Alabama, adopted a provisional constitution for the Confederate States of America, and five days later elected Jefferson Davis of Mississippi provisional president and Alexander H. Stephens of Georgia provisional vice president. On February 18, delegates from the South inducted both men into office. On March 6, President Davis called for a hundred thousand volunteers to be equipped for service in the field. For two of his six cabinet members he appointed former senators who had recently been embroiled in defending the actions of the plucking board, Judah P. Benjamin of Louisiana as attorney general and former U.S. Senator Stephen R. Mallory of Florida as secretary of the Confederate Navy. Neither man liked Maury. The feeling was mutual.

On March 4 Abraham Lincoln took office as president of the United States, and Gideon Welles became secretary of the navy. After meeting Welles, Maury wrote, "The new Secretary promises finely as compared to Toucey, the most corrupt and mean official I have ever known."

Though disconcerted by the turmoil of secession, Maury returned to the observatory and tried to concentrate. He immersed himself in an effort to finish two nautical monographs: *The Barometer at Sea* and *The Southeast Trade Winds of the Atlantic*. Both followed an earlier monograph, *The Winds at Sea*, and served as refinements to the knowledge he had accumulated while charting the tracks of the oceans. He tried to distract himself from the troubles brewing in South Carolina over Major Anderson's occupation of Fort Sumter by proposing an international expedition to explore Antarctica, but he found few listeners. By April, everyone he met talked only of war. Maury expected the worst, and on April 18 he hurried to the Government Printing Office the final edit of *The Southeast Trade Winds of the Atlantic*, a work he described as "one of the most valuable contributions that I have ever made to navigation." No officer in the United States Navy could know the consequences of a publication like that, as well as others, being in the hands of the new enemy.

The glue still holding together any prospect of a peaceful settlement were Virginia's delegates, who on April 4 voiced their sentiment and voted 88 to 45 against secession. Eight days later South Carolina's militia fired on Fort Sumter and on the following day forced Major Anderson to surrender. Events then moved swiftly. President Lincoln called for seventy-five thousand troops to restore to the Union those states in secession, but his first concern involved the defense of the capital. If Maryland and Virginia seceded, Washington would be surrounded by states of the Confederacy.

On April 17 the Virginia Convention called a secret session to consider what action to take. Maury saw all hopes for reconciliation dashed, writing, "Things are rapidly developing and we may soon be seeking shelter indeed . . . for as soon as Virginia declares she's out, I'll follow." Virginia voted to secede that day, but because of the closed session, Maury did not receive the dreaded news until April 19.

Maury troubled over the possibility of secession, and his worries escalated after John Brown's raid of the Harpers Ferry federal armory in October 1859. States' rights still dominated the politics of particularly the South, and in the view of most southerners, one of those inalienable rights included the right to secede, as the colonies had done in 1776. Maury had only to look at the Constitution to see that the nation had been created for one country, not two. Being a Virginian who had spent most of his youth in Tennessee compelled Maury to cast his lot with the South. He had to make such an important decision rationally, not emotionally. It was his nature to take sides, especially on political issues. He did not believe that the South should become subjects of the North merely because the latter now had more congressional votes. He feared those votes would be used to disrupt or destroy the southern economy. Maury did not give his views on whether South Carolinians firing upon Fort Sumter demonstrated a dignified withdrawal.

Maury marked April 20, 1861, as the blackest day in his career. It would be his last day in the navy to which he had given his life. He fussed through the hours clearing his desk, bringing his records up to date, and transferring all public property into the hands of Lieutenant William Whiting, his second in command. He could not bring himself to write his letter of resignation and asked his secretary of twenty years, Thomas Harrison, to prepare it. Swept by grief, Harrison scratched a few indecipherable words and handed Maury a nearly blank sheet of paper. In a quavering voice, Harrison said, "I cannot write it, sir!" He knew it would be the death of Maury's scientific life, and he could not pen the warrant that "would paralyze and kill him in his pursuit after the knowledge of . . . nature's laws." So Maury wrote his own resignation and forwarded it to President Lincoln. Secretary Gideon Welles never acknowledged Maury's resignation but "dismissed" him from the service. After Maury's departure, Welles made Bache happy by transferring the superintendency of the observatory to Commander James M. Gilliss. Having cherished the post for more than ten years, Gilliss expressed his disdain for Maury by discontinuing the charts and observations on which the merchant marine so unanimously depended. Bache finally had his own man in the observatory.

In early April Maury had sent his family back to Fredericksburg. Now he followed them, dressed in a plain black suit. He left behind an admirable and glorious career and one to which he could never return. He had no illusions about abandoning his life's work, and a tragic sadness enveloped him as he departed from the observatory. He made no effort to hide his sorrow when he stepped into a carriage to begin his journey into an unpredictable future. Within a year he would tell an in-law that he felt "quite indifferent to life."

In Richmond, Maury offered his services directly to the governor. Letcher placed him on the Advisory Council of Three to aid in mobilizing the state to defend against an invasion of its shores. The post suited Maury. When the Virginia militia captured the Norfolk Navy Yard, he learned that the hull of the frigate USS *Merrimack* lay in shallow water where she had been scuttled and burned by retreating Union forces. He knew the ship could be raised and advised doing so. In less than a year, the ship would start a second life as the 275-foot ironclad ram CSS *Virginia*.

On May 29, 1861, President Jefferson Davis moved the Confederate government to Richmond, bringing with him his cabinet. On June 10 Governor Letcher transferred the newly established Navy of Virginia to the Confederacy. Lacking ships of war, Secretary of the Navy Mallory demoted a number of officers to a lower grade. Maury retained his rank as commander, not because Mallory liked him, but because of his position on Letcher's Advisory Council. Mallory did not know what to do with Maury any more than Maury knew how to satisfy his new boss. So Maury began work on a project to protect the coastline of the Confederacy from attack by blowing up Union vessels using underwater explosive devices called "torpedoes." During his experiments he nearly blew up himself. Maury's torpedoes were an early form of submersible mines operated from shore by electric cables connected to galvanic batteries. After searching and finding no insulated wire anywhere in the South, Maury sent an agent to New York to buy some. When the agent failed in this mission, Maury turned to experimenting with mechanically triggered torpedoes. The work would keep him busy during much of the war.

Though the war brought a halt to Maury's scientific work on navigation, the Confederacy turned this knowledge to its advantage. During the years before Maury began charting the seas, American merchantmen had followed their own courses, unaware that a better route lay but fifty or a hundred miles to port or starboard. By 1861 every vessel sailed the same tracks, diligently guiding their vessels by Maury's charts. American skippers had developed so much confidence in the charts that they no longer thought of sailing by any other route. And now that a state of war existed between the North and the South, no skipper wanted to be at sea any longer than necessary to get from one port to another. Speed meant greater profits and greater safety. Every merchant and shipmaster wanted to cash in on the probability of a short war. Since 1856, owners had been slowly liquidating their fleets. Merchants no longer wanted the rich cargoes that once went to San Francisco and Australia. Shipbuilders launched only six extreme clippers in 1854, and not one was ever again laid down in America. War gave merchants their last rich opportunity to revive their wealth, and because the Confederacy had no ships, there would be no enemy vessel to stop them. Flawed thinking sometimes produces disastrous results. Every commander in the Confederate navy had contributed in some way to building Maury's data base, and many of them knew as much about Maury's charts and sailing directions as the shipmasters of the merchant fleets. Secretary Mallory realized that the Confederacy could capitalize on this mutual knowledge with a few armed cruisers.

On March 13, 1861—nine days after Jefferson Davis called for a hundred thousand volunteers—Mallory began looking for steamers to arm for service on the high seas. He needed steamers specially rigged with full sets of sails because the Confederacy had no coaling stations and would be dependent upon sympathetic neutral nations for fuel. International law allowed a belligerent vessel to purchase coal no more than once a month from the same neutral country, forcing Confederate skippers to become more reliant on the sailing qualities of their ships. If Mallory expected to overmatch the U.S. Navy on the open sea, he could not succeed with inferior vessels.

At the beginning of the Civil War the American carrying trade, guided for fourteen years by Maury's charts and sailing directions, had outcompeted and eclipsed the great merchant fleet of Great Britain. During those years, worldwide trade had increased 300 percent, and 70 percent of that trade went into American bottoms. Around the globe, sailing ships flying the Stars and Stripes dotted the seas. The British wanted to see them gone, and so did the Confederacy.

Though the South lacked naval vessels, Mallory did have a surplus of experienced officers who had learned their trade in the U.S. Navy. When agents located the steam packet ship *Havana* moored off New Orleans, Mallory bought it and ordered Commander Raphael Semmes to fit it for service at sea. Semmes rigged her as a barkentine, mounted six guns on the deck, and renamed her CSS *Sumter*, the first Confederate cruiser. At 520 tons she did not make much of a cruiser, especially when clipper ships with four times her displacement still roamed the seas. But *Sumter's* guns gave her a bite, and once Semmes cleared for sea, he gave her quite a ride.

Semmes had followed Maury's work at the observatory with great interest. Studying natural history had become one of his most enjoyable pastimes, and when Maury began publishing his charts and sailing directions, Semmes adopted them for even the shortest of voyages.

To get out of the Mississippi Delta and into the Gulf of Mexico, Semmes had to outmaneuver the three-thousand-ton, twenty-four-gun screw steamer USS *Brooklyn*, a feat he narrowly succeeded in accomplishing on June 30, 1861. He wisely stayed away from Havana, Cuba, and sailed to the southern side of the island. During the next six days *Sumter* captured eight American merchantmen before disappearing into the Caribbean. After two weeks at sea, Semmes realized that he did not have a very seaworthy ship. It leaked badly and burned coal at an excessive rate. Nevertheless, he headed into the tracks of the sugar traders and picked up two more prizes on the way to Brazil. Learning that the U.S. Navy had dispatched several ships to put him out of business, Semmes crossed back and forth through Maury's sea lanes, never staying in one place for any length of time. After six months in and out of neutral ports for repairs, he crossed the Atlantic during the winter and in January 1862 brought the broken-down minicruiser into port at Gibraltar, where he eventually abandoned her. News of *Sumter's* eighteen prizes greatly embarrassed Gideon Welles and his navy and threw insurance underwriters into a panic. At times Welles had as many as six warships combing the seas for Semmes, but they never once sighted *Sumter*. The raids worried Welles: he envisioned them as only the beginning.

The South operated no shipyards for building the sailing steamers Mallory needed for commerce raiding, but Great Britain did. Knowing English merchants resented losing cargoes and commissions to the more efficient American sailing ships, Mallory devised a plan to have his cruisers built in Europe. Fast British steamers were already active in the practice of delivering arms and supplies to the Confederate army by running the

Union blockade. So, Mallory decided, why not use English shipyards to build the Confederacy's warships?

During the time when Semmes was still on the Mississippi fitting *Sumter* for sea, Mallory sent Commander James Dunwoody Bulloch to Liverpool with instructions to hire firms willing to build cruisers equipped for long voyages at sea. Because of Britain's proclamation of neutrality, no English shipbuilder could legally build an armed vessel for either belligerent. Bulloch secretly hired British agents to screen his activities. They engaged William C. Miller and Sons to build a vessel for an undisclosed Italian owner in Palermo. The disguise went undetected until the ship neared completion, at which time Bulloch hurried the so-called *Oreto* to sea before the vessel could be impounded by British authorities.

Englishmen sailed the vessel to Nassau in the Bahamas and turned it over to Lieutenant John Newland Maffitt of the Confederate States Navy. Maffitt spirited the unarmed vessel out of Nassau, renamed it the CSS *Florida*, and after much difficulty ran the Union blockade off Mobile Bay and brought her safely under the guns of Fort Morgan.

On October 3, 1862, work began on the cruiser to fit her for commerce raiding. At seven hundred tons displacement, she was nearly half again the size of *Sumter*, but with a hull cut to the lines of a clipper. Under steam and sloop-rigged sail she could cruise at twelve knots, but the Union Navy had many ships of equal and greater speeds. Armed at Mobile, she carried two 7-inch Blakely rifled cannon in pivot and six rifled 32-pounders in broadside, making her a vessel ideally suited for commerce raiding but not especially powerful as a ship of war.

On the dark, blustery early morning of January 17, 1863, *Florida*, with 20 officers and 116 men, escaped from Mobile Bay. With adept sailing, Maffitt eluded his Union pursuers. Once free to roam as he pleased, he captured and burned three quick prizes off the north coast of Cuba before taking the Gulf Stream into the Atlantic. Maury could not have laid out *Florida*'s track any better had he been on board. Maffitt swept down the shipping lanes to the West Indies, doubled back, crossing the lanes between New York and Brazil, and sailed east into the lanes between the Cape of Good Hope and New York. He returned to Brazil for coal, made a second cruise through the route between the Cape of Good Hope to New York, and then crossed the North Atlantic to Brest, France, where he put the vessel into port for repairs. By then he had tallied twenty-four prizes, five of them clipper ships. He commissioned one prize, *Clarence*, armed her with a single howitzer, put Lieutenant Charles W. Read in command, and sent the vessel into the shipping lanes off the coast of the United States. Read took twenty-one prizes before being captured off Portland, Maine.

Deprived of southern ports, Confederate captains offered no quarter when it came to disposing of prizes. Maffitt burned nineteen vessels and bonded four, using them as cartels to carry prisoners to port. *Clarence* (the so-called tender) burned fifteen and bonded five.

At Brest, Maffitt fell ill, so Lieutenant Charles M. Morris took command of *Florida*. In leaving port he escaped from USS *Kearsarge* and hurried the cruiser back to sea. Morris went right back into the same tracks hunted so successfully by Maffitt. Among American-built vessels he began to find fewer of them registered to merchants of the Unites States—a certain sign that Union shipowners were either selling their vessels to other nationalities or seeking refuge by transferring title to foreign registers. Frustrated by the absence of American shipping, Morris cruised off Bermuda, taking a small number of prizes. From prisoners, Morris learned that most American ships were now avoiding Maury's sea lanes and taking alternate routes. With this in mind Morris sailed *Florida* into the waters off the American East Coast and in three days captured seven prizes. Knowing the U.S. Navy would engage in a pursuit, he headed back to sea. During the next three months *Florida* tracked in and out of southern sea lanes but captured only two more prizes. Morris finally took the ship into Bahia, Brazil. Thinking nothing bad could befall her in a neutral port, he paid a price for poor vigilance. USS *Wachusetts*, under Commander Napoleon Collins, forced her to surrender during the dead of night, hauled her out of Bahia, and took her into Hampton Roads, Virginia, where she mysteriously sank.

Morris added to Maffitt's toll on American shipping by burning ten, scuttling one, and bonding two more prizes. During *Florida*'s career, she and the prize-turned-raider, *Clarence*, captured sixty vessels worth $4,617,144, and the Union Navy spent $3,325,000 searching for her. The consequences of Maury's scientific work were beginning to have a telling effect on the American carrying trade.

Another product of British shipyards soon overshadowed *Florida's* enormous destruction of Union shipping. Even before English builders launched *Florida* into the waters of the Mersey, Commander Bulloch had engaged Birkenhead shipbuilders John and William Laird for a second cruiser. Together they formulated the design of *Alabama*, the most powerful of all the Confederate cruisers. The Lairds produced a warship displacing 1,040 tons that combined the highest standards and latest technology used by the Royal Navy. Though Bulloch intended *Alabama* as a commerce raider, he armed her with a 7-inch 100-pounder Blakely pivot gun, an 8-inch smoothbore, and six 6-inch 32-pounders in broadside, thereby providing her with enough firepower to contend with any United States warship looking for a fight. Bulloch disguised *Alabama* as a vessel intended for a Spanish buyer and managed to get her to sea just hours before British authorities issued orders to detain her.

Bulloch planned from the beginning to command *Alabama*, but after Semmes abandoned *Sumter* at Gibraltar, he yielded to the more experienced captain. Semmes took command in the Azores, and during the next eleven days captured ten prizes, mostly whalers on their way home after four-year voyages. During that time of year, Maury's charts showed the presence of whales among the Azores, and every vessel with a few barrels to fill passed through the islands for a final hunt on their way home. Semmes looked for them, and the unsuspecting whalers fell into his trap.

Departing from the Azores, Semmes took the track of vessels sailing outbound from New England, putting *Alabama* into the face of the prevailing westerlies. He not only carried Maury's charts and sailing directions, his library afloat also contained a recent copy of *The Physical Geography of the Sea*. After Semmes entered the Gulf Stream, he captured seven more prizes during a twelve-day rampage before slipping away from coastal waters. He never stayed in one place long enough to be caught by prowling Union warships. He navigated the seas with shrewdness, slipping into busy sea lanes, snatching a few prizes, and outwitting pursuers by disappearing into another section of the ocean. He could use steam in the calms and wind in the trades, and Maury's *Sailing Directions* showed him exactly where to find the weather he wanted.

When referring to Maury's sailing directions, Semmes once wrote:

> And when we reach the equator, there is another crossing recommended to the mariner, as being most appropriate to his purpose. This it is, that the roads upon the sea have been blazed out, as it were—the blazes not being exactly cut upon forest-trees, but upon parallels and meridians. The chief blazer of these roads, is an American, of whom all Americans should be proud—Captain [sic] Maury. . . . He has so effectually performed his task in his "Wind and Current Charts" that there is little left to be desired. The most unscientific and practical navigator, may, by the aid of these charts, find the road he is in quest of. . . . He has saved every Yankee ship, by shortening her route, on every distant voyage she makes, thousands of dollars. The greedy ship-owners pocket the dollars, and abuse the philosopher.

Semmes calculated the annual savings for American shipowners at $2,250,000 a year. Those were the very vessels he sought to destroy. On one day he counted seven vessels bound in line for Europe, all "jogging along, in company, following Maury's blazes like so many passengers on a highway. *Alabama* stood like a toll-gate before them, and though we could not take toll of them, as they were all neutral, we made each traveler show us his passport as he came up." A few days later Semmes reached the equator and wrote: "We were at the 'crossing' blazed by Maury, and with the main topsail at the mast, were reviewing, as it were, the commerce of the world. We were never out of sight of ships. They were passing, by ones, and twos, and threes, in constant succession, wreathed in rain and mist, and presenting frequently the idea of a funeral procession. The honest traders were all there, except the most honest of them all—the Yankees—and they were a little afraid of the police [*Alabama*]. Still we managed to catch a rogue now and then."

During *Alabama*'s career as a commerce raider, the only Union gunboat to sight Semmes at sea was USS *Hatteras*, and Semmes sank her in the Gulf of Mexico. His search for prizes took *Alabama* down the east coast of Brazil, around the Cape of Good Hope, through the Roaring Forties to

Australia, north to Singapore, across the Bay of Bengal and into the Indian Ocean, down the eastern coast of Africa, back around the Cape of
Good Hope, and finally, on June 11, 1864, the worn commerce raider
limped into port at Cherbourg, France, for repairs. By then, she had taken
sixty-six prizes worth $5,176,164, a sum American claimants boosted to
$19,021,428. The only mistake Semmes made was issuing a challenge to
USS *Kearsarge*, commanded by Captain John A. Winslow. In preparing for
battle, Semmes transferred his trophies to a British vessel—perhaps the
largest collection of chronometers in any single place—for he had removed the precision clocks from every prize. Then, in the Civil War's only
great contest at sea, *Kearsarge* sank *Alabama* in the English Channel.
Maury had provided nothing in his *Sailing Directions* to cover such con-
tingencies.

BY June 1862, Maury had struck a new emotional low. The most powerful men in the Confederate government—Jefferson Davis, Stephen Mallory, and Admiral Franklin Buchanan, the latter having been a prominent member of the plucking board—all seemed to be against him. Maury
believed he had once been deprived of a captaincy in the U.S. Navy because of the enmity of these same fellows, and all the signs pointed to him
being denied again. In a recent conversation with Mallory, he had asked in
what capacity he might be of most benefit to the South. Mallory told him
blandly that, "He thought I would be of use doing nothing." Maury needed
to be wanted. He needed to be recognized for his talents. He needed to feel
accomplished and that he was contributing something essential to the
preservation of the Confederacy. With his family and country suffering
the scourge of war, he felt for the first time in many years an irresolvable
helplessness. He shared his agonies with Franklin Minor, writing, "I feel
quite indifferent to life. I would cultivate this fashion were it not cow-
ardly, mean, and selfish."

    After *Alabama* escaped to sea during the summer of 1862, Commander
Bulloch's efforts to build more cruisers fell under closer scrutiny from the
British. Because of the success of *Florida* and *Alabama*, Mallory wanted

more commerce raiders, so he augmented Bulloch's efforts by sending Commander Maury to Great Britain to buy them. Davis and Mallory welcomed the opportunity to ship Maury off to England for the publicized purpose of studying submarine warfare and to buy articles for building submersible mines—such items as magnetic exploders, insulated wire, and underwater detonation caps.

On a dark night mixed with light rain, the steamer *Herald* crept through the Union blockade off Charleston and carried Maury and his thirteen-year-old son, Matthew Jr., to sea. *Herald*'s captain had spent his life in the coasting trade between Charleston and Florida, and when a gale struck the vessel, he lost his bearings. For several days he steamed about the Atlantic looking for Bermuda. Thinking he had sailed right by the island, he finally went to Maury and asked for help. At 10 P.M. on the sixth day out, Maury took a sextant and, while lying on his back, scanned the skies. After finishing his calculations, he gave the captain a course to steer and told him to look for the light at Port Hamilton at 2 A.M. As one observer on *Herald* wrote:

> No one turned into his bunk that night except the commodore [sic] and his little son; the rest of us were too anxious. Four bells struck and no light was in sight. Five minutes more passed and still not a sign of it; then grumbling commenced, and the passengers generally agreed with the man who expressed the opinion that there was too much d——d science on board and that we should all be on our way to Fort Lafayette in New York Harbor as soon as day broke. At ten minutes past two the masthead lookout sang out, "Light ho!"—and the learned old commodore's [sic] reputation as a navigator was saved.

Lieutenant James Morris Morgan sailed with Maury on the *Herald* and spent many hours chatting with him during the voyage to England. Morgan recalled that Maury "had been many years in the navy, but had scarcely ever put his foot on board of a ship without becoming seasick, and through it all he never allowed it to interfere with his duty. He was the only man I ever saw who could be seasick and amiable at the same time. . . . I remember once entering his stateroom where he was seated with a Bible on his lap and a basin alongside of him. I told him that there was a ship in sight, and between paroxysms he said, 'Sometimes we see a ship, and sometimes ship a sea!' "

A highly regarded scientist with an international reputation, Maury quickly renewed old friendships when he disembarked at Liverpool on November 23, 1862. Admirers in the maritime trade still called him "the great Lieutenant Maury," ignoring his promotion to commander since the Brussels conference. When he reached London, strings of carriages with coronets on their doors pulled up to his house on Sackville Street, the occupants paying their respects to a man much more appreciated in Europe than in his native land. The emperor of Russia offered to make him an admiral with a salary of $30,000 a year. As a sweetener, he also promised to build an observatory at any site in Russia of the admiral's choice. Maury thanked the czar for the flattering offer but demurred, explaining that he wanted to devote his energies to the cause of the South.

With help from colleagues like Captain Marin H. Jansen of the Royal Netherlands Navy and Lieutenant William Lewis Maury, a distant cousin in England, Maury purchased two steamers and renamed them CSS *Georgia* and CSS *Rappahannock*, both of which needed to be sent elsewhere to be armed. Neither vessel met the high standards demanded by Bulloch, but *Georgia* managed to get to sea. For a few months she posed a third threat to American shipping during a time when *Florida* and *Alabama* still roved the sea. *Georgia* captured nine prizes worth about $406,000, but *Rappahannock* never got farther than Calais, where French authorities refused to let her sail.

While in Great Britain, Maury observed a number of thick sheets of armor being rolled for British warships built entirely from iron. Maury predicted that for the navies of the world, the day of the sailing warship had ended, "and thus perished the wooden walls of Old England." Steam and iron would change the maritime industry, but for many years to come, there would still be sailing ships among the merchant fleets.

No cruiser depended on Maury's charts and sailing directions more than CSS *Shenandoah*, the last of the Confederacy's British-built commerce raiders. After USS *Kearsarge* sank *Alabama* in the English Channel, Mallory asked Bulloch to find some way to build or buy one more powerful cruiser. Bulloch could no longer build anything, but once more, using the cleverest of tactics, he bought the steamer *Sea King* through an English friend. With help from confederates, he loaded arms and ammunition on a tender, picked a rendezvous point, and sent both steamers to sea. Lieutenant James I. Waddell took command of the vessel, renamed her CSS *Shenandoah*, and started her on a cruise that circumnavigated the globe.

Waddell sailed into the South Atlantic sea lanes to hunt for homebound vessels. He found prizes scarce, the Yankee ships having been driven off the ocean by *Alabama, Florida,* and *Georgia.* The last great American fleets still roving the seas in concentrated numbers were the whaling vessels, and Maury's whale charts depicted exactly where and in what season the massive migrating mammals could be found. Waddell rounded the Cape of Good Hope, crossed through the South Indian Ocean to Melbourne, picked up an occasional prize, and, toward the end of the Australian summer, started north through the South Pacific. Not until June 1865 did he find the whaling fleet quietly going about its bloody business in the far stretches of the Bering Sea between Alaska and Siberia. The War Between the States had ended, but the news did not reach Waddell until after he had captured, burned, or bonded twenty-four whalers. To investigate rumors he heard about the war ending, he departed from the Bering Sea, and when off California he received confirmation that in April the war had indeed ended. His cruiser now became a renegade and a pirate ship. Against the wishes of many of his crew, who preferred the safety of Australia, he sailed her back to England. Maury's charts not only tracked the shipping lanes, they also provided information for the sailor who did not want to be seen. From California, Waddell sailed the vessel around Cape Horn, wound her through the Atlantic, and at night brought her into Liverpool unobserved. Nobody was more astonished or embarrassed to see old *Sea King* back in port than the British who had let her get away.

During *Shenandoah's* thirteen-month career, she captured thirty-eight prizes and added another $1.3 million in damages to the toll of ships taken by the cruisers. Of that number, Waddell captured twenty-four whalers during a period of six days while cruising in the midnight sun through the far northern reaches of the Bering Sea. Maury never intended that his work be

Maury around 1860 in a Mathew Brady portrait photo. Within a year he would abandon his life's work at the Naval Observatory to offer his services to the Confederacy. He sent his resignation to President Lincoln on April 20, 1861, two days after submitting for publication his monograph The Southeast Trade Winds of the Atlantic, *which he called* "one of the most valuable contributions that I have ever made to navigation."

Ann Hull Herndon Maury in 1877, four years after her husband's death.

Maury and his wife, Ann Hull Herndon Maury, sat for this portrait in London in 1868. Standing behind Maury is his friend and supporter Marin Jansen of the Netherlands Royal Navy. Jansen is flanked by several Maury children: Eliza, 21; Lucy, 17; Mary, 23; Matthew Jr., 19, and Diana, 30 or 31. Diana's child, Nannie, is corralled between her grandfather and grandmother. Maury returned to America later that year to learn that he had been pardoned by President Andrew Johnson. He died at home in Virginia, less than five years after sitting for this photograph.

used to destroy the American whaling fleet, but it did. Before the war, one observer had written Maury, "The Whale Chart is a precious jewel; it seems to have waked up the merchants and masters to the practical utility of your researches on their behalf." Seven years later, *Shenandoah's* depredations may have given the writer cause to reflect on the negative aspects of the "precious jewel" that in the summer of 1865 lured Waddell from England to the North Pacific whaling grounds.

The United States blamed Great Britain for building the cruisers that led to the devastation and decline of the American carrying trade. Seven years after the war, Britain agreed to pay the United States the flat sum of $15,500,000 in gold as reparations for damages caused by commerce destroyers built in English shipyards. By then, the United States government could no longer find all the claimants entitled to a share of the settlement.

For seventeen years Maury had plotted the tracks of the seas, always searching for the swiftest and safest passage for every vessel plying the oceans. His efforts created the century's greatest work on the science of navigation. His concept of international cooperation led the world in thought and practice. He never envisioned that his greatest contribution to navigation would be used for commerce raiding—the burning, bonding, and scuttling of 237 of the very vessels he tried most to protect. The American carrying trade continued but never completely recovered. Science, though often altruistic in endeavor, does not always work for the benefit of mankind.

One might think that the Civil War would have brought an end to commerce raiding by ships of sail, but during World War I Count Felix von Luckner took the famous *Seeadler*, an auxiliary sailing ship, through the Allied blockade and destroyed what little remained of the once great commercial sailing fleet, whose masters still carried copies of Maury's old charts. His ruse was every bit as clever as devices used by Semmes to deceive the enemy while hunting his prey. After hiding all the ship's arms below and stacking the deck with rough lumber, Luckner hoodwinked a British boarding party into believing, during nips from the whiskey bottle, that his vessel was a harmless Norwegian trader. He spoke fluent Norwegian, as did several members of his crew. He went so far as to dress a seventeen-year-old boy as his "wife," and to add to the facade of a family outing, had him lan-guish seductively on a settee in the saloon. Had the Royal Navy Reserve officer in charge of the British boarding party been more inquisitive or more knowledgeable about sailing ships, he might have recognized *Seeadler* as an auxiliary vessel and searched her more thoroughly. Instead, he de-parted feeling delightfully tipsy, returned to his ship, and signaled Luck-ner "happy voyage."

Luckner wasted no time getting away on his "happy voyage," sailing quickly south from the North Atlantic and into the horse latitudes and the doldrums, where nobody would look for him. Commercial sailing vessels still followed Maury's tracks, and Luckner deceived and captured them with the same guile and rapidity as did Semmes fifty years earlier. Unlike German submarine commanders, who would sink a vessel and sometimes kill the surviving crew, Luckner felt an affinity for captured seamen. He eventually sent them off to safety, using as cartels captured, sluggish sail-ers headed for some distant port. In its own way, World War I brought to an end most of those sailing traders Luckner did not destroy.

In today's world, modern navies and commercial fleets have drastically changed, as have the instrumentation and technology that guide and pro-pel them through the seas. But the work started by Lieutenant Maury in the 1840s still progresses. The U.S. Hydrographic Office continues to make surveys and collect data from around the world, helped along by oceano-graphic centers of other nations, just as Maury had proposed in 1852.

A man ahead of his time is seldom appreciated by those who have no vi-sion, especially if he happens to be an aging lieutenant in a decaying navy.

LOAVES AND FISHES

ON May 2, 1865, the day he set sail from England on the steamer *Atrato* with his youngest son, Matthew Jr., Maury became a man without a country, but he did not know it yet. On reaching Havana twenty days later he learned that on April 26 General Joseph E. Johnston had surrendered the last Confederate army to Union General William T. Sherman. He also reacted with shock at the news that Abraham Lincoln had been assassinated, leaving the presidency in the hands of Andrew Johnson of Tennessee. While Johnson's policy toward Confederates remained unclear, Maury knew well what Lincoln's position had been. On December 8, 1863, President Lincoln had stipulated six provisions qualifying a person for a grant of amnesty. Because Maury served as a "diplomatic officer or agent for the confederated government," had been a naval officer above the rank of lieutenant, and had resigned his commission in the U.S. Navy and afterward aided the rebellion, he could not apply for amnesty. Therefore he decided to send young Matthew alone to New York to reunite with the family. Maury, alone again, reboarded *Atrato* and sailed for Mexico.

En route he wrote a letter of surrender and held himself as a prisoner of war, asking the same terms as those granted to General Lee and his officers.

Thus ended Maury's career as a man of the navy. Being too vigorous to remain idle and deeply in need of money, Maury took refuge in Mexico City. He wrote to his wife, Ann, and son Richard, asking them to join him.

A simple woman of plain tastes, Ann did not relish the idea of living in a country where no one spoke her native tongue, so Maury sent the family to England. Ann also did not entirely agree with her husband's plan to colonize Mexico with Confederate officers who had lost their plantations during the war, even though Maury had convinced the Austrian-born Emperor Maximilian and Empress Carlotta that good, intelligent men of the South would be beneficial to the regime. Maury proved to be a good promoter, and he dearly wanted to continue certain aspects of his scientific work. Maximilian named him imperial commissioner of colonization and director of the Astronomical Observatory, yet to be constructed.

On September 18, 1865, Maximilian appointed Maury an honorary counselor of state, in addition to being a trusted counselor to the emperor and the empress. Five days later Maximilian naturalized Maury as a citizen of Mexico. All this troubled the growing number of dissidents.

Maximilian, a former commander-in-chief of the Austrian navy and brother of Austria's emperor, would not send a ship to sea without Maury's charts and sailing directions. He also had been influential in securing for Maury the Austrian gold medal of arts and sciences. As Maximilian's imperial commissioner, Maury induced a number of officers of the former Confederate army to take land in Mexico, among them his son Richard.

Maury privately predicted the overthrow of Maximilian's government, and in March 1866 he left for a reunion with his wife and four youngest children in England. Two months later Mexican insurgents executed their emperor.

During Maury's self-imposed exile from the United States, another race between two clippers occurred that would have captured his attention. Though nearly a decade had passed and work had not resumed on his charts, he would have been gratified to know that sailors still used his work with the same interest as before. Two medium clippers of equal sailing qualities, *Prima Donna* and *Governor Morton*, competed in one more voyage to California. Neither vessel expected to set records for speed, but their skippers did agree to sail from Sandy Hook at precisely the same hour. They also agreed to adhere strictly to Maury's charts and sailing directions, now many years old, throughout the voyage. Both vessels set sail at exactly the same time on February 14, 1867, their routes marked out identically on their charts. One hundred and twenty-three days later, both vessels passed through the Golden Gate, *Governor Morton* ahead by only three hours. The twin voyages testified to the exactness of the science Maury had created—the science his successor at the observatory, James Gilliss, chose to ignore.

When Maury reached London, his youngest daughter, Lucy, did not recognize him and cried, "This is not my papa! This is an old man with a white beard!" The feelings of husband, wife, and children were mixed—they felt happy to be together again, but the reunion revived long-suppressed grief for the loss of their son and brother John during the war. Maury readily found work in Europe teaching naval officers from several countries how to make and operate electric torpedoes. Knowing Maury's financial plight, distinguished men of science created a fund and presented him with $15,000, money the family direly needed. The loaves he had cast upon the waters in the 1840s began flowing back as cash.

Maury longed for his native Virginia, but friends in America cautioned him to wait. Northern animosity still existed toward former Confederate officers, and his Mexican naturalization only made matters worse.

During the winter of 1867–68, Maury received several job offers from southern universities: professor of astronomy at the University of Virginia; vice-chancellor (equivalent of president) at the University of the South in Sewanee, Tennessee; and professor of meteorology and physics at the Virginia Military Institute. Although some friends still feared for Maury's safety if he returned to the United States, his own misgivings were allayed when he learned that General John B. Magruder, who had assisted in the recent colonization of Mexico, returned home without being arrested.

On July 1, 1868, after receiving a degree of Doctor of Laws from Cambridge University and saying good-bye to young Matthew, who remained in England to study, Maury sailed for home with his wife and two daughters, Mary and Lucy. Having accepted a professorship of meteorology and physics at the Virginia Military Institute in Lexington, Virginia, he hoped for the best. On reaching New York he learned that President Andrew Johnson had pardoned many more Confederate officers, among them himself. He passed through customs without a problem.

The Virginia Military Institute treated Maury royally. They built a home for his family, where he entertained such notable guests as General Robert E. Lee, the president of Washington College (later Washington and Lee University), also in Lexington. Once established at VMI, Maury undertook a physical survey of Virginia, lectured occasionally, and wrote several books on the sea, including a student's simplified edition of *The Physical Geography of the Sea*. He also revived an old theme and advocated the building of a railroad to connect Virginia to the West, a proposal endorsed by General Lee.

Throughout the early 1870s Maury's health began a slow decline. He suffered in particular from advanced rheumatism and a worrisome gastric condition. Occasionally he fainted, and often he moved on crutches, owing to pain in his foot. New propositions arrived. The University of Alabama offered him the presidency at $3,500 a year. The University of Tennessee offered the same position, though at a higher annual salary and including a house. He declined them all, being no longer able to maintain a strenuous life.

He found the energy to once again promote an old interest: an international conference for meteorological research, this time including land observations to aid agriculture. He also revived his old proposal for a national weather service. Joseph Henry at the Smithsonian still threw roadblocks in the way. Maury no longer had the strength to vigorously pursue such matters in the nation's capital, so he attempted to fight the battle from VMI, asking for a congressional land grant to provide additional facilities for the college. This, too, failed. Then came an invitation from the *Boston Daily Globe* to speak to the Farmers Club. He journeyed north, comforted by the knowledge that at last the wounds of the war seemed healed, for Boston in 1861 had labeled him a traitor but now welcomed him back as a celebrated scientist, a learned and respected man who with his knowledge of weather could help not only the sailor, but the farmer, too.

After the Boston trip Maury headed for New York for conferences with his publisher. Feeling reinvigorated, he planned to journey on to St. Louis to speak at an agricultural fair. Accompanied by his daughter Eliza, he

Maury late in life, possibly around 1870. When Maury left Mexico in 1867 to be reunited with his family in London, his youngest daughter Lucy cried, "This is not my papa! This is an old man with a white beard!"

A 1929 monument to Maury, "Pathfinder of the Seas," in Richmond, Virginia.

made it as far as Fredericksburg, Virginia, where his strength gave out. Eliza telegraphed her father's regrets to Missouri, and Maury solemnly returned to Lexington, announcing to his wife, Ann, "My dear, I am come home to die."

On Saturday, February 1, 1873, the sixty-seven-year-old lay in bed during his final hours, while the family gathered around and sang his favorite hymns. He grew weary and asked them to leave, all but his two sons, Dick and Matthew, and his two sons-in-law (Diana's and Mary's husbands). To Dick, he asked, "Do I seem to drag my anchors?" The son replied, "They are sure and steadfast." A sailor to the end, Maury replied, "All is well!"

Maury's body lay in state at the Virginia Military Institute for three days. Obituaries and eulogies appeared in newspapers and magazines around the world for the man who had made a science of the ocean, both above and beneath its surfaces. On the day of his funeral, the churches of Lexington rang their bells and shopkeepers closed their doors. After the service in Grace Episcopal Church, a full battalion of cadets followed the hearse, drawn by four horses, to a vault opposite the tomb of General Thomas "Stonewall" Jackson. To an intermittent firing of cannon, Maury's body came to rest.

Seven months later Ann took her husband's casket to Richmond, followed by the cadets of VMI and General Francis H. Smith, the institute's president. At Goshen Pass the family paused to pick laurel and rhododendron, bedecking their father's casket with the spring flowers he loved so well. On September 27, 1873, Matthew Fontaine Maury came to his ultimate resting place on a private knoll in Richmond, not far from the graves of President John Tyler and President James Monroe. There he laid down his final track, leaving to others the tracks to follow.

❧

MAURY did not live to witness and appreciate the thousands of men at sea and on land who continued his work. But his charts and sailing directions lived on. Before leaving the observatory in 1861, his eighth edition of *Explanations and Sailing Directions* had been divided into two volumes containing thirteen hundred pages packed with the knowledge of navigation.

He apologized for such lengthy volumes, admitting that they were overly copious and somewhat disjointed, but organized, he said, for usefulness rather than symmetry. His last edition contained notices to mariners, letters from ship captains, extracts from logbooks, the first thrilling outlines for the practice of the new science of sailing, a treatise on the Gulf Stream, observations on ocean currents and on the general circulation of the atmosphere, data and methods for taking deep sea soundings, analysis of storms, clouds and the equatorial cloud rings, all this together with descriptions and explanations of the *Wind and Current Charts.*

After Maury departed from the observatory, Gilliss stopped further publication of the charts. By then, two hundred thousand copies of the *Wind and Current Charts* and twenty thousand copies of *Sailing Directions* had been distributed free to the masters of merchant vessels who participated in Maury's program.

Maury had never been completely satisfied with his pilot charts, and after the animosities of war subsided, the U.S. Navy Hydrographic Office resurrected his data and in 1883 began publishing the unfinished charts. In 1884 they republished his steamer and sailing ship routes across the Atlantic and to the equator. Once again, the work started by Maury in 1842 caught the attention of the merchant marine, and in 1885 the Hydrographic Office revived all of Maury's work, including a number of manuscripts he had left unfinished. New charts and sailing directions continued to pour forth until the Hydrographic Office finished the series in 1915, a time when sailing traders finally gave way forever to diesel and coal-powered vessels during World War I.

During the fifty years following the Brussels Marine Meteorology Conference in 1853, Dutch seamen turned in 3.5 million abstract logs, American seamen 5.5 million, British seamen 7.0 million, and German seamen more than 10.5 million. As one biographer noted: "The brittle pages of old logbooks studied by Maury in 1842 had multiplied into 'loaves and fishes' for the mariners of the world."

Each chart printed after 1883 contained a statement that read: "Founded upon the researches made in the early part of the nineteenth century by Matthew Fontaine Maury while serving as a lieutenant in the U.S. Navy." Today's charts, while containing all the information gained by modern oceanography, still acknowledge a debt to the man who first conceived them. The hundreds of sailing craft that ply the oceans today, from bluewater yachts to tall ships, still depend on and are guided by the pilot charts and sailing directions. Maury, who had fought so hard for recognition, would have been pleased by so lasting a memorial.

During his lifetime, Maury introduced more than a science to sailing; he imposed a priceless discipline on the seafaring nations of the world that slowly began to die after America's Civil War. Most sailors of the twentieth century probably never heard of Maury. Alan Villiers, who chronicled countless horror stories at sea, mentions Maury only vaguely, perhaps because those disasters involved shipmasters who knew nothing about the long-deceased navigator. A. B. C. Whipple, a contemporary author, understood Maury's worth and wrote of him profusely. Daniel Spurr, a modern sailor and author, believes that today's mariners "could use Maury's charts and *Sailing Directions* with the same assurance and reliability as a sailor in the mid-nineteenth century, but," he laments, "Maury's charts are not so easy to get anymore. Even his 'Scraps from the Lucky Bag' are hard to find, but part of it—the 'Lucky Bag' part—survived to become the name of the yearbook for the U.S. Naval Academy."

By the 1930s, the U.S. Navy and most of the world had forgotten about Maury. They were too busy building dreadnaughts, aircraft carriers, and heavy cruisers to worry about Maury's contributions to the maritime world of the nineteenth century. But Mrs. James Parmelee (Alice Woolfolk Maury), the long-deceased pathfinder's granddaughter and daughter of Elizabeth Maury, on April 14, 1932, paid a visit to the U.S. Naval Observatory on Embassy Row. She carried a magnificent bronze bust of Commander Maury, twenty-three inches high on a base fifteen and a half inches across. In a quiet ceremony that took place in the beautiful old library of the observatory, she presented the bust to Secretary of the Navy Charles Francis Adams. It is still there, a proud tribute to a proud man who put his heart and hands upon the waters and gave the world tracks in the sea.

A witness to the ceremony, Captain J. F. Hellweg of the U.S. Navy, reported:

> To this day, all mariners of all nationalities religiously obey without question the orders which were issued many years ago by that famous American naval officer. It is doubtful if there is another instance in history where the orders of an officer are obeyed many years after his death with such faithfulness as are the instructions of the "Pathfinder of the Seas," Lieutenant Matthew Fontaine Maury, United States Navy.

After seventy-one years of separation from the service he most dearly loved, the great navigator of the seas had come home to rest in the hallowed chambers of the building he loved, the United States Naval Observatory.

NOTES

NOTES can include paragraphs preceding or following the highlighted paragraph. The number at the beginning of the note is the page number on which the highlighted paragraph begins.

Abbreviations

AJS   *American Journal of Science*

LC   Library of Congress

NA   National Archives

RG   record group

SIA   Smithsonian Institution Archives

SLM   *Southern Literary Messenger*

USNIP   U.S. Navy Institute *Proceedings*

UV   Alderman Library, University of Virginia

Introduction

3 **Maury had a . . .** Matthew F. Maury, *The Physical Geography of the Sea*, 8th ed., ed. John Leighly (Cambridge, Mass.: Belknap Press/Harvard University, 1963), 307. This Belknap Press edition is a reissue of the 1861 edition. There were many printings of *The Physical Geography* without edition numbers, making it difficult for a researcher to identify the correct edition. All citations to *Physical Geography* are from the above 8th ed. unless specified otherwise.

Chapter One. The Trackless Seas

6 **In the decades . . .** The track of Columbus is analyzed from "The Journal of Christopher Columbus," reprinted in N. C. Wyeth, ed., *Great Stories of the Sea and Ships* (New York: David McKay, 1940), 58–69, and M. F. Maury, *Explanations and Sailing Directions to Accompany the Wind and Current Charts* (Philadelphia: E. C. & J. Biddle, 1855), 7th ed., plates 6 and 18, 37–39.

6 **Navigators shared . . .** Alan Villiers, *Wild Ocean: The Story of the North Atlantic and the Men Who Sailed It* (New York: McGraw-Hill, 1957), 86.

7   **When out of** . . . Nathaniel Bowditch, *Bowditch's Coastal Navigation* (New York: ARCO, 1979), 13; Ralph D. Paine, *The Ships and Sailors of Old Salem* (Chicago: A. C. McClure, 1912), 291.

7   **Columbus discovered** . . . Robert F. Marx, *Shipwrecks of the Western Hemisphere, 1492–1825* (New York: David McKay, 1971), 366–67.

9   **Barely a year** . . . Ibid., 209–13.

9   **After other nations** . . . Ibid., 19–20, 198.

10 **Though latitude** . . . Bowditch, *Coastal Navigation*, 8; Winston B. Lewis, "Bowditch," 1802–1952," *USNIP* 78, no. 6 (June 1952): 653.

14 **After four months** . . . The first edition of Harrison's account of "The Melancholy Narrative Of The Distressful Voyage and Miraculous Deliverance Of Captain David Harrison Of The Sloop *Peggy*" is in the Library of Congress and reprinted in Donald P. Wharton, *In the Trough of the Sea* (Westport, Conn.: Greenwood Press, 1979), 259–78.

14 **For nearly two** . . . Paine, *Ships and Sailors*, 292–93.

15 **Two years after** . . . Bowditch, *Coastal Navigation*, 13; Sam McKinney, *Bligh: A True Account of Mutiny Aboard His Majesty's Ship* Bounty (Camden, Maine: International Marine, 1989), 11.

16 **At the time** . . . Bowditch, *Coastal Navigation*, 32, 44, 45. For the history of the chronometer, see Dava Sobel, *Longitude: The True Story of the Lone Genius Who Solved the Greatest Scientific Problem of His Time* (New York: Walker, 1995); McKinney, *Bligh*, 9.

16 **In late December,** . . . McKinney, *Bligh*, 16–17.

16 **For instruments,** . . . Ibid., 8, 9, 35.

17 **When Bligh reached** . . . Ibid., 34–39.

17 **Later, following** . . . Samuel Eliot Morison, *The Maritime History of Massachusetts, 1783–1860* (Boston: Houghton Mifflin, 1921), 114.

18 **In 1790** . . . McKinney, *Bligh*, 81–108.

18 **But even if one** . . . Morison, *Maritime History*, 115, 116; G. W. Logan, "Nathaniel Bowditch," *USNIP* 29, no. 7 (July 1903): 928–29.

20 **No reliable** . . . David Porter to William Bainbridge, March 23, 1813, Captains' Letters, vol. 4, no. 139, NA (M125, roll no. 25); David Porter, *Journal of a Cruise Made to the Pacific Ocean in the U.S. Frigate* Essex, *in the Years 1812, 1813, and 1814*, 2 vols. (Philadelphia: Bradford & Inskeep, 1815), 1:32, 55; Loyall Farragut, *Life and Letters of Admiral D. G. Farragut* (New York: D. Appleton, 1879), 20–21.

Chapter Two. The Lure of the Sea

25 **That Richard Maury** . . . Patricia Jahns, *Matthew Fontaine Maury and Joseph Henry: Scientists of the Civil War* (New York: Hastings House, 1961), 11–12.

26 **Being too young** ... Ibid., 12–13; Frances Leigh Williams, *Matthew FontaineMaury, Scientist of the Sea* (New Brunswick: Rutgers University Press, 1963), 13.

26 **Richard Maury worked** ... Williams, *Maury*, 2–11.

27 **Soon after the** ... Ibid., 16–21.

27 **Late in 1811** ... Diana Fontaine Maury Corbin, *Matthew Fontaine Maury, U.S.N. and C.S.N.* (London, 1888), 10–12.

29 **During the summer** ... Corbin, *Maury*, 12–13; Charles Lee Lewis, "Our Navy in the Pacific and the Far East Long Ago," *USNIP* 69, no. 6 (June 1943): 857–64. For the cruise of the *Essex*, see David Porter, *Journal of a Cruise*, 2:19–163.

30 **Wanting to learn** ... Mary Maury Werth to her children, July 26, 1879, Maury Papers, vol. 42, LC.

30 **In 1818,** ... Williams, *Maury*, 28–29.

31 **Apart from** ... Jahns, *Maury and Henry*, 23; Dabney H. Maury to Maury, January 25, 1872, Maury Papers, vol. 44, LC.

32 **Casting aside** ... Maury to Rutson Maury, and Memorandum to Rutson Maury, August 31, 1840, Maury Papers, vol. 2, LC. See also Mary M. Werth to her children, July 26, 1879, ibid.

32 **Without the knowledge** ... Maury to William C. Ventress, November 13, 1825, Maury Papers, vol. 1, LC.

33 **The trip also** ... Maury to Rutson Maury, August 31, 1840, Maury Papers, vol. 2, LC.

34 **To reach the** ... Mary Maury Werth to her children, July 26, 1879, Maury Papers, vol. 42, LC.

35 **After meeting with** ... Maury to Rutson Maury, August 31, 1840, Maury Papers, vol. 2, LC.

35 **On July 9,** ... Howard I. Chapelle, *The History of the American Sailing Navy: The Ships and Their Development* (New York: Bonanza Books, 1988), 336, 534; Log of *Brandywine*, June 17, July 1, 1825, NA; Auguste Levasseur, *Lafayette in America in 1824 and 1825; or, A Journal of a Voyage to the U.S.*, trans. John D. Godman, 2 vols. (Philadelphia: Garden & Thompson, 1829), 2:255–56. Lafayette had been on a twelve-month tour of the United States with his son, George Washington Lafayette, and his secretary, Auguste Levasseur.

36 **Now officially** ... Williams, *Maury*, 41, 42.

36 **Attired in his** ... Ibid., 42; Maury to Rutson Maury, August 31, 1840, Maury Papers, vol. 2, LC; Chapelle, *American Sailing Navy*, 417–18.

Chapter Three. The Education of a Sailor

37 **Maury soon** ... George Jones, *Sketches of Naval Life with Notices of Men, Manners and Scenery on the Shores of the Mediterranean in a Series of Letters from the Brandywine and Constellation Frigates*, 2 vols. (New Haven, 1829), 1:5–12.

38 **Maury easily made** . . . Williams, *Maury*, 44–45; *Navy Rules, Regulations and In structions for the Naval Service of the United States, 1818* (Washington, D.C.: Department of the Navy, 1818.), 68.

38 **Probably nobody on** . . . Villiers, *Wild Ocean*, 63.

38 **With Lafayette soon** . . . Jones, *Sketches of Naval Life*, 1:37; Log of *Brandywine*, August 14, 1825, NA.

39 **At dawn the** . . . Log of *Brandywine*, September 8, 9, 1825, NA; Jones, *Sketches of Naval Life*, 1:15; Williams, *Maury*, 46–48.

40 **Once at sea,** . . . Log of *Brandywine*, September 10–14, 1825, NA; Jones, *Sketches of Naval Life*, 1:17–18, 22.

40 **Maury's first voyage** . . . Jones, *Sketches of Naval Life*, 1:20–21, 27–28; Log of *Brandywine*, October 3, 4, 26, 1825, NA; Charles Lee Lewis, *David Glasgow Farragut: Admiral in the Making* (New York: Arno Press, 1980), 174–75.

41 **Concluding that Bowditch's** . . . Mary Maury Werth to her children, July 26, 1879, Maury Papers, vol. 42, LC.

41 **From Sailing Master** . . . Matthew Fontaine Maury, "Scraps from the Lucky Bag," *Southern Literary Messenger* 6, no. 5 (May 1840): 316, hereinafter "Scraps," *SLM*; Jones, *Sketches of Naval Life*, 1:94.

41 **Jones's task was** . . . Maury, "Scraps," *SLM* 6, no. 5 (May 1840): 316; Jones, *Sketches of Naval Life*, 1:263–64.

41 **Shore leave in** . . . Log of *Brandywine*, December 26, 1825, through February 21, 1826, NA; Jones, *Sketches of Naval Life*, 1:86; Maury, "Scraps," *SLM* 6, no. 5 (May 1840): 315.

42 **Maury made one** . . . Maury, *Physical Geography*, 174–75.

42 **On February 21** . . . A better track for *Brandywine* is deduced from comparing the Log of *Brandywine*, February 21–April 26, 1826, NA, with Maury's Wind and Current Chart, no. 6, series A, for the North Atlantic, NA; Jones, *Sketches of Naval Life*, 1:88–90.

43 **Maury continued his** . . . Maury to Rutson Maury, August 31, 1840, Maury Papers, vol. 2, LC.

43 **On April 30,** . . . Samuel L. Southard to Maury, April 27, 1826, and Maury to Southard, May 2, 1826; orders for leave in Appointments, Orders, and Resignations, RG 45, NA, vol. 13:284, 303.

43 **On June 1** . . . William D. Gordon to Southard, June 16, 1826, Captains' Letters, May–June, 1826, RG 45, NA; Richard C. McKay, *South Street: A Maritime History of New York* (Riverside, Conn.: 7 C's Press, 1969), 136–37.

44 **A walk down** . . . Howard Irving Chapelle, *The History of American Sailing Ships* (New York: Bonanza, 1935), 116; Arthur H. Clark, *The Clipper Ship Era* (New York: G. P. Putnam's Sons, 1910), 47.

47 **During the weeks** . . . McKay, *South Street*, 52–53, 175–79, 273–74; Clark, *Clipper Ship Era*, 47–49.

48 **Maury did not** ... Williams, *Maury*, 58–60, 62; Log of *Brandywine*, September 3, 1826, NA. In 1837, the rank of master commandant was changed to commander.

48 **He hoped to** ... Maury, "Scraps," *SLM* 6, no. 5 (May 1840): 315.

48 **For Maury,** ... William Francis Lynch, *Naval Life; or, Observations Afloat and on Shore* (New York: Charles Scribner, 1851), 18–22; Log of *Brandywine*, October 25–27, 1826, NA; Charles Samuel Stewart, *A Visit to the South Seas in the U.S. Ship* Vincennes *during the Years 1829–1830*, 2 vols. (New York, 1831).

48 **The uneventful voyage** ... Jacob Jones to Samuel L. Southard, November 17, 1826, Captains' Letters, October–November 1826, RG 45, NA; Log of *Brandywine*, November 18, 1826, NA.

49 **In describing his** ... Log of *Brandywine*, December 5–24, 1826, NA; Matthew F. Maury, "On the Navigation of Cape Horn," *American Journal of Science and Arts* 26 (July 1834): 54–61.

50 **Maury's arrival at** ... Log of *Brandywine*, December 26, 1826, January 6, 1827, NA; Corbin, *Maury*, 10–12.

50 **While** *Brandywine* **remained** ... Chapelle, *American Sailing Ships*, 116; Chapelle, *American Sailing Navy*, 501; Stewart, *Visit to the South Seas*, 1:140; Maury, "Scraps," *SLM* 6, no. 5 (May 1840): 315; Maury to W. C. S. Ventress, June 18, 1829, Maury Papers, vol. 1, LC.

51 **What caused this** ... Maury to Rutson Maury, August 31, 1840, Maury Papers, vol. 2, LC; Maury to James H. Otey, February 29, 1829, and Maury to W. C. S. Ventress, June 18, 1829, Maury Papers, vol. 1, LC.

52 **Farther north,** ... Log of *Vincennes*, July 4, 1829, NA; Stewart, *Visit to the South Seas*, 1:209–10.

53 **Unlocking the mysteries** ... Maury, *Physical Geography*, 253.

53 **Captain Finch picked** ... Log of *Vincennes*, July 28, 29, 1829, NA; Stewart, *Visit to the South Seas*, 1:277–81, 346–352; Maury to N. P. Willis, September 24, 1859, Maury Papers, vol. 8, LC.

54 **Not much had** ... Stewart, *Visit to the South Seas*, 1:352.

54 **One day while** ... Maury, *Physical Geography*, 129, 131.

54 **Another experience** ... Log of *Vincennes*, August 17, 1829, NA; Stewart, *Visit to the South Seas*, 2:7, 15, 42–50.

55 **While in the heated** ... Stewart, *Visit to the South Seas*, 2:100–105, 171–234.

55 **A month later,** ... Maury, *Physical Geography*, 187–88.

55 **On New Year's** ... Log of *Vincennes*, January 1, 1830, NA; Charles Oscar Paullin, *Diplomatic Negotiations of American Naval Officers, 1778–1883* (Baltimore, 1912), 183.

56 **Later, Finch** ... Paullin, *Diplomatic Negotiations*, 170–72, 183–85; Stewart, *Visit to the South Seas*, 2:294–96.

56 **On January 22** ... Log of *Vincennes*, January 22, 29, 1830, NA; Stewart, *Visit to the South Seas*, 2:300–320.

56 **Leaving Manila** ... Log of *Vincennes*, February–March, 1830, NA; Corbin, *Maury*, 17; William Leigh to Mary H. Maury, September (n.d.), 1873, Maury Papers, vol. 44, LC.

57 **On one occasion,** ... Williams, *Maury*, 81.

57 **When passing down** ... Log of *Vincennes*, April 7, 19, May 1, 1830, NA; Stewart, *Visit to the South Seas*, 2:323–27, 334–37.

57 **The ancient Phoenicians** ... Villiers, *Wild Ocean*, 36–41.

58 **During the voyage** ... Maury, *Physical Geography*, 363, 328.

58 **On June 8,** ... Log of *Vincennes*, June 8, 1830, NA.

59 **When joining the** ... Maury to James H. Otey, February 18, 1829, Maury Papers, vol. 1, LC.

Chapter Four. A Thirst for Knowledge Unheeded

61 **In 1830** ... Maury to Mary Maury Werth, August 7, 1873, and Dabney H. Maury to Mary H. Maury, August 7, 1873, Maury Papers, vol. 44, LC.

62 **Maury reported for** ... Charles Lee Lewis, *Matthew Fontaine Maury: Pathfinder of the Seas* (Annapolis, Md.: Naval Institute Press, 1927), 21.

62 **Release from the** ... McKay, *South Street*, 172–79; Carl C. Cutler, *Greyhounds of the Sea* (New York: Halcyon House, 1930), 77–78.

62 **But speed had** ... McKay, *South Street*, 383–84. To see the immense mercantile growth along South Street, see 432–50.

63 **The other matter** ... Dabney H. Maury to Mary H. Maury, August 7, 1873, Maury Papers, vol. 44, LC.

64 **On March 3,** ... Maury, "Scraps," *SLM* 6, no. 12 (December 1840): 120; William O. Stephens and C. Alphonso Smith, "Two Early Proposals for Naval Education," *USNIP* 39, no. 1 (March 1913): 127; Lewis, *Matthew Fontaine Maury*, 21.

65 **The role of sailing** ... Corbin, *Maury*, 20, 164, 23.

65 **When the cruise** ... Log of *Falmouth*, July 5, 1831, NA; Lawrence Fasano, *Naval Rank: Its Inception and Development* (New York: Horizon House, 1936), 69–75; Jahns, *Maury and Henry*, 47.

66 **The incident made** ... Maury, "On the Navigation of Cape Horn," *AJS* 26 (July 1834): 60–61, 56, 61.

67 **Maury's experiences** ... Williams, *Maury*, 93–94.

67 **In faraway places** ... Maury to Richard L. Maury, November 17, 1831, April 10, 1833, Maury Papers, vol. 1, LC.

67 **As dejected as** ... William B. Whiting to John M. Brooke, May 31, 1873, Maury Papers, vol. 44, LC.

68 **In 1833 Maury** ... Jones, *Sketches of Naval Life*, 2:271; Williams, *Maury*, 98; Corbin, *Maury*, 23.

68 **On August 21, . . .** Log of *Dolphin*, August 21, 1833, NA; Journal of *Potomac*, November 22, 1833, February 10, 1834, NA.

68 **The homeward voyage . . .** Log of *Potomac*, March 10–16, 1834, NA; Journal of *Potomac*, March 10–16, 1834, NA.

69 **On May 24, . . .** Log of *Potomac*, May 24, 1834, NA.

69 **Maury reached Laurel . . .** Dabney H. Maury to Mary H. Maury, August 7, 1873, Maury Papers, vol. 44, LC; John W. Wayland, *The Pathfinder of the Seas: The Life of Matthew Fontaine Maury* (Richmond, Va.: Garrett & Massie, 1930), 39–40; Maury to Betty Maury, November 26, 1856, in Corbin, *Maury*, 162.

69 **As an unexpected . . .** Maury, "Navigation of Cape Horn," 54–63; Matthew Fontaine Maury, "Plan of an Instrument for Finding the True Lunar Distance," *AJS* 26, no. 6 (July 1834): 63–65.

70 **As a robust, . . .** Matthew Fontaine Maury, *A New Theoretical and Practical Treatise on Navigation; together with a new and easy plan for finding diff. lat., course and distance, in which the auxiliary branches of mathematics and astronomy, comprise of algebra, geometry, variation of the compass, etc. are treated. Also the theory and most simple method of finding time, latitude and longitude* (Philadelphia: Key & Biddle, 1836), hereinafter cited as Maury, *Navigation*; Maury to cousin Ann Maury, January 19, 1836, Maury Collection, UV; Maury to James Maury, November 19, 1834, Maury Papers, vol. 1, LC; Williams, *Maury*, 103.

70 **Maury worked assiduously . . .** Maury to James Maury, November 19, 1834, Maury Papers, vol. 1, LC.

70 **To promote his . . .** Alexander D. Bache to Maury, April 14, 1835, and Nathaniel Bowditch to Maury, April 2, 1835, both quoted in Maury, *Navigation*, 337.

71 **Late in April . . .** Maury to cousin Ann Maury, June 12, July 15, 1835, Maury Collection, UV.

71 **He also deluded . . .** Maury to Richard L. Maury, October 29, 1835, Maury Papers, vol. 1, LC.

72 **During the mid-1830s . . .** Maury to cousin Ann Maury, June 18, 1836, Maury Collection, UV; *A New Theoretical and Practical Treatise on Navigation by M. F. Maury, passed midshipman, U.S. Navy*, copyright April 29, 1836, Maury Papers, vol. 1, LC.

72 **Now thirty years . . .** Maury to Ann Maury, May 11, 1836, Maury Papers, vol. 1, LC.

72 **Unlike "granny" Dickerson, . . .** Letters of endorsement in Maury, *Navigation*, 2d ed., 338–40.

73 **On July 10, . . .** Maury to Richard Maury, September 9, 1836, Maury Papers, vol. 1, LC; Williams, *Maury*, 111–13.

73 **Since 1828 . . .** Maury to Richard L. Maury, September 9, 1836, Maury Papers, vol. 1, LC.

74 **In the muddle . . .** Maury to cousin Ann Maury, September 23, 1836, Maury Collection, UV.

74 **Maury worked with** ... Maury to Thomas A. Dornin, September 18, 24, 26, 29, October 9, 1836, Maury Papers, vol. 1, LC.

74 **With the spring** ... Maury to cousin Ann Maury, July 5, 1837, Maury Collection, UV.

75 **On June 25** ... Ibid.; Maury to Thomas A. Dornin, September 19, 1837, Maury Papers, vol. 1, LC.

75 **Never trusting** ... Maury to Thomas A. Dornin, September 19, 1837, Maury Papers, vol. 1, LC; Maury to Secretary Dickerson, October 23, 1837, in *Report on the Exploring Expedition*, 25th Cong., 2d sess., 1838, H. Doc. 147, 498–99, hereinafter *Exploring Expedition*.

75 **For the beginning** ... Quotes in *Exploring Expedition*, 74, 76, 503, 560–62.

76 **On November 29** ... Ibid., 324, 583–85, 595, 599–601.

76 **Many years later** ... Charles Wilkes, *Autobiography of Rear Admiral Charles Wilkes, U.S. Navy, 1798–1877*, ed. William James Morgan et al. (Washington, D.C.: Department of the Navy, 1978), 323, 324. Wilkes is best known for creating the *Trent* Affair during the Civil War, when he forcibly removed two Confederate agents from the British steamer *Trent* and caused the Federal government much diplomatic embarrassment.

77 **The battle between** ... *Exploring Expedition*, 10, 600–601, 603.

77 **President Martin Van Buren,** ... Maury to Thomas A. Dornin, March 23, 1838, Maury Papers, vol. 1, LC; Maury to cousin Ann Maury, January 25, 1872, Maury Papers, vol. 42, LC; Maury to cousin Ann Maury, April 5, 1838, Maury Collection, UV; Maury to Dickerson, June 9, 1838, Maury Papers, vol. 1, LC.

77 **Meanwhile, Wilkes held** ... Wilkes, *Autobiography*, 294, 327, 367–68.

78 **The newspaper editorials** ... Williams, *Maury*, 119.

78 **Six months passed** Maury to cousin Matthew Maury, January 4, 1839, Maury to sister Ann, December 12, 1838, and Maury to cousin Ann Maury, August 25, 1838, January 26, 1839, all in Maury Collection, UV.

79 **In late January** ... See various letters dated November 6, 1839, to January 26, 1840, in Maury Collection, UV; Maury to cousin Ann Maury, December 16, 1839, Maury Papers, vol. 2, LC; Williams, *Maury*, 121–24.

Chapter Five. Setting the Navy Straight

81 **In mid-February** ... Maury to cousin Ann Maury, February 15, 1840, Maury Collection, UV.

81 **By March he felt** ... Maury to cousin Ann Maury, March 29, 1840, Maury Collection, UV; Maury, "Scraps," *SLM* 6, no. 4 (April 1840): 233.

82 **Few people knew** ... Maury to cousin Matthew Maury, March 3, 1840, and Maury to cousin Ann Maury, May 24, 27, 1840, Maury Collection, UV; Maury, "Scraps," *SLM* 6, no. 4 (April 1840): 234–35.

82 **In another article** ... Maury, "Scraps," *SLM* 6, no. 5 (May 1840): 318–19.

83 **Months passed without** ... Maury to cousin Matthew Maury, January 30, 1840, and Maury to cousin Ann Maury, February 15, 1840, Maury Collection, UV.

83 **Not until late** ... Records of the Office of the Judge Advocate General for "The Case of Lieut. M. F. Maury, Naval Court of Inquiry, No. 1," Courts of Inquiry, Act of Jan. 16, 1857, vol. 21, 35–39, RG 125, NA; hereinafter "Courts of Inquiry." Richard L. Maury was born on October 9, 1840.

83 **While in Washington,** ... Maury, "Scraps," *SLM* 6, no. 4 (April 1840): 234.

83 **This time the** ... Maury, "Scraps," *SLM* 6, no. 12 (December 1840): 786–800; Fasano, *Naval Rank*, 150–51; Maury to cousin Ann Maury, June 21, 1841, Maury Collection, UV; Paolo E. Coletta, *American Secretaries of the Navy*, 2 vols. (Annapolis, Md.: Naval Institute Press, 1980), 1:220–21; Henry Francis Sturdy, "The Establishment of the Naval School at Annapolis," *USNIP* 71, no. 1 (January 1945): 1–11.

84 **Most navy men** ... Maury to cousin Ann Maury, June 21, 1841, Maury Collection, UV. For Maury's articles, see "Scraps," *SLM* 7, no. 1 (January 1841): 3–25; *SLM* 7, nos. 5–6 (May–June 1841): 345–79; *SLM* 7, no. 10 (October 1841): 724–29; "Lieutenant M. F. Maury of the U.S. Navy" by "A Brother Officer," *SLM* 7, no. 7 (July 1841): 560–63; Charles Morris, *The Autobiography of Commodore Charles Morris, U.S. Navy* (Boston: Little, Brown, 1880), 110.

85 **At the age of** ... Maury to cousin Ann Maury, January 10, 1841, Maury Collection, UV; "Reply to Harry Bluff by C.S.," *SLM* 7, no. 3 (March 1841): 209–13.

85 **By July 1841,** ... "Lieutenant M. F. Maury of the U.S. Navy" by "A Brother Officer," *SLM*, 7, no. 7 (July 1841): 560–63.

85 **With the cat** ... Maury to cousin Ann Maury, June 21, July 4, August 14, October 10, 1841, Maury Collection, UV; Maury to George E. Badger, June 10, 1841, Maury Papers, vol. 2, LC.

86 **Maury's friends,** ... Corbin, *Maury*, 39; Abel P. Upshur to Maury, November 15, Maury to Upshur, November 18, and Upshur to Maury, November 22, 1841, Maury Papers, vol. 2, LC.

86 **Maury knew little** ... Quoted in Coletta, *American Secretaries*, 1:179.

86 **Meanwhile, Maury's** ... Williams, *Maury*, 139–40.

87 **Upshur soon discovered** ... Coletta, *American Secretaries*, 1:180–81.

88 **Dismayed by the** ... Maury to Rutson Maury, February 20, 1842, Maury Collection, UV; Maury to John B. Minor, January 28, 1856, Maury Papers, vol. 5, LC.

88 **Because Congress muddled** ... Maury to cousin Ann Maury, May 28, 1842, Maury Collection, UV; Coletta, *American Secretaries*, 1:180–82.

88 **On Independence Day,** ... Maury to cousin Ann Maury, August 4, 1842, Maury Collection, UV; Coletta, *American Secretaries*, 1:166; clipping from *Navy Register*, 1841, in Maury Papers, vol. 6, LC.

89 **Since its formation** ... Maury to cousin Ann Maury, August 4, 1842, Maury Collection, LC.

89 **Because of his** ... Cutler, *Greyhounds of the Sea*, 89, 111, 112.

89 **Officers at the** ... Maury to John Quincy Adams, November 17, 1847, printed in *SLM* 14, no. 1 (January 1848): 9. See also Gustavus A. Weber, *The Hydrographic Office: Its History, Activities, and Organization* (Baltimore: Institute for Government Research, 1926), 17.

90 **Maury found no** ... Maury to John Quincy Adams, November 17, 1847, printed in *SLM* 14, no. 1 (January 1848): 9; Williams, *Maury*, 29; Weber, *Hydrographic Office*, 17–18.

90 **When Maury had** ... Williams, *Maury*, 147–48; Hildegarde Hawthorne, *Matthew Fontaine Maury: Trail Maker of the Seas* (New York: Longmans, 1943), 82–87.

91 **Because so many** ... Maury to cousin Ann Maury, August 4, 1842, Maury Collection, UV; Morris, *Autobiography*, 110. For Upshur's reforms, see Coletta, *American Secretaries*, 1:186–89.

91 **Crane had become** ... *Dictionary of American Biography*, ed. Allen Johnson et al., 22 vols. (New York, 1943), 4:510; Maury to William M. Blackford, November 19, 1843, Maury Papers, vol. 3, LC.

91 **Soon after moving** ... Lewis J. Darter Jr., "The Federal Archives Relating to Matthew Fontaine Maury," *American Neptune* 1 (April 1941): 154; Maury to John Y. Mason, November 18, 1844, RG 37, Letters Sent, NA.

92 **Sailing masters entered** ... Orrin E. Klapp, "Matthew Fontaine Maury, Naval Scientist," *USNIP* 71, no. 11 (November 1945): 1,317.

92 **His own experience** ... Log of *Falmouth*, July 2–August 20, 1831, NA; Corbin, *Maury*, 53; Maury to William M. Blackford, November 19, 1843, Maury Papers, vol. 3, LC.

93 **Because of the** ... Maury to William M. Crane, November 9, 1842, RG 37, Letters Sent, NA.

93 **The analysis of** ... Maury, *Physical Geography*, 6th ed., v, vi.

93 **He believed that** ... Clipping from Navy Register, 1841, in Maury Papers, vol. 6, LC; Klapp, "Matthew Fontaine Maury," 1,317.

94 **Maury harbored concerns.** ... Quoted in Williams, *Maury*, 151.

Chapter Six. Tracking the Winds and Currents

95 **Having drafted his** ... Klapp, "Matthew Fontaine Maury," 1,317.

96 **Maury had been** ... Maury to cousin Ann Maury, February 16, 1843, Maury Collection, UV.

97 **She also remembered** ... Wayland, *Pathfinder of the Seas*, 132–33.

97 **His young subordinates** ... Maury to cousin Ann Maury, February 16, 1843, Maury Collection, UV.

97   **Soon after Maury** . . . Maury to William M. Crane, March, 13, 16, 1843, RG 37, vol. 1, Letters Sent, NA; *Army-Navy Chronicle and Scientific Repository*, March 30, 1848, 365.

98   **He did not expect** . . . *Army-Navy Chronicle and Scientific Depository*, May 25, 1843, 637–38; Matthew Fontaine Maury, "Blank Charts of Board Public Cruisers," *SLM* 9, no. 8 (August 1843): 458.

101 **This Bureau is** . . . Quoted in Klapp, "Matthew Fontaine Maury," 1,317.

101 **Maury listed the** . . . Ibid., 1,317–18; Maury, "Blank Charts," 458.

101 **Setting bottles adrift** . . . Maury, *Physical Geography*, 43–44; Villiers, *Wild Ocean*, 19.

102 **Not all navy captains** . . . Maury to Francis G. Gregory, August 29, 1843, and Maury to Samuel Barron, November 14, 1843, RG 37, vol. 1, Letters Sent, NA.

102 **He feared the** . . . Maury to William M. Crane, September 25, 1843, RG 37, vol. 1, Letters Sent, NA.

102 **Maury's remarkable ability** . . . Maury to cousin Ann Maury, November 4, December 6, 1843, September 11, 1844, Maury Collection, UV.

103 **For more than** . . . Villiers, *Wild Ocean*, 20–21; Maury, *Physical Geography*, 1st ed., 59–64; Matthew Fontaine Maury, "The Gulf Stream and Currents of the Sea," *SLM* 10, no. 7 (July 1844): 393–409; Maury to Lucien Minor, June 15, 1844, Maury Papers, vol. 3, LC.

104 **There is an equatorial** . . . Quoted in Wayland, *Pathfinder of the Seas*, 81–82.

104 **Three-quarters of** . . . Villiers, *Wild Ocean*, 25, 30.

104 **Some early scientists** . . . Maury, *Physical Geography*, 6th ed., chapt. 11.

105 **He refuted many** . . . Ibid.

106 **Maury became an** . . . Williams, *Maury*, 155.

106 **Two years had passed** . . . Maury to William M. Blackford, November 19, 1843, Maury Papers, vol. 3, LC; Maury to cousin Ann Maury, September 12, 1844, Maury Collection, UV; Williams, Maury, 147.

107 **On October 1,** . . . Maury to William M. Crane, October 12, 1844, RG 37, vol. 1, Letters Sent, NA; James C. Dobbin to Charles Morris, December 12, 1854, RG 45, Letters Sent, vol. 3, NA.

107 **It was a short** . . . This description is in Jahns, *Maury and Henry*, 7–8.

108 **The observatory presented** . . . Gilliss to Secretary of the Navy, November 3, 1843, RG 37, vol. 1, Letters Sent, NA. Description of the observatory is in Jahns, *Maury and Henry*, 7–8.

108 **Twenty-three feet** . . . Described in Jahns, *Maury and Henry*, 7–8.

111 **While the staff** . . . Maury to William M. Crane, October 12, 1844, Maury to F. A. P. Barnard, December 23, 1844; Maury to Benjamin Pierce, March 20, 1845, all in RG 37, vol. 1, Letters Sent, NA.

111 **Former president** ... John Quincy Adams, *Memoirs of John Quincy Adams*, 12 vols. (Philadelphia: 1876–77), 12:195; Maury to Builders, April 24, 1845, RG 37, Letters Sent, NA; Corbin, *Maury*, 151–52; Mary Maury Werth to children, July 26, 1879, Maury Papers, vol. 42, LC.

112 **During his first** ... Maury to John Quincy Adams, November 14, 1847, quoted in *SLM* 14, no. 1 (January 1848): 5, 7; see also review of *Astronomical Observations: Made under the Direction of M. F. Maury* in Notice of New Works, *SLM* 13, no. 4 (April 1847): 251–52; Maury to William M. Blackford, January 1, 1847, Maury Papers, vol. 3, LC.

112 **In 1846, war** ... Maury to George Bancroft, May 11, 1846, RG 37, Letters Sent, NA; Maury to cousin Ann Maury, September 30, 1847, Maury Collection, UV.

112 **Toward the end** ... William B. Whiting to John M. Brooke, May 31, 1873, Maury Papers, vol. 44, LC.

113 **With the first** ... Maury to John Quincy Adams, November 14, 1847, quoted in *SLM* 14, no. 1 (January 1848): 9–10.

114 **The periodical winds** ... Quoted in Wayland, *Pathfinder of the Seas*, 83–84.

114 **Because the war** ... Maury to John Quincy Adams, November 14, 1847, quoted in *SLM* 14, no. 1 (January 1848): 9–10.

115 **We were two months** ... Villiers, *Wild Ocean*, 13.

116 **He also discovered** ... Maury, *Physical Geography*, 82, 83–85, 90, 152–53, 307, 309, 310, 311, 319, 329.

116 **Maury further observed** ... Ibid., 322–23.

119 **From Australia to** ... Ibid., 328.

120 **The difference between** ... Ibid., ix–xi; John Lyman, "The Centennial of Pressure-Pattern Navigation," *USNIP* 74, no. 3 (March 1948): 309–10; Matthew F. Maury, *Explanations and Sailing Directions to Accompany Wind and Current Charts*, 4th ed. (Washington, D.C.: C. Alexander, 1852), 304–5, hereinafter cited as *Sailing Directions* (other editions are noted).

120 **Conventional wisdom** ... Maury, *Sailing Directions*, 288–91, 306.

121 **After so many** ... Ibid., 41–42; Lyman, "Centennial of Pressure-Pattern Navigation," 310.

121 **By sea, following** ... Maury, *Sailing Directions*, 2 vols., 8th ed., vol. 1 (Washington, D.C.: William Harris, 1858), vol. 2 (Washington, D.C.: Cornelius Wendell, 1859), 2:146; Maury, *Physical Geography*, 306.

Chapter Seven. Sailors and Whalers

123 **With every set** ... Matthew F. Maury, "On the Winds and Currents of the Ocean," *AJS*, 6, no. 19 (November 1848): 399–401; Maury, *Sailing Directions*, 19, 412–13.

124 **Navigators who are** ... Maury, *Sailing Directions,* 289–91. George Manning had become one of Maury's most faithful agents in charge of distributing the *Wind and Current Charts* to merchant shippers.

124 **Some vessels sent** ... Maury to William M. Blackford, July 17, 1848, Maury Papers, vol. 3, LC; Maury, *Sailing Directions,* 305; Maury, *Physical Geography,* 307; Lyman, "Centennial of Pressure-Pattern Navigation," 310.

126 **During the year** ... Maury to Matthew Maury, July 14, 1848, Maury Collection, UV; Maury to Mrs. William Maury, January 22, 1848, Maury Papers, vol. 3, LC. Sarah Mytton Maury, after being widowed, married William Maury, who lived in Liverpool. In writing *The Statesmen of America in 1846,* she included a flattering account of Matthew Maury, who, as a lieutenant, would not normally be listed among men recognized as statesmen. See Sarah Mytton Maury, *The Statesmen of America in 1846* (Philadelphia: n.p., 1847), 167–68.

126 **In 1848, Maury** ... Maury to cousin Ann Maury, April 19, June 10, August 25, 1848, Maury Collection, UV.

127 **Maury's plans for** ... Maury to William M. Blackford, March 12, July 17, 1849, Maury Papers, vol. 3, LC; Maury to Rutson Maury, March 17, 1848, Maury Collection, UV; L. Heflin, "Comments and Notes," *USNIP* 74, no. 6 (June 1948): 759.

127 **Toward the end** ... Maury to cousin Ann Maury, April 19, 1848, Maury Collection, UV; Heflin, "Comments and Notes," 759.

127 **Then, at the newly** ... *American Association for the Advancement of Science Proceedings and Reports, 1848–1851* (Washington, D.C.: C. Alexander, 1852), 7, 67.

128 **In 1852 Maury** ... Maury, *Sailing Directions,* 193–230; Maury to William M. Blackford, March 12, 1849, Maury Papers, vol. 3, LC; W. H. Beehler, "The Origin and Work of the Division of Marine Meteorology, Hydrographic Office," *USNIP* 19, no. 3 (July 1893): 268–69.

132 **In tracking the** ... Maury, *Physical Geography,* 183.

132 **Maury discovered that** ... Villiers, *Wild Ocean,* 4–5.

Chapter Eight. The California Clippers

133 **Using the best** ... Octavius T. Howe and Frederick C. Matthews, *American Clipper Ships, 1833–1858,* 2 vols. (New York: Dover, 1986) 1:v, 11–12.

134 **In 1844 New York** ... Ibid., 2:501.

134 **Enormous trade** ... Ibid., 300–301; A. B. C. Whipple, *The Clipper Ships* (Alexandria, Va.: Time-Life Books, 1980), 45.

135 **Publication of the** ... Maury to Secretary of the Navy, 32d Cong., 1st sess., [date], S. Doc. 1, 60–61; Maury, *Sailing Directions,* 125–27.

135 **These voyages often** ... Matthew Fontaine Maury, "The Isthmus Line to the Pacific," *SLM* 15, no. 5 (May 1849): 441–57; *National Intelligencer,* November 4, 1849;

Maury to William M. Blackford, November 20, 1849, Maury Papers, vol. 3, LC.

136 **In 1850 the first** ... Clark, *Clipper Ship Era*, 145; Howe and Matthews, *American Clipper Ships*, 1:53, 274; 2:378, 650.

136 **The competitors did** ... Clark, *Clipper Ship Era*, 145–46.

137 **Though the first** ... Log of *Helena*, May 19, 1843, RG 78,NA.

137 **The remainder of** ... Clark, *Clipper Ship Era*, 145–46; Ibid., 146; Maury to Secretary of the Navy William A. Graham in *Annual Report of the Secretary of the Navy for 1851* (Washington, D.C.: Government Printing Office, 1851), 13, 61.

138 **Though Maury had** ... Maury, "Navigation of Cape Horn," 63; Maury, *Physical Geography*, 324, 398, 399–400.

138 *Flying Cloud* **wore** ... Howe and Matthews, *American Clipper Ships*, 1:190; Clark, *Clipper Ship Era*, 153, 155.

139 *Flying Cloud* **arrived** ... Cutler, *Greyhounds of the Sea*, 160–61; Clark, *Clipper Ship Era*, 156.

140 **With two other** ... Howe and Matthews, *American Clipper Ships*, 1:54–56, 190; 2:569–70, 658; Clark, *Clipper Ship Era*, 365; Cutler, *Greyhounds of the Sea*, 61, 103, 105, 137–40.

140 *Flying Cloud* **sailed** ... Howe and Matthews, *American Clipper Ships*, 1:190–91; Whipple, *The Clipper Ships*, 58.

141 *Challenge* **departed from** ... Howe and Matthews, *American Clipper Ships*, 1:56–57; 2:658.

141 **By 1851 Maury** ... A. B. C. Whipple, *The Challenge* (New York: William Morrow, 1987), 96, 140, 144.

142 **With** *Flying Cloud* ... Whipple, *Challenge*, 220–21; Clark, *Clipper Ship Era*, 366.

142 **In 1851, there** ... Clark, *Clipper Ship Era*, 365–66.

142 **Maury took as much** ... Howe and Matthews, *American Clipper Ships*, 1:55–56.

145 **On the stretch** ... Clark, *Clipper Ship Era*, 189–92; Jaquelin Ambler Caskie, *Life and Letters of Matthew Fontaine Maury* (Richmond, Va.: Garrett & Massie, 1928), 38.

145 **Though sixteen days** ... Clark, *Clipper Ship Era*, 192.

146 *Arthur,* **from New York,** ... Ibid., 193.

146 **Although clipper ships** ... Ibid., 193–94.

147 **Maury took special** ... Corbin, *Maury*, 57.

148 **The focus of** ... Howe and Matthews, *American Clipper Ships*, 1:54, 103, 204, 304; 2:649–50, 669, 705; Whipple, *Clipper Ships*, 104, 105; Cutler, *Greyhounds of the Sea*, 240.

149 **The race about** ... Howe and Matthews, *American Clipper Ships*, 1:204–5, 304; 2:669–70, 705–6; Whipple, *Clipper Ships*, 104, 105.

149 **Unlike the 1851** ... Maury, *Physical Geography*, 2d ed., 363.

151 **Because Nickels sailed** ... Ibid., 263–64; see also Wayland, *Pathfinder of the Seas*, 68–72.

Notes

_[263]_

151 **Trade Wind sailed** . . . Howe and Matthews, _American Clipper Ships_, 2:670; Clark, _Clipper Ship Era_, 226.

153 **When Putnam reached** . . . Maury, _Physical Geography_, 2d ed., 264–65; Wayland, _Pathfinder of the Seas_, 72–75.

153 **At the equator** . . . Maury, _Physical Geography_, 2d ed., 266; Clark, _Clipper Ship Era_, 365–70; Howe and Matthews, _American Clipper Ships_, 1:7–8.

153 **John Gilpin, though** . . . Howe and Matthews, _American Clipper Ships_, 1:103, 198, 206, 304; 2:670, 706.

154 **The public generally** . . . Ibid., 2:448; Lyman, "Centennial of Pressure-Pattern Navigation," 310.

154 **After studying the** . . . Maury, _Physical Geography_, 2d ed., 266–67, 270.

155 **Maury provided McKay** . . . Howe and Matthews, _American Clipper Ships_, 2:594–96; Clark, _Clipper Ship Era_, 217–18.

155 **Sovereign had not** . . . Howe and Matthews, _American Clipper Ships_, 2:597.

156 **Most of the crew** . . . Ibid., 2:598; Clark, _Clipper Ship Era_, 220; Cutler, _Greyhounds of the Sea_, 251–52. Maury actually underestimated _Sovereign_'s run, thinking McKay had made only 427.6 statute miles compared with a later study that showed a run of 472.92 statute miles.

156 **Over time, Sovereign** . . . Howe and Matthews, _American Clipper Ships_, 2:598–99; Clark, _Clipper Ship Era_, 220–21.

157 **So fast and able** . . . Cutler, _Greyhounds of the Sea_, 147, 173–74, 477.

157 **From the early 1850s** . . . Columbus O. Iselin, _Matthew Fontaine Maury (1806–1873), Pathfinder of the Seas: The Development of Oceanography_ (New York: Newcomen Society, 1957), 8; Whipple, _Clipper Ships_, 45; Howe and Matthews, _American Clipper Ships_, 2:552; Hugh McCulloch Gregory, _The Sea Serpent Journal_, ed. Robert H. Burgess (Charlottesville: University Press of Virginia, 1975), 27, 52.

157 **By 1855 the average** . . . Maury to Secretary of the Navy William A. Graham in _Annual Report of the Secretary of the Navy for 1851_, 13, 61; Maury, _Physical Geography_, 2d ed., viii, 263; Clark, _Clipper Ship Era_, 365–69; Maury to Walter P. Jones et al., July 14, 1853, RG 37, vol. 9, Letters Sent, NA.

158 **Other honors followed.** . . . Quoted in Williams, _Maury_, 215, 545 n. 97; Wayland, _Pathfinder of the Seas_, 86, 175, 176.

Chapter Nine. Disasters and Discoveries

159 **On November 19,** . . . Maury to Crane, November 13, 1851, RG 37, vol. 7, Letters Sent, NA; quotes from Williams, _Maury_, 192.

160 **The cutters followed** . . . Whipple, _Clipper Ships_, 43; Maury to F. W. Beechey, Maury to Adolphe Quetelet, January 7, 1853, and Maury to Charles Morris, January 12, 1853, RG 37, vol. 8, Letters Sent, NA; Maury, _Physical Geography_, 2d

ed., 57–58; Corbin, *Maury*, 57; Cutler, *Greyhounds of the Sea*, 303–4.

161 **Maury's track down** ... U.S. Navy, *Annual Report of the Secretary of the Navy, 1854* (Washington, D.C.: Government Printing Office, 1854), 401–2; Cutler, *Greyhounds of the Sea*, 299–300; Wayland, *Pathfinder of the Seas*, 86.

161 **In 1854 Maury** ... McKay, *South Street*, 381–83; Howe and Matthews, *American Clipper Ships*, 1:210.

162 **The experiences recorded** ... Maury statement, April 17, 1856, RG 37, vol. 13, Letters Sent, NA.

163 **Maury had more** ... Lewis, *Matthew Fontaine Maury*, 118; Caskie, *Life and Letters of Maury*, 119.

164 **Both Herndon and** ... William Lewis Herndon, *Exploration of the Valley of the Amazon* (New York: McGraw-Hill, 1952) ix, xii, xiii, xiv, xxii–xxvi, 7–9, 12, 149–50. See also *Exploration of the Valley of the Amazon*, vol. 1, 32d Cong., 2d sess., 1853, S. Doc. 36, and Matthew F. Maury, *Report of Lt. Matthew F. Maury on the Loss of the U.S. Mail Steamer* Central America *under the Command of Commander William Lewis Herndon (written October 19, 1857)* (Washington, D.C.: Government Printing Office, 1884). Maury, *Physical Geography*, 323.

165 **Herndon, a balding** ... Herndon, *Exploration of the Valley*, xiv, 34; Gary Kinder, *Ship of Gold in the Deep Blue Sea* (New York: Atlantic Monthly Press, 1998), 24; Charles Neider, ed., *The Autobiography of Mark Twain* (New York: Harper & Brothers, 1959), 98.

165 **Maury, however, became** ... Matthew Fontaine Maury, *Valley of the Amazon and the Atlantic Slopes of South America* (Washington, D.C.: Frank Taylor, 1853), 22; Wayland, *Pathfinder of the Seas*, 76–80; Herndon, *Exploration of the Valley*, xix; Kinder, *Ship of Gold*, 23.

166 **In 1855 William** ... Herndon, *Exploration of the Valley*, xx; Kinder, *Ship of Gold*, 20–21. See also Cedric Ridgely-Nevitt, "The United States Mail Steamer *George Law*," *American Neptune* 4, no. 3 (October 1944): 305–7. The S.S. *Central America* was originally named *George Law*. In the 1850s, U.S. mail steamers were commanded by naval officers. Ridgely-Nevitt states that *George Law* carried 423 persons.

166 **During the previous** ... Marx, *Shipwrecks of the Western Hemisphere*, 206–9; Kinder, *Ship of Gold*, 21.

167 **At daybreak on** ... Kinder, *Ship of Gold*, 26–31.

168 **To feed the furnaces,** ... Here and following quoted in ibid., 30–36 and passim. Kinder's source material here is Cedric Ridgely-Nevitt, "The United States Mail Steamer *George Law*," *American Neptune* 4, no. 1 (October 1944), 304–17 (the *Central America* was originally named the *George Law*).

171 **During the final** ... Kinder, *Ship of Gold*, 127; Herndon, *Exploration of the Valley*, xx.

172 **The public's howls** ... James P. Delgado, "Murder Most Foul: San Francisco Re-

acts to the Loss of the S.S. *Central America*," *Log of the Mystic Seaport* 25, no. 4 (spring 1983): 3–15.

172 **Affectionate in disposition,** . . . Maury to Isaac Toucey, October 19, 1857, RG 37, vol. 15, Letters Sent, NA.

172 **Hurricanes were not** . . . Maury, *Physical Geography*, 70–71.

174 **Nobody, however,** . . . Ibid., 327, 376, 381, 387, 388, 70–71.

175 **In 1853, Maury** . . . Ibid., 195–99.

176 **The *Advance* was** . . . Maury to Alexander Keith Johnston, November 2, December 13, 1853, RG 37, vol. 10, Letters Sent, NA; Maury to Elisha K. Kane, November 26, 1852, February 3, 1853, October 7, 1856, RG 37, vol. 8, Letters Sent, NA.

Chapter Ten. Organizing the Nations

177 **In 1847, Joseph** . . . Maury to Charles Morris, November 21, 1851, RG 37, vol. 7, Letters Sent, NA; Maury, *Sailing Directions*, 63; Matthew F. Maury, *On the Establishment of a Universal System of Meteorological Observations by Sea and Land* (Washington, D.C.: C. Alexander, 1851), 1–5.

177 **Maury planned to** . . . Maury, *Establishment of Universal System*, 6–8.

178 **Maury's appeal for** . . . Ibid., 9–10, 13; Maury to various ministers, December 10, 1851, to January 3, 1852, and Maury to various scientists, December 29, 1851, to April 10, 1852, RG 37, vol. 7, Letters Sent, NA; Maury to Joseph Henry, January 14, 1852, ibid.

179 **Joseph Henry had become** . . . Joseph Henry Memorial, 60, 492, SIA; quoted in Jahns, *Maury and Henry*, 73.

179 **During his years** . . . Jahns, *Maury and Henry*, 74.

179 **Though Bache had** . . . Maury, *Navigation*, 337; Maury to Bache, March 6, July 28, 1846, RG 37, vol. 2, Letters Sent, NA; Williams, *Maury*, 174.

180 **In 1852, Bache** . . . Maury to Benjamin Peirce, January 26, 1846, RG 37, vol. 2, Letters Sent, NA; Maury to Charles Henry Davis, December 20, 1850, March 11, 1851, RG 37, vol. 6, Letters Sent, NA; Charles H. Davis, *Life of Rear-Admiral Charles Henry Davis* (Boston: Houghton Mifflin, 1899), 84; Maury to Lewis Warrington, March 1, 1847, RG 37, vol. 2, Letters Sent, NA.

180 **Back in the early** . . . Davis, *Charles H. Davis*, 75–89.

183 **Jefferson Davis had** . . . Thomas Coulson, *Joseph Henry, His Life and Work* (Princeton: Princeton University Press, 1950), 236, 282; Merle M. Odgers, *Alexander Dallas Bache, Scientist and Educator* (Philadelphia: University of Pennsylvania Press, 1947), 102, 149; Henry to Bache, October 25, 1851, Joseph Henry Letters, SIA.

183 **Maury's first trouble** . . . Maury to Alexander D. Bache, March 11, July 1, 1847, and Maury to Joseph Henry, September 20, October 20, November 15, 1847, RG

37, vol. 2, Letters Sent, NA; Coulson, *Joseph Henry*, 91, 93, 106, 146–47.

184 **Secretary of State** ... Maury to Joseph Henry, January 22, 1852, RG 37, vol. 7, Letters Sent, NA; Joseph Henry Journal, March 2, May 2, 1852, SIA.

184 **As a consequence** ... Maury to John P. Kennedy, November 6, 1852, RG 37, vol. 8, Letters Sent, NA; Maury's invitations to scientists, February 21, 1853, RG 37, vol. 8, Letters Sent, NA.

185 **Because the Royal** ... Maury to James C. Dobbin, June 18, 1853, and Maury to foreign ministers and Royal Navy, June 27, 28, 29, 1853, RG 37, vol. 9, Letters Sent, NA.

186 **Although Great Britain** ... Corbin, *Maury*, 155; Maury, *Sailing Directions*, 8th ed., 2:591; Herndon, *Exploration of the Valley*, xii.

186 **Parliament could no** ... Maury to George Minor, August 14, 1853, RG 37, Letters Received, NA; George Minor to Maury, September 8, 1853, RG 37, Letters Sent; Maury, *Sailing Directions*, 6th ed. (1854), 54–88; Maury, *Establishment of Universal System*, 14–16.

186 **Already aware of** ... Derek House and Michael Sanderson, *The Sea Chart* (New York: McGraw-Hill, 1973), 124–25.

186 **Eleven men from** ... Maury, *Sailing Directions*, 6th ed., 55–88; Beehler, "Origin and Work of the Division of Marine Meteorology," 269–70.

187 **For two weeks** ... Maury, *Sailing Directions*, 6th ed., 88–96; 8th ed., 1:332–56, 593; Maury, *Physical Geography*, 2d ed., 272–73, 8th ed., 201; Klapp, "Matthew Fontaine Maury," 1,320.

188 **This meeting was** ... George Minor to Maury, September 8, 1853, RG 37, vol. 9, Letters Received, NA, and Maury to Adolphe Quetelet, February 9, 1854, RG 37, vol. 10, Letters Sent, NA; Maury, *Physical Geography*, 2d. ed., xiii.

188 **On October 21** ... George Minor note dated October 21, Maury to James C. Dobbin, October 22, 1853, RG 37, vol. 9, Letters Sent, NA; Maury, *Sailing Directions*, 8th ed., 1:xi, 2:870.

189 **Maury's presentation** ... See Maury's letters to Adolphe Quetelet and other delegates, December 12, 1853, to February 9, 1854, RG 37, vol. 10, Letters Sent, NA.

189 **Maury could have** ... Corbin, *Maury*, 291–92.

190 **Maury's grand vision** ... Maury to Quetelet, May 3, 1858, RG 37, vol. 15, Letters Sent, NA.

190 **Maury firmly believed** ... Clipping from *New York Daily Tribune*, December 25, 1855, Maury Papers, vol. 5, LC.

190 **Henry did not** ... U.S. *Agricultural Society Journal for 1856*, part 1, vol. 3, Journal of the 4th Annual Meeting, January 1856 (Boston: U.S. Agricultural Society, 1856), 48, 51–53; *Washington Daily Star*, January 10, 1856.

191 **After the conference,** ... Jahns, *Maury and Henry*, 133; Maury to B. Franklin Minor, January 11, 1856, Maury Papers, LC; Maury quoted in Klapp, "Matthew

Fontaine Maury," 1,324. See also Vest's speech in Caskie, *Life and Letters of Maury*, 108–9.

Chapter Eleven. The "Indefatigable Investigator"

193 **Exactly when Maury** ... Maury to Alexander von Humboldt, November 10, 1853, RG 37, vol. 10, Letters Sent, NA; Maury, *Physical Geography*, 1st ed., xiii.

194 **Having reviewed the bulky** ... Dabney H. Maury, *Recollections of a Virginian in the Mexican, Indian, and Civil War* (New York: Charles Scribner's Sons, 1894), 18; Dabney H. Maury to Mary Maury, August 7, 1873, Maury Papers, vol. 44, LC.

194 **From his charts** ... Maury to cousin Ann Maury, June 21, December 1, 12, 1854, Maury Collections, UV.

195 **Much of the material** ... Maury, *Physical Geography*, xvi, xvii. This 8th edition from Belknap Press included review quotes from earlier editions.

195 **In 1855, ...** Ibid., 2d ed., 217–29, 231–43, 257–61, 244–56, plates 8, 9; Klapp, "Matthew Fontaine Maury," 1,322; Wayland, *Pathfinder of the Seas*, 99–100; Humboldt's great work in 1845–47, titled *Kosmos*, contained scant treatment of oceanographic topics; Maury, *Physical Geography of the Sea*, 8th ed. (New York: Harper, 1858). Tracking the number of editions of *Physical Geography of the Sea* is almost an exercise in futility because there appear to be editions both in the United States and aboard containing no edition number and falling between numbered editions. How many editions were actually printed would be a good topic for an extended international research project.

195 **While preparing** ... Quoted in Klapp, "Matthew Fontaine Maury," 1,322–23.

198 **Had Bache and Henry** ... Frank Waldo, "Some Results on Theoretical Meteorology in the United States," *Report of the International Meteorological Congress held at Chicago, Ill., Aug. 21–24, 1893* (Washington: U.S. Weather Bureau, 1894), bulletin no. 11,319.

199 **He then went** ... Maury, *Physical Geography*, 285–86. Maury discovered that the descent of the ball slowed as it reached greater depths, and by determining the time taken for the ball to run a hundred feet off the reel, he could closely estimate the depth of the water.

199 **In 1852–53, ...** Ibid., 6th ed., 153–54, 200–16; Maury, *Sailing Directions*, 5th ed., 125–40, 174–77, 187–90, and plates 14 and 15; Maury to Isaac Toucey, September 4, 1854, RG 37, vol. 16, Letters Sent, NA.

200 **Berryman's samples** ... Maury, *Physical Geography*, 206–7; Maury to Isaac Toucey, September 4, 1858, and Maury to James C. Dobbin, February 22, 1854, RG 37, Letters Sent, NA; Klapp, "Matthew Fontaine Maury," 1,321; Arthur C. Clarke, *Voice across the Sea* (New York: Harper & Brothers, 1958), 22.

203 **Maury knew more** ... Maury to Cyrus Field, February 24, April 21, and Maury to Samuel F. B. Morse, February 23, 1854, RG 37, vol. 10, Letters Sent, NA; Wayland, *Pathfinder of the Seas*, 106–7.

203 **Naval cooperation** ... Maury to James C. Dobbin, May 5, 1856, RG 37, vol. 13, Letters Sent, NA; Odgers, *Bache*, 146, 158, 210. See also A. D. Bache Papers, vol. 1, LC; Williams, *Maury*, 241–43.

204 **Much effort still** ... Herndon, *Exploration of the Valley*, xiii; Cyrus Field to Maury, March 7, 1857, RG 37, Letters Received, NA; Maury to Cyrus Field, February 28, March 28, May 7, 1857, RG 37, vol. 14, Letters Sent, NA. At Bache's request, Berryman used a new metered device that had never been tested or calibrated for deep-sea soundings. At depths over 1,500 feet, readings off the apparatus became increasingly unreliable.

205 **Field then listened** ... Maury to Adolphe Quetelet, July 9, 1857, RG 37, vol. 14, Letters Sent, NA; Henry Martyn Field, *The Story of the Atlantic Telegraph* (New York, 1892), 162–74.

206 **The happy moment** ... *New York Times*, November 3, 1858; Maury to Isaac Toucey, September 24, 1858, RG 37, vol. 16, Letters Sent, NA. Field's quote is from McKay, *South Street*, 271; Clarke, *Voice across the Sea*, 47–77.

207 **With Maury's vast** ... Matthew F. Maury, *Lanes for the Steamers Crossing the Atlantic* (New York: Board of Underwriters, 1855), 1–12; Maury to Walter R. Jones, November 8, and to Robert Bennett Forbes, December 14, 1854, RG 37, vol. 9, Letters Sent, LC.

207 **Forbes reported** ... Maury, *Sailing Directions*, 8th ed., 2:71–73.

208 **Maury worked at** ... Ibid., 73–80; Maury, *Lanes for the Steamers*, 1–12; Maury to James H. Otey, November [date], 1860, RG 37, vol. 18, Letters Sent, NA.

208 **Some steamship captains** ... Wayland, *Pathfinder of the Seas*, 87–88, 92.

208 **Maury had barely** ... Maury, *Sailing Directions*, 8 and passim; Maury to Charles Morris, January 11, 1855, RG 37, vol. 11, Letters Sent, NA; Maury to B. Franklin Minor, December 25, 1855, Maury Papers, vol. 5, LC.

209 **Maury looked forward** ... See *Astronomical Observations Made during the Year 1848 at the U.S.N. Observatory, Washington, Under the Direction of M. F. Maury, LL.D., U.S.S., Superintendent*, vol. 4 (Washington, D.C.: A. O. P. Nicholson, 1856); Matthew F. Maury, *Abstract Log for Men of War* (Philadelphia: E. C. & J. Biddle, 1855).

210 **Yet there were those** ... Caskie, *Life and Letters of Maury*, 51.

210 **Since the days** ... Maury to Stephen R. Rowan, January 15, 1853, RG 37, vol. 8, Letters Sent, NA; *New York Herald*, February 3, 1855.

211 **The Navy Retiring Board** ... See "Correspondence Relating Primarily to Lt. M. F. Maury, U.S.N., and the 'Plucking Board' of 1855," RG 45, vol. 1, no. 45, NA,

hereinafter, "Maury and Plucking Board"; James C. Dobbin to Maury, September 17, 1855, Maury Papers, vol. 4, LC.

211 **If Maury had not ...** Maury to James C. Dobbin, September 20, and Dobbin to Maury, September 24, 1855, RG 37, vol. 12, Letters Sent, NA; Maury to William Blackford, September 25, 1855, Maury Papers, LC; see also Maury to James H. Otey, September 20, 1855, quoted in Caskie, *Life and Letters*, 69–71.

212 **Maury would not ...** James C. Dobbin to Maury, September 24, and Maury to Secretary Dobbin, October 1, 1855, RG 37, vol. 12, Letters Sent, NA; Maury to cousin Ann Maury, November 3, 1855, Maury Collection, UV.

212 **Scientists can be ...** James C. Dobbin to Maury, November 9, Maury's letters to board members, November 8, and James S. Biddle to Maury, November 13, 1855, all in RG 37, Letters Received, vol. 12, NA; Maury to Congress, December 1, 1855, RG 45; "Maury and Plucking Board," no. 45, NA.

213 **Dobbin not only ...** *National Intelligencer*, October 5, 1855, in Caskie, *Life and Letters of Maury*, 65–66; *New York Herald*, December 15, 1865.

213 **Dobbin's actions ...** Corbin, *Maury*, 113; for Mallory's defense of the Naval Affairs Board, see Joseph T. Durkin, *Stephen R. Mallory, Confederate Naval Chief* (Chapel Hill: University of North Carolina Press, 1954), 70–83. The many honors and medals coming from abroad are summarized in Wayland, *Pathfinder of the Seas*, 176–77.

213 **By November, ...** Maury to Franklin Minor, November 15, 1855, Maury Papers, LC. For the debate in the Senate, see Durkin, *Stephen R. Mallory*, 70–83, which presents one view, and Williams, *Maury*, 280–81, 286–93, for a more balanced view.

214 **On March 6, 1857, ...** *National Intelligencer*, July 18, 1856; see James C. Dobbin to Captain E. A. F. Lavalette, February 12, 1857, in RG 125, "Courts of Inquiry," 2–10; Maury to Isaac Toucey, October 15, 1857, RG 37, vol. 15, Letters Sent, NA.

214 **Letters from skippers ...** McLaughlin to Maury, April 22, 1856, quoted in Frederick C. Matthews, *American Merchant Ships, 1850–1900*, 2 vols. (New York: Dover, 1987), 1:154–55.

217 **A log came into ...** Cutler, *Greyhounds of the Sea*, 327, 472, 473.

217 **On November 25, ...** James C. Dobbin to Maury, September 17, 1855, Maury Papers, LC; Maury to Isaac Toucey, October 10, 1857, RG 37, vol. 15, Letters Sent, NA; Toucey to Maury, October 13, 1857, RG 125, "Courts of Inquiry," 15–18; Caskie, *Life and Letters of Maury*, 69.

217 **Maury believed the ...** Testimony in RG 125, "Courts of Inquiry," 35–52, passim, 58, 58A and B, 285, 291; Isaac Toucey to Maury, January 29, 1858, Maury Papers, LC.

Chapter Twelve. Maury's Charts Go to War

219 **By 1860 Maury's . . .** Maury to Edouard Vaneechout, March 12, 1860, RG 37, vol. 17, Letters Sent, NA.

219 **After dedicating . . .** Maury wrote many letters to friends to preserve the Union, among them Maury to B. Franklin Minor, December 30, 1859, October 22, 1860, Maury Papers, LC; Maury to Robert Fitz Roy, August 4, 1861, Maury Collection, UV.

220 **While in England, . . .** Maury to William C. Hasbrouck, December 7, 1860, Maury Papers, vol. 10, LC; Maury to Adolphe Quetelet, December 7, 1860, RG 37, vol. 18, Letters Sent, NA.

220 **Maury returned . . .** *The War of the Rebellion: A Compilation of the Official Records of the Union and Confederate Armies*, 130 vols. (Washington, D.C.: Government Printing Office, 1880–1901), ser. 1, 1:99–125, 134–37; F. N. Boney, *John Letcher of Virginia: The Story of Virginia's Civil War Governor* (University: University of Alabama Press, 1966), 102–5; Mark M. Boatner III, *The Civil War Dictionary* (New York: David McKay, 1959), 729.

220 **During the nation's . . .** Corbin, *Maury*, 183–84; Maury to B. Franklin Minor, January 16, and to W. C. Whithorne, January 4, 1861, Maury Papers, vol. 10, LC; Maury to Lord Wrottesley, January 28, and Maury to W. C. Whithorne, March 21, 1861, Maury Papers, vol. 11, LC. See also several letters from Maury to the Virginia Convention, January 16 to February 7, 1861 in Maury Papers, vols. 11 and 12, LC; Boatner, *Civil War Dictionary*, 729.

221 **On February 4, 1861, . . .** Boatner, *Civil War Dictionary*, 170, 729.

221 **On March 4 Abraham . . .** Maury to B. Franklin Minor, March 26, 1861, Maury Papers, vol. 13, LC.

221 **Though disconcerted . . .** Maury to B. Franklin Minor, February 11, 14, 1861, and Maury to William C. Hasbrouck, May 12, 1861, Maury Papers, vol. 13, LC.

222 **On April 17 . . .** Boney, *John Letcher*, 111–14; Boatner, *Civil War Dictionary*, 299–300; Roy Basler, ed., *The Collected Works of Abraham Lincoln*, 9 vols. (New Brunswick: Rutgers University Press, 1953–55), 4:331–32; Maury to cousin Ann [Mrs. B. Franklin Maury], April 17, 1861, Maury Papers, vol. 14, LC.

223 **Maury marked April . . .** Corbin, *Maury*, 190; Maury to Abraham Lincoln, April 20, 1861, RG 37, Letters Sent, vol. 18, NA; Beehler, "Origin and Work of the Division of Marine Meteorology," 275.

223 **In early April . . .** Maury to B. Franklin Minor, June 8, 1862, Maury Papers, vol. 16, LC.

223 **In Richmond, . . .** Williams, *Maury*, 365, 370.

224 **On May 29, 1861, . . .** Maury to B. Franklin Minor, June 11, 1861, Maury Papers, vol. 14, LC.

225 **On March 13, 1861** ... Cutler, *Greyhounds of the Sea*, 311; J. Thomas Scharf, *History of the Confederate States Navy* (New York: Rogers & Sherwood, 1887), 33.

225 **At the beginning** ... Chester G. Hearn, *Gray Raiders of the Sea: How Eight Confederate Warships Destroyed the Union's High Seas Commerce* (Camden, Maine: International Marine, 1992), 1.

225 **Though the South** ... Raphael Semmes, *Memoirs of Service Afloat during the War between the States* (Baltimore: Kelly, Piet, 1869), 89–94; *Official Records of the Union and Confederate Navies in the War of the Rebellion*, 30 vols. (Harrisburg, Pa.: National Historical Society, 1987), ser. 1, 1:613, 614, ser. 2, 1:268.

226 **Semmes had followed** ... W. Adolphe Roberts, *Semmes of the Alabama* (Indianapolis: Bobbs-Merrill, 1938), 17; *Official Records of the Navy*, ser. 2, 1, 48; Semmes, *Service Afloat*, 114–18; Hearn, *Gray Raiders*, 15–42 passim, 311.

226 **The South operated** ... Hearn, *Gray Raiders*, 52–53.

227 **During the time** ... Frank W. Owsley Jr., *The CSS Florida: Her Building and Operations* (Philadelphia: University of Pennsylvania Press, 1965), 19–20.

227 **Englishmen sailed** ... Hearn, *Gray Raiders*, 55–66.

227 **On October 3, 1862,** ... *Official Records of the Navy*, ser. 2, 1:252; Owsley, CSS *Florida*, 34.

227 **On the dark,** ... Maffitt's Journal, *Official Records of the Navy*, ser. 1, 2:667; Hearn, *Gray Raiders*, 70–101, 311–13; Royce Shingleton, *High Seas Confederate: The Life and Times of John Newland Maffitt* (Columbia: University of South Carolina Press, 1994), endmaps; Owsley, CSS *Florida*, 78–91.

228 **Morris added to** ... Hearn, *Gray Raiders*, 118–28, 142–51, 312; *Papers Relating to the Treaty of Washington: Geneva Arbitration*, 3 vols. (Washington, D.C.: Government Printing Office, 1873), 3:583–90, hereinafter *Treaty of Washington*; Robert G. Albion and Jennie Barres Pope, *Sea Lanes in Wartime* (New York: W. W. Norton, 1942), 172.

229 **Another product of** ... *Official Records of the Navy*, ser. 2, 1:247; James D. Bulloch, *The Secret Service of the Confederate States in Europe; or, How the Confederate Cruisers Were Equipped*, 2 vols. (New York: Putnam's, 1883), 1:56, 59–61, 227, 229.

229 **Bulloch planned from** ... Semmes, *Memoirs*, 423–44; Hearn, *Gray Raiders*, 161–71.

230 **And when we reach** ... Semmes, *Memoirs*, 580.

230 **Semmes calculated** ... Ibid., 580, 583, 588.

230 **During *Alabama's*** ... Maury to Marin Jansen, July 23, 1864, Maury Papers, vol. 20, LC. For the cruise of *Alabama*, see Semmes, *Memoirs*, 370–788, and Hearn, *Gray Raiders*, 161–236, 315–16.

231 **By June 1862,** ... Maury to B. Franklin Maury, June 5, June 8, 1862, Maury Papers, vol. 16, LC; Jahns, *Maury and Henry*, 202.

231 **After *Alabama* . . .** Maury to wife Ann Maury, September 17, 18, 1862, Maury Papers, vol. 16, LC; Stephen R. Mallory to Maury, November 7, 1862, *Official Records of the Union and Confederate Navies in the War of the Rebellion*, 30 vols. (Washington, D.C.: Government Printing Office, 1894–1922), ser. 2, 2:295.

232 **No one turned . . .** James Morris Morgan, *Recollections of a Rebel Reefer* (Boston: Houghton Mifflin, 1917), 98–100.

232 **Lieutenant James Morris Morgan . . .** Ibid., 101–2.

233 **With help from . . .** Ibid., 107; Maury to wife Ann Maury, November 30, December 5, 1862, Maury Papers, vol. 17, LC; Hearn, *Gray Raiders*, 239–49, 314.

233 **While in Great . . .** Maury to Marin Jansen, April 21, 1863, Maury Papers, vol. 18, LC.

234 **Waddell sailed into . . .** For the cruise of *Shenandoah*, see James I. Waddell, CSS *Shenandoah: The Memoirs of Lieutenant Commanding* James I. Waddell, ed. James D. Horan (New York: Crown, 1960), 20–182; Hearn, *Gray Raiders*, 251–301.

234 **During *Shenandoah's* . . .** Hearn, *Gray Raiders*, 316–17; quote from Klapp, "Matthew Fontaine Maury," 1,320.

237 **The United States . . .** Caleb Cushing, *The Treaty of Washington, Its Negotiation, Execution, and the Discussions Relating Thereto* (New York: Harper & Brothers, 1873), 280.

237 **For seventeen years . . .** Hearn, *Gray Raiders*, 311–17.

238 **Luckner wasted no . . .** Villiers, *Wild Ocean*, 283–85.

Chapter Thirteen. Loaves and Fishes

240 **On September 18, . . .** Corbin, *Maury*, 292.

240 **Maury privately . . .** Boatner, *Civil War Dictionary*, 441, 520; Maury to B. Franklin Minor, May 19, 20, 1865, Maury Papers, vol. 21, LC; Basler, *Works of Lincoln*, 7:53–56; Wayland, *Pathfinder of the Seas*, 121–24.

240 **During Maury's self-imposed . . .** Howe and Matthews, *American Clipper Ships*, 1:249, 2:486–87.

242 **The Virginia Military Institute . . .** Wayland, *Pathfinder of the Seas*, 125–29.

242 **Throughout the early . . .** Joseph H. Speed to Maury, April 15, 1871, Maury Papers, vol. 37, LC; Maury to Francis W. Tremlett, February 2, 1872, vol. 39, Maury Papers, LC.

242 **He found the energy . . .** See Maury's Memorial of the Academic Board of the Virginia Military Institute to the Legislature of Virginia in vol. 50, Maury Papers, LC.

242 **After the Boston . . .** Quoted in Corbin, *Maury*, 284.

245 **On Saturday, . . .** Quoted in Wayland, *Pathfinder of the Seas*, 151–52. Maury's second son, John, affectionately called "Davy Jones," became an officer in the Con-

federate Army and died mysteriously during the fighting around Vicksburg in 1863 "as if he had been swallowed up by the sea" (134).

245 **Seven months later** . . . Williams, *Maury*, 478–79.

246 **After Maury departed** . . . Beehler, "Origin and Work of the Division of Marine Meteorology," 269. For a brief history of the post–Civil War Hydrographic Office, see 276–80.

246 **Maury had never** . . . Ibid., 272; Klapp, "Matthew Fontaine Maury," 1,321.

246 **During the fifty years** . . . Williams, *Maury*, 221.

246 **Each chart printed** . . . Lyman, "Centennial of Pressure-Pattern Navigation," 310.

248 **To this day,** . . . J. F. Hellweg, "The Pathfinder of the Seas," *USNIP* 59, no. 1 (January 1933): 93–97. A photo of the Gilriss Library at the U.S. Naval Observatory with a view of the location of Maury's bust (on left) can be seen at the USNO Web site, www.usno.navy.mil/library/history/Library-1.jpg.

INDEX